REMINISCENCES
POLITICAL AND PERSONAL

REMINISCENCES
POLITICAL AND PERSONAL

By

SIR JOHN WILLISON

MᶜCLELLAND & STEWART
PUBLISHERS - TORONTO

PRINTED IN CANADA

CONTENTS

SIR JOHN MACDONALD

LIST OF ILLUSTRATIONS

REMINISCENCES
POLITICAL AND PERSONAL

CHAPTER I

MY FIRST POLITICAL MEETING

The house in which I was born in the township of Stanley, in Huron county, stood in a "clearing" of a few acres, and all around was bush, in which no axe had ever swung. As a child I often wandered among thick underbrush and picked wild flowers along streams that ceased to murmur long ago. The trees were beech and maple, ash and elm, basswood and hemlock. But chiefly that was a maple country, where the sap ran in the spring and sugar-making was a happy, if mysterious, festival. In the summer there was something intimate and companionable in the forest. One thinks of climbing moss and trailing vine and tangled thicket. The woodpecker beat his tattoo. The squirrel chirped and gambolled in leafy branches. Plaintive voices whispered from the underbrush or came faintly from the tree-tops. The birds sang the songs that are never new nor ever old. There were open spaces where the sun shone upon a stretch of natural meadow or shimmering water. Near was the long tamarack marsh where we gathered cranberries. We knew that the bush could be loud and angry, for we had heard the great trees wail and seen them thrash their arms in the storm. But for the most part we looked into deep and friendly silences. We saw the earth, unspoiled by human arti-

9

fice, as when "God saw everything that He had made, and, behold, it was very good."

In those days the sound of the axe was heard all through the winter. The great trees were felled, the brush piled in heaps for burning, and the trunks cut into "lengths" for logging. Blazing brush heaps across many acres like "the watch-fires of a hundred circling camps," revealed as did nothing else the ruthless warfare of the pioneers against the forces of nature. In the "logging bee" there was as much of sport as of conflict. "The captains of tens" strove against one another, and that "gang" which first logged its width across the field turned homewards in triumph. I fear there was a "grog boss," whose jug was not neglected. Rude times, perhaps, but men were neighbourly, limbs were strong, and hearts were sound. How women bore and reared children, and did the cooking and choring, the making and mending of those days, only God who pities and strengthens understands. This is not so much a man's world as it was, and no doubt men toiled long and hard to make homes in the bush, but when one thinks that women nursed babies, washed dishes, swept and scrubbed, cooked and served, milked cows and fed calves and pigs, spun and wove, made and mended for all the household, and sometimes helped with the harvest, one feels there was an unequal division of labour and bows the head in reverence for the mothers of half a century ago. But whether men or women, the pioneers of Upper Canada fought the battle of the wilderness with high courage, endured and conquered. They sleep well in their quiet beds on the hillsides, and we "enter into their labours."

But one may love the woods and the fields and not

like farming. I got away from the farm as soon as I could, and I have not wanted to return. Nor have I ever heard that there was any desire that I should. It is often said that a good farmer has been spoiled to make a poor lawyer or a poor doctor. Whether or not I am a good journalist, no one who knows will suggest that I was likely to become a good farmer. The fashion changes. It is a sure word of prophecy that the movement towards the cities has spent itself. Moving pictures, rural mail delivery, good roads, motors, bathrooms, house furnaces, and many other devices to save labour, enhance comfort and relieve isolation make the country ever more desirable, and better prices give the farmers an increasing but still inadequate return for their labour. In a democracy rooted in the soil lies the sanity and the stability of human institutions. But we cannot all be farmers, and to many of us a call comes that will not be denied. Whether we go to town or country, still blessed is he that findeth himself.

For thirty-six years I was engaged in political journalism in Canada. During all that time my pen was my only means of income. All my earnings were derived from reporting, editorial writing, or the editorial direction of newspapers. I have never bought a share of stock "on margin" or speculated in real estate. I have never received payment for any service done for a political leader or a government. So far as I know I have had no unholy alliance with "the interests." It is not pretended that there is any demand or justification for these Reminiscences. They are an intrusion, but they may be entertaining, possibly instructive. At least no journalist can have any ground of protest. All journalism is more or less of an intrusion, and even writers of history have no commission from the state or the public. But neither journalists nor historians need to justify themselves any more than do those who paint pictures or fabricate ornaments. If it be said that only great men may write Reminiscences it may be pleaded that a close, even if accidental, relation to great men or great events may give equal or better qualifications for dispassionate dealing with the forces by which events are directed or controlled, social and political institutions fashioned, and the destinies of peoples determined.

Unless Reminiscences have the flavour of egotism they illuminate nothing. Such a book must be a "human document," much as I dislike the phrase, and gladly as I would punish the author if one knew where he could be found and how put to shame and silence. There is a tradition that one must not write the life of a man still living. This is why there is truth in the old judgment that "history is a lie." In time we shall discover that contemporary writers speak with such knowledge and authority as later historians cannot possess. Many of the decisive facts and incidents which determine the course of human affairs are not contained in any documents that go down to posterity. There is much that the contemporary writer cannot divulge; but he is less hampered by reticence than will be the writer of fifty years hence by ignorance. I think of events within my own knowledge of which I can say little or nothing. Of the real pith, motive and bearing of these events neither this nor any other generation can have full or exact knowledge. What is not disclosed by contemporary writers will never be disclosed. Hence history never can be a true record, and the exact relation of public men to the causes in which they are concerned never can be determined. If there is reticence in the present and ignorance in the future, at best we can have only light in the darkness. The law from which no man can escape is that what he learns in a confidential relation he may not disclose to the discredit or injury of men still living. He is bound also to observe a decent discretion even when death has removed the actors from the stage where we all appear so often with painted faces and in borrowed attire. Subject to this law these Reminiscences will be frank and open, but, I trust, free from temper or malice, from detraction or adulation.

As long ago as 1872 I attended my first political meeting. I had walked four miles from my home near Hillsgreen, on the boundary between the townships of Hay and Stanley, in Huron county, to the village of Varna. I was just fourteen years of age, and to me Varna, with two general stores, a shoemaker, a blacksmith, a wagon-maker, a tavern, two churches and an Orange hall, was a considerable community. This day a rough frame hustings stood at the crossroads by the village tavern. A group of men sat upon the platform, and in front and around were a crowd of people with eyes fixed upon a man who was speaking. I knew at once that it was not a camp-meeting, for there was no suggestion of the fervour and solemnity which distinguished such events. There was occasional laughter and cheering, but I thought that some of those who listened did not like the behaviour of their neighbours. I was interested in the statement of the speaker that wherever he had gone throughout the county he found that someone else had been there, and that many calves and steers had been bought at very high figures.

13

Who was this mysterious person? Why should he buy
calves and steers? Why should be pay such high
prices? Finally the speaker sat down to much clapping
and cheering. Another man arose, and there was even
more cheering. As he spoke it was remarkable that he
agreed with nothing that the first speaker had said,
while those who had been silent now became happy and
demonstrative. But the light was breaking. I recalled
many a fireside controversy, and almost instinctively I
knew what game they were playing.

Before the second speaker had finished a buggy,
turning from the Bayfield road in a cloud of dust, stopped on the edge of the crowd, and a heavy figure, with
flowing mutton-chop whiskers, under a wide soft hat,
jumped to the ground and made his way to the platform. In a moment there were shouts of "Speak now,"
"Big Thunder," and a tempest of booing and cheering.
When he rose to speak the cries of "speak now" were
renewed with noisy and angry vehemence, and apparently by those who did not seem to be willing that he
should speak at all. I could not understand, but probably I alone among those who stood around the hustings
needed enlightenment. I gazed at the bulky figure on
the platform, I noticed that he had lost one arm, that
his dusty white vest was buttoned unevenly so that one
side hung below the other, and that in the teeth of the
shouting he was indomitably calm and unperturbed.
Finally the man who had first spoken made an earnest
appeal to the meeting to give the obnoxious stranger a
hearing, and the clamour subsided. And he spoke. His
voice thundered out over the cross-roads. His words
came with stormy fluency. There was tremendous
volume and vigour. The conquest was complete. He

had not gone far before there was tumultuous cheering. He seemed to sway the crowd as he would. Instead of division, there was unity; instead of dissent there was eager assent and a fervour of enthusiasm. Even "Big Thunder" could have had few greater personal triumphs on the platform.

The meaning of all this I had to learn later. But not so much later. From the day that I stood in the cross-roads at Varna forty-seven years ago I have loved political debate. I have had no interest in life comparable to the study and discussion of public questions. It seems to me that I had an instant birth into "politics." From that hour I saw the way along which I must go. Even now I can recall as many sentences spoken at that meeting as at any other that I ever attended. No other political event is so clear and vivid in my memory. The man whose voice I first heard from the platform at Varna was Mr. Thomas Greenway. He was standing as the Conservative candidate for the House of Commons for South Huron in the second election after Confederation. The Liberal candidate was Mr. M. C. Cameron, for so long the chief political figure of Huron county. In later years I knew both men well, and we were comrades in many a political contest. Mr. Cameron, who was returned for South Huron at Confederation, defeated Mr. Greenway in 1872, and again in 1874. He was, however, unseated, and in 1875 Mr. Greenway succeeded to the representation of the constituency. Although he was a Conservative candidate in two contests, and is described in *The Parliamentary Companion* for 1875 as an "independent Conservative," he gave a guarded support to the Mackenzie Government, and gradually established a working relation with the Liberal party. In fact, there was an agreement before he was returned by acclamation that he would support the Administration. He was one of the leaders in the movement of population from Huron and Bruce to Manitoba. Unable to resist the lure of politics, he entered the western Legislature and eventually became leader of the Liberal party and Premier of the Province.

In 1882 I met Mr. Greenway in London. He had established a weekly newspaper at Crystal City, in Manitoba, and was looking for an editor. The negotiations terminated when it was intimated that the editor would be required to furnish some capital. I met Mr. Greenway again in 1895 when he was Premier of Manitoba and I was editor of *The Globe*. For a day or two he was my guide throughout southern Manitoba. At his side I first looked wide and far across leagues of wheat yellow to the harvest, and knew that the confusion of the pessimists was at hand. For it was the year of the first "great crop," and the efflorescence of faith in the West. By the way, during that visit to the West my wife and I had to stay over night in a village near the "end of the track." Mr. George Ham told us at Winnipeg that there were two hotels in the place and that "if we stayed at either we would wish we had stayed at the other." He was right. There were flies enough around the supper-table for a second visitation to the children of Egypt.

The third speaker at the Varna meeting, so long ago, I never saw again. But I soon came to understand the significance of "speak now" and "Big Thunder." The orator whose swift and sounding sentences reduced the hostile element in the meeting to subjection was Hon.

E. B. Wood, of Brantford. He had been Treasurer in the Sandfield Macdonald Administration, which held office during the first Legislature under Confederation. But for reasons which have never been fully disclosed, perhaps partly personal and partly political, but not necessarily discreditable, he joined hands with Hon. Edward Blake against the sardonic, intractable, petulant, obstinate, incorruptible politician, who was incautious enough to meet the House with a group of constituencies unrepresented and confident enough in his own integrity to neglect the "fences," which, if properly guarded, would have protected the citadel against successful attack. Defeated by one vote on the Address, Mr. Sandfield Macdonald sought to adjourn the Legislature for a fortnight, but he could not prevail against the forces which had manœuvred so dexterously to accomplish his destruction.

During the contest in Ontario Sir John Macdonald was engaged in the negotiations which produced the Treaty of Washington. The Conservative leader was anxious to have the election delayed until his return to Canada, but Sandfield would not be advised, nor would he delay calling the Legislature together until the vacant seats were filled. In Pope's "Memoirs of Sir John Macdonald" there is a letter from the Federal leader which shows how fully he understood the situation in Ontario. "I hope," he said, "that nothing will happen to Sandfield or his Government. I am vain enough to think that if I were in his place just now, and had his cards, I could carry him through the first three weeks of the session (wherein alone there is any danger) triumphantly. I am not so sure that he will be able to manage it himself." Sir John Macdonald would

2

have used the surplus which Sandfield had accumulated, have created two or three new portfolios, and have delayed the session until he had a complete Parliament. But his advice was not taken. Mr. Sandfield Macdonald resigned, Mr. Blake took office, and for more than thirty years thereafter the Liberal party enjoyed an unbroken ascendancy in Ontario. All this because the counsel of the most consummate political strategist in Canadian history was rejected.

We do not know the exact relation of Hon. E. B. Wood to these events. We do know that he broke away from Sandfield Macdonald and united with Blake and Mackenzie to bring in a Liberal Administration. During the debates preceding Sandfield's downfall, a vigilant Conservative collected and pieced together the torn fragments of a note which Mr. Blake had sent across the House to Mr. Wood, and which said only "speak now." There is no need to elaborate an incident with which students of the period are familiar. It is clear there was an understanding between Mr. Blake and Mr. Wood and that Wood was ready to take the floor when his speech would be most destructive. He spoke, as has been said, with tremendous power and volume. Hence the sobriquet of "Big Thunder." It is curious that so many of the orators which Brant has produced or harboured had voices hardly less powerful than that which Mr. Wood possessed. Hon. A. S. Hardy was known as "Little Thunder." Hon. William Paterson could thunder as loudly as either Mr. Wood or Mr. Hardy. It is said that when Mr. Paterson first spoke in the House of Commons he was eager to have a word of commendation from Hon. Alexander Mackenzie. No man could have had less vanity than Mr. Paterson, but he courted his leader's approval. When the House rose he got alongside Mr. Mackenzie and whispered, "Do you think they heard me?" "Aye," said the Prime Minister, "they heard you at the Russell Hoose." The Russell House was three blocks away. With that doubtful compliment Mr. Paterson had to be content. Mr. Mahlon Cowan, who died the other day, with distinction at the Bar and in public life riper than his years, had, too, the voice and manner which seemed to be the peculiar product of Brantford. In this characteristic, however, they have no immediate successors. For the time the Grand River keeps its secret.

Many stories cluster about the name and fame of Mr. E. B. Wood. He lived in a less arid time and was not always neglectful of his opportunities. It is said that he and Mr. Edward Farrer were once opposing speakers at a series of political meetings. At one of these meetings a voice shouted as Mr. Wood was going in the full sweep and majesty of deliverance that he had been "drunk" the night before. Mr. Wood paused and uttered a grave and feeling protest against the accusation. Turning to Mr. Farrer he said: "There sits the man who has been opposing me from many platforms. He cannot desire to shield me, but I have faith that he will not do me injustice. After last night's meeting we spent the time together until we retired. We are opposed politically, but we respect each other and have friendly personal relations. I ask Mr. Farrer to answer my accuser." Mr. Farrer arose and declared with adequate emphasis that Mr. Wood had been just as sober as he was. The story, which may be purely apochryphal, although it is supported by the probabilities, is not revived to the discredit of either. Those days were not as these. It is true, however, as Dr. Johnson says, that all dealers in anecdote are tainted with mendacity.

Mr. E. B. Wood's speeches were freely garnished with Scriptural references and sounding passages from the orators and poets. He was not without learning, but his speeches gave an impression of learning greater than he possessed. Still, behind his roaring sentences and furious fluency there was appeal and logic that was moving and effective. When Mr. John Charlton was elected for North Norfolk, in 1872, he sent this congratulatory message: "Sing unto the Lord for He hath triumphed gloriously, the horse and his rider hath He thrown into the sea."

There is a vagrant story that Mr. Wood and Mr. Charlton were once holding meetings in Norfolk. For some days they had been in hostile territory and were depressed by the hardness and impenitence of the unbelievers. Argue and appeal as they would they felt that all was as "a wind that passeth away and cometh not again." Driving outward from this inhospitable neighbourhood after midnight one cold, dreary morning, over roads deep in mud and behind a horse as weary as the passengers, Mr. Charlton was struck in the ribs by the stump of Mr. Wood's missing arm and roused from fitful, uneasy slumber by the shout, "Wake up, John, wake up! We're back in God's country. Here's a Baptist church." Thus they were refreshed and proceeded on their journey. During one of the elections in South Ontario, in which Hon. T. N. Gibbs was the Conservative candidate, Mr. Wood is reported to have said from the platform: "Electors of South Ontario,—When I heard that you had elected Thomas Nicholson Gibbs to be your representative at Ottawa, I went into my closet, and I shut the door, and I took the Bible from the shelf, and swore—before Almighty God—that justice had fled the land. But, electors of South Ontario, when I hear, on Tuesday next, that you have rejected Thomas Nicholson Gibbs, by an overwhelming majority, I shall say, with Ahasuerus the king, Who is he, and where is he?"

Mr. Wood was appointed to the office of Chief Justice of Manitoba by the Mackenzie Government. It is, however, as an advocate rather than as a judge that he is distinguished. He was an incident rather than an influence in the life of Canada. But one feels that he had the native strength to rise higher and the gifts to achieve a more enduring reputation.

During the general election of 1874 I lived near the village of Greenwood, in South Ontario. I had begun to read *The Globe* and *The Mail*. At home we "took in" *The Toronto Leader,* which had all the respectability and at times all the dullness of orthodox Toryism, and *The Daily Telegraph,* which was neither so dull nor so respectable. In *The Daily Telegraph* Mr. Phillips Thompson appeared as Jimuel Briggs, a graduate of Coboconk University. For a time he reported the proceedings of the Police Court in verse. Here is a sample which I cannot forget:

> John Brown
> Went down
> Thirty days;
> Couldn't raise
> Three dollars,
> Peeler hollers,
> You clear
> Out of here;
> In that room
> Wait your doom.

21

REMINISCENCES

What curious fag-ends repose at the back of one's memory. As parliamentary correspondent of *The Daily Telegraph,* Jimuel Briggs described a debate on prohibition. He said that when the House rose the members descended to the restaurant below, where they "put down the curse of the country with great success." *The Daily Telegraph,* which ran from 1866 to 1872, was one of Mr. John Ross Robertson's ventures, and during its too short life displayed vigour, courage and originality. When I returned home in 1876, after an absence of four years, my father said that he was glad to have me back, but the fact that I brought a copy of *The Globe* did not add to his pleasure. This I submit as definite and final evidence that my father was a Conservative.

I found a treasure-house in the Greenwood Mechanics' Institute. Looking backward to those days, I have wondered if Mr. Andrew Carnegie would not have served the world better if he had endowed village and township libraries. We are too willing to carry water to the springs when it is needed in the parched places. From the Mechanics' Institute at Greenwood I had all the English poets, and no one ever read Pope and Dryden and Campbell and Goldsmith, Tennyson and Longfellow and Whittier, and even Mrs. Hemans and Eliza Cook more faithfully or with greater reverence of soul. There, too, I had Don Quixote, and that was a task; Dickens, whom I still love, sneer the intellectuals as they may, Thackeray, who is not for youth, and Scott, who is for all ages and for all time. This village library had also a few standard biographies and histories, and somewhere I got Eugene Sue's "Wandering Jew" and Samuel Smiles's "Self Help." Upon that last book we now bestow a smiling and tolerant patronage, but many a thirsty youth has had the first draughts of the water of life from its pages. I recall, too, that at this time I found in an upper room of the farm-house where I lived two or three volumes of *Harper's Weekly,* with Nast's cartoons, much serious and instructive reading, and a noble poetical tribute to Garibaldi, verses of which never have been erased from my memory. One doubts if there is now a weekly periodical in America of higher standard than was *Harper's Weekly* under the editorship of Mr. George William Curtis fifty years ago. This at least I know, that none of its issues ever were read more greedily than those which I discovered in the farm-house at Salem's Corners. Henceforth *The New York Ledger* and the dime novels of Beadle and Munro were treated with "salutary neglect." But who would forget "Hardskull, the Avenger" and "The Terror of the Gulch" or the dread fascination of desperate adventures in "The Dark and Bloody Ground." Who would deny his devotion to Richard Lewis, and Mrs. Southworth and Sylvanus Cobb, Junior; to Fanny Fern and John G. Saxe. Milk for babes and meat for strong men. If we do not take the milk the appetite for meat may not develop.

There was a happy day, long ago, while I was still under my father's roof, when with a dollar in my pocket I walked fourteen miles to Clinton, bought ten dime novels, had another "thrown in" because I took so many, and walked all the way home again, richer than I have ever been in all the years that have since settled on my head. As was his habit, my father scolded his erring son, made his choice out of the collection, and one by one read first all the "trash" that I had accumulated.

This is a digression, but Reminiscences are chiefly digression and disconnection. No man serves a youth so well as he who lures him into reading what wise men have said, and foolish men have thought and vain men have dreamed. I think with gratitude of Mr. Fred Meen, who established the Mechanics' Institute at Greenwood, as I confess a lasting debt to Hon. David Mills and Mr. Edward Farrer, who opened to me the books out of which they drew strength and inspiration, and which at least I have loved for their solid counsel, their beauty, authority and integrity.

In 1874, when I lived at Greenwood, the country was convulsed by the "Pacific scandal." Even the village school was broken into factions. Reared in a Tory household, and in worship of John A. Macdonald, I clung to the faith as it was received from the fathers. But I fear that I wavered as I found life-long Conservatives falling away from the standard. At school those who held to the Conservative leader were denounced as "Charter-sellers." I cannot recollect that the taunt was supported by fact or argument. Nor was there any better support for the retort of youthful Conservatives that all Reformers were "rebels." But if there was comedy in the schoolyard, there was an element of tragedy in the position of many Conservatives. Grieved to the soul over the "scandal," they turned sadly from the leader who had commanded their complete sympathy and devotion. This was long before we had manhood suffrage and many of those who deserted Sir John Macdonald were old men whose loyalty to the leader and the party had become a tradition and almost a religion. Not only did they forsake the old allegiance, but they became active working members of Liberal committees. There is nothing in the political history of Canada to justify the notion that Conservatives submit more readily than Liberals to the bondage of party.

The Conservative candidate in South Ontario in 1874 was Hon. T. N. Gibbs, who had been admitted to the Cabinet in 1873, a few months before Sir John Macdonald resigned office. Of fine presence and high character, and with influential social and business connections throughout the riding, he was formidable in the canvass and on the platform. It was Mr. Gibbs who defeated Hon. George Brown in 1867, in a contest in which, if rumour was not unjust, there was expenditure of money as lavish as ever fertilized a Canadian constituency. The charge of corruption always lies against the victor, but there is reason to think Mr. Brown was not empty-handed. Thought of that achievement still brings a flush of pride to the furrowed cheeks of Conservative veterans in South Ontario. But I think of more than one gray-haired Conservative who resolutely resisted Mr. Gibbs's personal appeal, and of at least one woman who shed bitter tears over the contumacy and recreancy of her husband. Hon. Malcolm Cameron, of Perth, famous in early political battles in Lambton and Kent, was brought into the riding to oppose this strong local candidate. He was called "The Coon" in contemporary political writing. Once when George Brown appeared as a candidate in Kent, Cameron wrote a letter urging the "clear Grit" wing of the Liberal party to give Brown "a coon-hunt on the Wabash." From this he was "The Coon" while he lived. A pioneer temperance agitator, Mr. Cameron had many anecdotes which he told with good effect. At

Brougham, referring to the regard in which Mr. Gibbs had been held by Conservatives throughout the riding, and declaring that he had forfeited this esteem by adherence to an unworthy leader, the Liberal candidate emphasized the contention by the story of a shepherd who had two sons, one wise and one otherwise. The foolish youth had a pet lamb, and when the shepherd came to divide his flock he put the pet lamb in one enclosure and all the rest of the sheep in another. Then he called upon the foolish one to choose between the lamb and the flock. At once "the saftest of the family" ran to the lamb, put his arms about its neck and sobbed, "I loved you, Billy. We have had happy days together, and parting is painful. But you have got into bad company and I must leave you there." And he chose the flock.

Mr. Gibbs was not unequal to the occasion. Recalling that Mr. Cameron had been imported from outside the constituency and brought back into public life from a retirement which became his years, to contest South Ontario, Mr. Gibbs said he was reminded of the farmer who sternly but unsuccessfully opposed the construction of a railway across his farm. He had a favourite bullock, which, under the impulse of instinctive sympathy, got on the track and braced himself to meet the inaugural train as it came rushing across the country. The consequence, as Mr. Gibbs said, was "a dead bullock." The farmer solemnly contemplating the carcase and looking sadly after the disappearing train, said, "Buck, I glory in your spunk, but d—— your judgment." Mr. Gibbs reminded the meeting that the people of South Ontario had not heard Hon. George Brown, and as long ago as 1854 had rejected Mr. Abram Farewell, of

Whitby, and he quoted St. Luke, 16:29-31: "But Abraham saith: They have Moses and the prophets, let them hear them. And he said, Nay, father Abraham; but if one go to them from the dead they will repent. And he said unto him, if they hear not Moses and the prophets, neither will they be persuaded if one rise from the dead."

But they did hear him who rose from the dead, and Mr. Gibbs, with many another gallant man, fell on that cold 22nd of January, 1874. It was not long, however, before he recovered his kingdom. Mr. Cameron died in 1876, and in a memorable bye-election Mr. Gibbs defeated Mr. J. D. Edgar and returned to the House of Commons. I was among those who gathered in the telegraph office at Greenwood on the night of the general election of 1874, when the Mackenzie Government carried the country by an overwhelming majority. It was known at an early hour that all the Toronto seats had been taken by the Liberal party and until midnight victory followed victory. There was a faint cheer from the stricken Conservatives when it was announced that Sir John Macdonald had carried Kingston. The incident of the night which I chiefly remember was the picturesque declaration of a gloomy and profane Conservative when this news was received, that he hoped not another candidate of the party would be elected since "John A." alone would be a match for all the d—— Grits that could be crowded into the Parliament Buildings. It is curious now to recall the settled conviction among Liberals that Sir John Macdonald never could rise again. For the moment he was discredited, and almost dishonoured. There is reason to think that his removal from the position of Parliamentary leader was considered. But he had the patience, the wisdom and the resource to repair his broken fortunes. He had not wholly alienated the affection for himself which lay deep in the hearts of Conservatives, while among the stable elements of the country there was always a strong reserve of confidence in his prudence and patriotism. In Canadian history there is no other such illustration of the charm of a man, the resource of a politician and the camaraderie of human nature as the restoration of Sir John Macdonald affords.

In the summer of 1875 I drove alone from Greenwood to Markham, across twelve miles of country, to attend a Conservative demonstration. Since I had begun to think that I was a Liberal I was not inspired to make the journey by devotion to the Conservative party. But among the speakers announced were Dr. Charles Tupper and Hon. William McDougall, and I was anxious in those days to hear the political leaders of both parties. As I stood in the street at Markham and for the first time saw the leaders ride by in cabs, followed by marching men and bands of music, I have no doubt I felt as did Tom Sawyer at church when the minister told of the blessed day when the lion and the lamb should lie down together and a little child should lead them, and Tom said to himself that he wished he could be that child if it was a tame lion. I remember nothing of what was said that day by either Dr. Tupper or Mr. McDougall. I have no better recollection of what was said by Mr. T. N. Gibbs or Sir Matthew Crooks Cameron, the leader of the Conservative party in the Legislature, who were also among the speakers. Dr. Tupper had come from Nova Scotia to address the meeting, and I do remember *The Globe* said next day

28

that there was nothing surprising about the event, except that the "War-horse of Cumberland" should have come so far to say so little. These were the only political speeches that I ever heard from McDougall or Cameron, although a year or two afterward I heard Cameron, who had become Chief Justice of Ontario, charge the jury at Guelph in a famous trial for abduction. It was not the fortune of Sir Matthew Crooks Cameron, who was a high Tory, nor of his successor, Sir William Meredith, who was a progressive radical, to command a majority in the Legislature, but for private virtue and public integrity there are no more shining names in the political annals of Ontario.

The speech at Markham which made the chief impression upon my mind was that delivered by Hon. William McDougall. In his comparatively unfruitful career I have had a deep and enduring interest. His contemporaries agree that he was a speaker of singular charm and lucidity. He had distinction of style; he was clear, impressive and logical. Those who read his address before the Reform Convention at Toronto in 1867 must admit that he gave reasons for remaining in the Cabinet of Sir John Macdonald, after Confederation was accomplished, as convincing as the arguments which Hon. George Brown advanced to justify his own withdrawal. But in a convention hostile to Macdonald, embracing Liberals who at best gave a sullen sanction to the project of union, exulting over Brown's separation from Macdonald, eager to reunite all elements which had constituted the Liberal party before Brown entered the coalition, and submissive to the great personal authority which Brown exercised, it was, perhaps, inevitable that judgment should go against Mc-

Dougall. Still even if George Brown was right, Mc-
Dougall was not necessarily insincere nor guilty of any
deliberate betrayal of the Liberal party. Sir John
Macdonald himself admitted in Parliament that Brown
and McDougall were among the first advocates of the
incorporation of the Northwest Territories into the
Dominion. They were influential advocates of Confederation before Macdonald regarded the project as politically practicable, and there is ground for thinking that
Brown saw the light through the clearer vision of Mc-
Dougall. Much of the legislation of the Mackenzie
Government was foreshadowed in *The North American,* which McDougall edited before he and the paper
were absorbed by *The Globe.* George Brown said that
McDougall was indolent and unreliable; Edward
Blake said that he was unstable. But he was more of a
prophet than either, and like other prophets was not
greatly honoured in his own time and has had scant justice in history. Even if one feels that McDougall made
the bed upon which he rested so uneasily the notion per-
sists that there is quality unrecognized and honour withheld. It is the fate of the journalist, and McDougall
was pre-eminently a journalist, to praise Caesar and
feed Caesar and take the crumbs and the boards.

Forty years ago joint political meetings were common throughout Canada. I have understood that Hon.
Edward Blake, after he succeeded to the leadership of
the Liberal party, set himself against the custom. He
issued no edict, but the impression became general
among Liberals that he doubted if such meetings produced the best results. Even if he was right, one may
still envy the fathers who were less grievously afflicted
by the amenities of a higher civilization. I recall

"one crowded hour of glorious strife" in South Ontario. Upon the death of Hon. Malcolm Cameron, a bye-election became necessary. Hon. T. N. Gibbs, as I have said, was again the Conservative candidate, while Mr. J. D. Edgar, later to be Speaker of the House of Commons and to receive knighthood, was the choice of the Liberal Convention. In the throes of a severe commercial depression, the country was disposed to hold the Mackenzie Government responsible for the ordinances of Divine Providence. The Conservative party was moving towards the "National Policy," and all the conditions were favourable to the propagation of protectionist teaching. A Government upon the defensive is a Government in distress. The Opposition, under Sir John Macdonald, displayed singular resource and energy. There has been nothing in Canadian politics more effective than the "demonstrations" which the Conservative leaders organized throughout the country. They were continually on the platform, exploiting the "existing discontents," establishing or manufacturing "scandals," charging extravagance and maladministration, and producing unrest among the industrial and agricultural classes. "Reciprocity of trade, or reciprocity of tariffs," which was the Conservative watchword, made its appeal to the workers with low wages and scarcity of employment, to the farmers whose products were fetching low prices, to the manufacturers who were exposed to the destructive competition of American industries, and to the producers who were excluded by high duties from access to American markets. Whether or not the Government understood, the "Conservative reaction" was flowing strongly when Mr. Gibbs and Mr. Edgar appeared as the protagonists of the parties in South Ontario.

But I am not so much concerned with the issues which entered into the contest as with a joint meeting in Whitby, at which the speakers were Alexander Mackenzie and Dr. Tupper. As arranged, each spoke for an hour, while the Liberal Prime Minister, who spoke first, had fifteen minutes in which to answer the arguments of his opponent. On the night before the meeting at Whitby Dr. Tupper had met Hon. L. S. Huntington at Oshawa and achieved a signal triumph. Mr. Huntington had a face and head as classic as the model of a sculptor. His voice was melodious and resonant. He had a gracious dignity, the language of a scholar and the studied deliverance of an actor. Except Sir Wilfrid Laurier I have seen no finer or more impressive figure on a political platform in Canada. But Mr. Huntington's addresses were laboured and polished. He was as concerned for the form of the message as for the message itself. He was not supple in controversy. He was easy in smooth water, but troubled in the rapids. Over such an opponent, before an eager and excited meeting, the vehemence, confidence, daring and energy of Dr. Tupper were bound to prevail. Moreover, Conservatives never forgot that Mr. Huntington had secured the private letters which produced the "Pacific scandal," and they pursued the man with savage joy and merciless ferocity. How often in politics the author of an "exposure" dies, while the victim survives.

Many of those who saw Mr. Huntington overcome at Oshawa attended the meeting at Whitby. The Conservatives were happy and exultant, the Liberals depressed and anxious. But Mr. Macknzie had resource in debate such as few men of his time possessed. Sir Wilfrid Laurier has said that when he was "on his legs" he had no peer in the House of Commons. There was little or nothing of the finish of oratory in his speeches. There were few ornate or elegant sentences. There was no elaborate preparation or dependence upon memory for felicitous phrases or orderly sentences. His strength was in facts, simplicity of statement, and complete knowledge of the subject. Of stern aspect and without natural gaiety of spirit, he yet had a penetrating humour and was fertile in illustration and anecdote. If he was austere he was just, and seldom sour or intemperate. Mr. Mackenzie's first speech was a quiet, orderly, logical defence of the acts and policies of his Administration. There was frequent cheering, but the Prime Minister's statement did not lessen the desire to hear Dr. Tupper. Nor did Dr. Tupper face an audience in which there was a predominant feeling of personal or political hostility. He was well received and quickly won the favour of the meeting. In those days Dr. Tupper was in full physical vigour. He spoke with tremendous energy. His vocabulary of denunciation was equal even to his own conception of the ineptitude and depravity of his opponents. On this occasion he was— himself. He held the Government responsible for drought and blight, for excessive heat and extreme cold, for the blasted corn and the barren fig-tree. The Conservatives warmed by degrees into sympathy, jubilation and confidence. Long before he had finished the meeting seemed to have gone hopelessly against Mr. Mackenzie. But the Prime Minister had fifteen minutes for reply. As the last word fell from Dr. Tupper's lips he sprang to the front of the platform. He stood, stern and unsmiling, while the long cheering for the Conservative spokesman died away. Then with swift, impetuous

33

3

sentences he fell upon Dr. Tupper. He wasted not a word or a moment. He struck blow after blow with such direct force that the whole structure which Dr. Tupper had reared with such superb assurance and confidence seemed to fall column by column into ruin. I have heard many speeches since that day, but nothing so trenchant and destructive. Of what was said by either speaker I have little recollection. I know that Dr. Tupper was merry over the inconsistencies and "broken pledges" of the Government, and that Mr. Mackenzie met the accusations with the history of a measure that Dr. Tupper had fathered and abandoned. He was guilty, Mr. Mackenzie said, of "the horrible crime of infanticide." He had "not only slaughtered his own child, but trampled on the remains." I was young when Mr. Mackenzie and Dr. Tupper met at Whitby so long ago. To youth wonder and enthusiasm come easily. But, I repeat, that I have heard nothing since from any platform as powerful, destructive and overwhelming as Mr. Mackenzie's reply. Conservatives around me who never had and never would cast a vote for a Liberal candidate rose to their feet and cheered with delight over the performance. That I have seen once only. Recalling such a glorious encounter one regrets that joint political meetings have been abandoned.

> Dim is the rumour of a common fight,
> Where host meets host, and many names are sunk,
> But of a single combat fame speaks clear.

Once again I heard Mr. Mackenzie before the day of his strength had passed. I drove—again alone— from the home of my boyhood to Clinton to hear the Prime Minister, Hon. L. S. Huntington, Hon. Oliver

Mowat, and Hon. T. B. Pardee. Two things said at that meeting have lived in my memory. Mr. Huntington, then Postmaster-General, was defending Mr. Mackenzie's purchase of steel rails on what was thought to be a rising market, and out of which transaction the Conservatives developed a "scandal," when a voice from the audience asked with rough asperity, "What about the post-office?" Mr. Huntington retorted to the confusion of the heckler and the joy of the Liberals, "The post-office is an organization for the transmission of intelligence to men who can read and write. I don't suppose you can do either." Justifiable, perhaps, but the blow that wounds is best withheld. I remember also Mr. Mackenzie's grave warning, spoken so the elect would not be misled, that "the heart of the average Tory was deceitful above all thengs and desperately wecked." I knew Mr. Mackenzie well when his frame was wasted by disease, and a faltering tongue could seldom give expression to the strong and restless spirit which the eye revealed. But during the years that I was in the Press Gallery he did not utter half a dozen sentences in Parliament. There was pathos in his patient, faithful, enduring attendance upon debates in which he could not engage.

Mr. Mackenzie was attacked with unrelenting vigour and often with sheer malignity. Of all the charges urged against his Government not one will command the respect of posterity or would now receive serious consideration by any dispassionate judge or jury. No matter how confident he may have been in his own patriotism and integrity, the Prime Minister must have been deeply wounded by the tongue of slander that would not be still and the vindictive savagery of continuous attack. But the Mackenzie Government, like all other Governments in Canada, had greedy mercenaries hanging upon its skirts, bent upon pillage and crafty beyond the wit of man in devising means to get at the treasury by dubious contracts or skilful alienation of the public resources. In 1896 *The Globe* published a letter by Mr. Mackenzie, to Mr. Thomas Hodgins, master at Osgoode Hall, and Liberal member for West Elgin in the Ontario Legislature from 1871 to 1879, whose name, however, was not disclosed, which shows how sorely he was beset by the spoilsmen and how sternly he resisted their demands. "Friends (?) expect to be benefited by offices they are unfit for, by contracts they are not entitled to, by advances not earned. Enemies ally themselves with friends and push the friends to the front. Some attempt to storm the office. Some dig trenches at a distance and approach in regular siege form. I feel like the besieged lying on my arms night and day. I have offended at least twenty parliamentary friends by defence of the citadel. A weak minister here would ruin the party in a month and the country very soon."

Mr. Mackenzie did guard the treasury, but the struggle was unceasing and the strain beyond endurance. The fault of the Liberal party was voluble virtue. It actually believed that it was the "party of purity." All its organs and leaders pursued Sir John Macdonald as the arch-master of electoral corruption, but after 1874 twenty or thirty Liberal members who had cried to the gods against the "Pacific scandal" were unseated for improper practices. Men scoffed and forgot that the masses of the Liberal party were wholesome and sincere people and their leaders able and faithful public servants. But Mr. Mackenzie's letter reveals that in the Liberal party, as in the Conservative party, the forces of interest and plunder are never asleep and the records of the courts show conclusively that one party is as good or as bad as the other. It was not because the Liberal party was excessively virtuous that Canada had honest government from 1874 to 1878, but because its leader had the resolution and the courage to require honest administration by the public departments and frugality in the public expenditures.

For his resistance to protection Mr. Mackenzie gets more praise than he deserves. He was ready to raise the duties from seventeen and one-half to twenty per cent. So were Hon. George Brown and Sir Richard Cartwright and Hon. Edward Blake, and other leading Liberals of Ontario and Quebec. Principle does not concern itself with percentages. If Hon. A. G. Jones and the near-sighted, contumacious, anxious Liberal group from the Eastern Provinces, who were possessed by the delusion that they could not carry their constituencies if duties were increased, had not gone into revolt against Mr. Mackenzie he would have raised duties to twenty per cent., and once committed in Parliament and on the platform to the defence of higher customs taxation who can be certain that the Canadian Liberal party would not have become entrenched in the fortress of protection. There is reason to believe that if the Mackenzie Government had committed itself to higher duties the Conservative Opposition would have adhered to low tariff. The common story is that when Sir Richard Cartwright arose to deliver the budget speech of 1876 it was not known if he would declare for or against higher duties, while Tupper, who was to follow, knew only that he would not agree with Cartwright.

REMINISCENCES

In a speech at St. Mary's in 1893, Mr. D'Alton Mc-Carthy said: "There is no doubt in the world that we were out of power and by going in for the National Policy and taking the wind out of Mr. Mackenzie's sails we got into power. We became identified with the protection policy, but if Mr. Mackenzie had adopted the protective policy we should have been free-traders." Mr. W. F. Maclean, M.P., whose father was one of the most convincing writers of protectionist literature at this period, has said that Sir John Macdonald was "timid unto death of protection," and "had to be bullied into it, led into it, committed to it by others." Mr. Goldwin Smith declares that when he warned Sir John that "Protection would never do for Canada" he was assured, "You need not fear that I am going to get into that hole." One does not understand how Mr. Goldwin Smith could give any such warning, for he was opposing the Mackenzie Government, petting Hon. Edward Blake as the repressed believer in a more liberal commercial policy, and cultivating close personal and political relations with the Conservative leader. In a letter to *The Toronto News* in 1901 Mr. Nicholas Flood Davin said: "Now as regards Sir John Macdonald's opinion, he is on record quite early in his career on the side of protection. On the other hand, in 1876, I was in *The Mail* office talking to the late Mr. Charles Belford, who was then editor under Mr. Patteson, who was manager and editor-in-chief, when Sir John Macdonald entered and said: 'Belford, what do you mean by that article on protection? I'm not a protectionist.' Belford replied: 'It doesn't commit you or the paper. It is marked "communicated." But that policy is taking hold of the public mind, and that is the question on

which you will have to go to the country.' The policy
of protection was preached on platforms and advocated
in *The Mail* before Sir John Macdonald took it up
heartily. He had undoubtedly gone over to free trade
with the Disraelian Conservatives, and was fully aware
what a hold belief in it had taken of the public mind.
He, however, took to studying protectionists' books,
and when he began to advocate protection he brought
to bear on its popularization his fine power of illustration, sometimes homely, sometimes whimsical, always
effective. It is the good fortune of the leading statesmen to get credit not only for the work, but the idea,
whereas they are never the first to conceive the idea."

What Mr. Davin, Mr. Maclean and Mr. Mc-
Carthy have said Mr. T. C. Patteson, who was the
editor of *The Mail* during that period, often admitted
and emphasized. But if it was the fortune of Mr. Mackenzie to take the wrong turning, this was not so much
through devotion to low tariff as through submission to
a wing of the Liberal party which by high concern for
principle or through zeal to save itself gave the whole
position to the enemy. After 1896 the common injunction among Liberals was to remember "Mackenzie's
mistakes."

CHAPTER II

EARLY DAYS IN JOURNALISM

From boyhood I thought of journalism as the pursuit to which I would like to devote myself. I do not say profession, because journalism is not exactly a profession, nor exactly a trade, nor always a means of livelihood. In confidential intercourse with my companions I often declared, not in sheer vanity or arrogance, that I would be editor of *The Globe*. Behind the conviction there was more of instinct than of conceit. So far as I know I come of a stock of writers and preachers and publishers. But I have never been interested in the pursuit of ancestry. That is not because I have read Bret Harte's "First Family of Tasajara," nor because I have been deterred by the experience of the man who paid £500 to discover his ancestors and £1,000 to have the facts suppressed. Who was it that said the vital question is not where you came from, but where you are going, not what you inherited from the past, but what you leave to the future?

Still we are directed by forces that are in our "bones and blood." There are voices within us that call across great distances. In a second-hand bookshop in Birmingham I found a book more than 200 years old by John Willison, M.A., "Late minister of the Gospel at Dundee," entitled "The Balm of Gilead for Healing a Disfeafed Land." One scoffs, but what is the true mission of the journalist, whether one confesses it or not, but to find this "Balm of Gilead" for the humours and distresses of his time? If one does not possess the evangelical spirit, and strive to make the world cleaner and better, what profit hath he "of all his labour wherein he laboureth under the sun." There may be the flavour of cant in the suggestion, but I do believe that the true journalist is most happy in the prosecution of movements which assail abuses and diffuse social blessings. If he thought chiefly of wealth or position he would not plant his ladder upon any such unstable foundation. It may be that occasionally there is the clink of dollars between the sobbings for "the people." In the business office there may be "wicked partners." If it were not so possibly the sheriff would forever hover in the offing.

My first contribution to a newspaper appeared in *The Whitby Chronicle,* then edited by Mr. W. H. Higgins, who like so many of the craft found his final refuge in the civil service. This was a poem of dejected spirit and portentous solemnity. Never was there a sadder message for a gray world, ailing by heredity, evil by tendency, and vicious by instinct and practice. At the moment I was under the inspiration of Swinburne, and if my verses were not as mellifluous as the master's they were as evasive and mysterious. It was not my fault that those who read would not understand nor "return from iniquity." Fortunately the verses had no gift of life, and I am comforted by knowledge that the fyles of *The Chronicle* have not been preserved.

I also imposed verses of flagrant sentimentality upon *The London Daily Herald. The Herald* departed this life long ago, and it may be that my verses contributed to its demise. The first letter on any public question that I offered for publication appeared in 1876 in *The*

Guelph Mercury. The Dunkin Act, which was the
forerunner of the Scott Act, was submitted in Wellington county. There was a hard contest and ultimate
defeat for the prohibitory measure. On some phase of
the controversy I expressed a weighty opinion, and *The
Mercury* was hospitable. I forget whether I wrote
over my name or as "Total Abstinence," "Pioneer,"
"Ratepayer" or "Pro Bono Publico." Any one of these
would have carried more authority than my own signature.

Many excellent speakers appeared in Wellington
during that contest. Among these were Mr. E. King
Dodds, Mr. Joseph Gibson, Mr. James Fahey, and
Mr. Marvin Knowlton. The chief protagonists were
King Dodds and Gibson. Generally they met each
other at joint meetings. Mr. Gibson was a ready, eager
and versatile debater with style and method greatly in
contrast with those which Mr. King Dodds adopted.
The champion of the prohibitionists was fluent, direct,
sincere and eloquent without tinsel or tawdriness. King
Dodds was verbose and torrential. He was a master of
all the artifices of platform advocacy. Fertile in sympathy or indignation, as the occasion required, he often
produced striking, immediate effects. The fashion of
oratory which King Dodds affected is passing as the
cause for which he contended has gone down to defeat.
It is the fortune of Joseph Gibson, in a serene and honourable old age, to rejoice in the victory for which he
fought so long with unquenchable ardour and unfalter-
ing courage. I like to think that between Mr. Gibson
and Mr. King Dodds on the platform there was conflict without acerbity and contention without detraction. When I asked Mr. Gibson if this was so he said:

"Yes, E. King Dodds and myself were on the best of terms. I can see no reason why public men who differ about some public question should allow the difference to affect their personal relations." In the old days the joint meeting was often a school of courtesy and, if there was much raillery and banter, accuracy and moderation of statement were essential if any permanent effect was to be produced. If sometimes joint meetings were disorderly and turbulent we know that the later fashion does not always ensure quiet and decorum.

On the night before the polling in Wellington county a meeting in the City Hall of Guelph was announced by the prohibitionists. Mr. James Fahey appeared as the champion of the opposing forces. There is reason to think that Mr. Fahey had deliberately settled upon the course that he would pursue. Whether the dispute that arose before the meeting could be organized was over the selection of a chairman or the time to be allotted to the various speakers I do not recollect, but it is certain that the meeting never was organized nor any speech delivered. With consummate strategy Mr. Fahey made objection to every proposal that was submitted by the temperance party, excited furious controversies on the platform and in the audience, and finally created a pandemonium of confusion and disorder. Before the hall could be cleared many benches were broken. There were actual physical collisions between the disputants, defiance of the police, and all the happy manifestations of riotous free men in a sanguinary combat.

We forget James Fahey. He ran well for a season, but health failed and the road became dark at mid-day. So far as one can learn he joined the staff of *The Guelph*

Mercury in 1879, and a year later became editor of *The Herald*. He and Mr. A. W. Wright were among the speakers for Mr. James Goldie, the Conservative protectionist candidate in the bye-election of 1876, which became necessary when Mr. David Stirton was appointed post-master at Guelph. In the contest Mr. Donald Guthrie, whose son now represents South Wellington, was the Liberal candidate, and even the "National Policy" could not prevail against a man of such solid ability and skill in debate as Mr. Guthrie. In this contest Mr. Fahey established his reputation as a speaker even in comparison with Mr. A. W. Wright, and that is a test to which few men were equal. They were formidable antagonists even for Mr. Donald Guthrie. Why do we shut Wrights and Faheys out of Parliament? To have youth, intellect, gifts of tongue and a residuum of independence almost closes the gateway to the Canadian House of Commons. No young man ever enters the Senate, and no old man ever leaves it. How much we "democrats" have to learn from the old mother of free communities where despite class and caste talent is recognized, youth may serve, and independent thinking is not always culpable eccentricity.

On the platform Mr. Fahey was brilliant alike in defence and in attack. He had little personal magnetism. His delivery was rapid and unrelieved by oratorical artifices. But his language was chaste, felicitous and impressive by its beauty and simplicity. One is told of a lecture by Mr. Fahey, entitled "The Literary Club," in which he wandered with Edmund Burke, Samuel Johnson, Joshua Reynolds, Oliver Goldsmith, David Garrick and other figures in that glorious company of immortals, revealing their wisdom and their folly, their virtues and their failings, with sympathy and insight and in language not so inferior to that of the old English essayists. He had gone to school to the masters. In political controversy Fahey was merciless; on the platform he could be unscrupulous. But he was ever intrepid and never common-place.

From Guelph he went to *The Stratford Herald,* but in a few years his health became so unsatisfactory that he was ordered to California. In a letter from Mr. J. P. Downey, superintendent of the Hospital for Feeble-minded at Orillia, who was among Mr. Fahey's successors on *The Guelph Herald,* and is himself an attractive and effective public speaker, it is said: "Fahey knew what it was to work hard for his wages and work harder to get them when they were earned. I think some of the wage cheques issued at that time by *The Guelph Herald* are still in circulation." But this condition of financial uncertainty was not peculiar to *The Herald* forty or fifty years ago, nor even in these days are newspapers always immune from the anxieties and vicissitudes which follow upon an empty treasury. There is a legend that once when Edward Farrer, George Gregg and Alex. Pirie were engaged upon a publication which suffered from a perennial shortage of the medium of exchange they loaded the safe upon a dray, drove to a pawnshop and secured enough cash from the dubious dealer in pledges to meet the unreasonable demands of printers who thought they should receive actual money for their labour.

For a time, towards the end, Mr. Fahey was on the editorial staff of *The Toronto World.* We were comrades in the Press Gallery of the old Legislative Buildings on Front Street, but the flame of his genius was not

45

burning with its early splendour. He was indifferent, not sour, listless, often weary. Among Canadian journalists we have had good paragraphers, but they have not been numerous. Few have had the quality which gives distinction to many American newspapers. We seem to labour over our humour. We seem to feel that if the blow is not struck with a club it will be taken for a caress. In the United States the editorial paragraphers are many and they are keen, incisive, stimulating, irreverent and delightful. In their work we have a key to the strength, sanity and audacity of the American character. It is curious, however, that of all the humourists of the new world only Haliburton in Sam Slick, Lowell in Hosea Bigelow, and Clemens as Mark Twain survive. And Haliburton was a Nova Scotian. Indeed, a Nova Scotian was the father of American humour. Petroleum V. Nasby, who so often brought healing to the soul of Lincoln, Mrs. Partington and Ike, Josh Billings, Artemus Ward, Bob Burdette and Bill Nye become shadowy memories. Lowell was a teacher as well as a humourist. Clemens was a fine craftsman and without humour would have had distinction among writers of English in America. Haliburton blazed the trail in which so many have sought fame and bread. The paragrapher must have humour. He cannot have immortality. But he contributes richly to the gladness of mankind. He gives the real impress of nativity to American journalism. The best paragrapher of his time in Canada was James Fahey. Nor can I think that he has any successor of equal polish and pungency. It is a pity that we have no memorial of Fahey. Nor, so far as I know, has any of his work been preserved. It is true that he wrote for the day only, but he said things that should not have perished.

Among other leaders of the Temperance movement whom it was my fortune to hear in the seventies were Mr. George W. Ross and Mr. Edward Carswell, of Oshawa. Of Mr. Ross there will be much to say later. Mr. Carswell I heard often in South Ontario from political and temperance platforms. In the press notices he was "the Canadian Gough." As one who heard John B. Gough I can testify that Mr. Carswell was not greatly his inferior in mimicry and anecdote, in moving appeal and homely argument. His hair was long and luxuriant, almost falling upon his shoulders, he was of commanding stature and altogether a picturesque figure. Once at a meeting in Whitby he was interrupted by the natural question, "Have you a barber in Oshawa?" The retort was instantaneous, "Yes, and we have a barbarian in the audience." The first time I heard Mr. George W. Ross was in 1875 at a meeting of the Grand Lodge of Good Templars at Guelph. He came as a fraternal delegate from the Sons of Temperance. The hotels were crowded and it had not been easy for Mr. Ross to secure accommodation. He had been married only a few days before and when he was introduced to Grand Lodge it was explained that he might have written that he had married a wife and therefore could not come, but since he had come they had done him all the honour possible under the circumstances; they had let him sleep with the Grand Chaplain. In reply Mr. Ross was flippant if not audacious in his references to the Grand Chaplain, and grimly but slyly humorous over the method adopted to atone for the separation from his wife and relieve the pressure on hotel accommodation. But he was seldom unready and never unhappy. Among the chief

causes of his successes on the platform were those flashes
of candour which were as much defiance as confession,
and which so provoked audiences to levity that they
could not pronounce judgment with sober faces. A
striking figure at this Grand Lodge meeting was Dr.
Oronhyatekha, who had not yet set his hand to the task
to which so much of his life was devoted. A discussion
arose as to whether or not prohibitionists in Federal
and Provincial elections should ignore all other considerations and support only candidates who were ab-
stainers and advocates of prohibitory legislation. De-
fining his own position Dr. Oronhyatekha explained
with severe gravity that when he had last voted he had
to choose between a sober Grit and a drunken Conservative, and that after anxious and mature consideration
he had given the Grit the benefit of the doubt.

Mr. Alex. Pirie, whom I have mentioned, had his
training on *The Guelph Herald,* while Mr. John R.
Robinson, his successor as editor of *The Toronto Evening Telegram,* began his career on *The Guelph Mercury.* Guelph seems to have been a school of journalism
as Brantford was a school of oratory. In 1887 Mr.
Pirie succeeded Mr. John C. Dent as editor of *The
Telegram.* For ten years he gave a pleasant humour
and a distinct individuality to its editoral columns. If
he was seldom aggressive he was adroit in controversy,
supple in defence and persuasive in argument. During
the parliamentary session of 1888 he represented *The
Montreal Star* in the Press Gallery at Ottawa. In 1890
he acquired *The Dundas Banner.* Gay, insouciant,
effervescent, irrepressible, Mr. Pirie was a stimulating
companion and a delightful after-dinner speaker. He
was often venturesome and occasionally audacious. I

would not say, as Bagehot said falsely of so great a man as Disraeli, that "his chaff was delicious but his wheat was poor stuff." His wheat was often the good seed of sound counsel, but his more serious performances were affected by his reputation as an entertainer. When Mr. James Johnson, of *The Ottawa Citizen,* was elected president of the Press Gallery, Mr. Pirie seized a pad of copy paper from the desk where Mr. Johnson was sitting, and giving the impression that Johnson had prepared an address for the occasion read several pages of extravagant gratitude for his election and absurd exaltation of the office to which he had been elected. It was done with becoming gravity and the sentences were so rounded and followed each other in such orderly sequence that it was not easy to believe he was fabricating every word as he proceeded. I have known few men who could equal Mr. Pirie at this sort of fooling.

In order that Mr. Johnson could attend the funeral of Hon. Thomas White at Montreal, Mr. Pirie, at this time his colleague in the Press Gallery, agreed to supply editorials for *The Citizen* during his absence. There never was a man with less hair on his head than James Johnson, and this suggested a subject to Pirie. He contributed an editorial on baldheads, and a paragraph on "Porridge as a Food." "Statistics," he said, "show that baldness is spreading in all civilized countries, and some of the distinguished scientists, who put their spectacles on their noses and look into these interesting subjects, assert that the time will inevitably come when the whole race will be baldheaded. This is not a pleasing outlook. 'Bald as a billiard-ball' has become a familiar simile by which people describe a baldheaded person. But who can look with equanimity to the coming of the time when people will be so bald that nothing but their ears will prevent their hats from slipping down upon their necks? Brain-workers grow bald at an early stage of their existence. This should teach us to reverence and respect bald-headed members of the community rather than to jeer at them and make them feel uncomfortable, as it is too much the custom of modern society to do. Some of the most profound thinkers the world has produced have been deficient in capillary adornment, and civilization has lost nothing in consequence. But taking a merely picturesque view of the case, it is a matter of regret that the tendency of the race to baldness should be as marked as it undeniably is." As to porridge, Mr. Pirie said: "The circumstance that the oatmeal mills of the country can, if worked to their full capacity, produce more oatmeal than is required for the porridge of the people is adopted by the Reform organs as an argument for Unrestricted Reciprocity. How the admission free of duty of cottons, woollens and other American manufactures can promote the consumption of porridge it is impossible to explain, except on the assumption that under the trade system the people will be reduced to an oatmeal diet. 'Much, of course, can be done with a little oatmeal'; but porridge is liable to become tiresome even to the sons of Scotland, if served up morning, noon and night."

While Mr. James Dickinson, for a time night editor of *The Globe,* and afterwards connected with weekly journals at Fort William and Windsor, was speaking at a meeting of the Canadian Press Association, Mr. Pirie intervened with a humorous observation. To the general surprise Mr. Dickinson intimated somewhat angrily that he did not want to be interrupted. Mr. Pirie arose and with infinite meekness declared that he would never speak to Mr. Dickinson again. Dickinson joined in the laughter. At a public dinner Mr. Pirie said that if he should print in *The Dundas Banner* such stuff as I allowed to appear in *The Globe* he would lose one if not both of his subscribers. Speaking at a dinner of the Canadian Press Association at which Sir Oliver Mowat was the guest of honour, Mr. Pirie explained that his contemporary at Dundas, which supported the Conservative Government at Ottawa, boasted that it got more public printing than his newspaper, which supported the Liberal Government at Toronto, and turning to the Premier with hand upraised and voice attuned between pleading and indignation he said: "I ask my honoured leader here and now to put me in a position to hurl back that slander." When Sir John Carling was Minister of Agriculture the members of the Press Gallery visited the Experimental Farm near Ottawa. At that time so many counties had adopted the Scott Act that prohibition prevailed over the greater portion of Ontario. At luncheon Mr. Pirie, proposing the health of the Minister, suggested that he should develop a grade of shorthorns for Scott Act counties. But Mr. Pirie was more than a jester. He had qualities of heart and mind which were seldom revealed and only to those who had his affection and confidence. These were few, for beneath apparent openness and spontaneity there was a reserve which was not easily penetrated. He got much out of life, but not all that he deserved nor all that he desired. Happy but often anxious and foreboding, aspiring but not

fully achieving, when I think of Pirie I recall what was
said of Shelley: "He passed through life like a strange
bird upon a great journey, singing always of the para-
dise to which he was travelling, and suddenly lost from
the sight of men in the midst of his song."

· I knew Mr. R. W. Phipps, one of the pamphleteers
of the protectionist movement, and the first Provincial
Superintendent of Forestry. He was a graceful and
exact writer and a very confident controversialist. His
confidence was not offensive, but he did sometimes seem
to suggest that "the creature was made subject to vanity." It is said he was profoundly persuaded that he
should have been taken into the first Conservative Protectionist Government. There is a story that he once
confided to Mr. Nicholas Flood Davin that he had
qualifications to govern Canada at least equal to any
that Sir John Macdonald possessed. Mr. Davin
agreed. "Phipps," he said, "if you had a secretary you
could govern the universe."

In the spring of 1880 I was in Toronto with empty
pockets and uncertain employment. Greatly daring,
I wrote a letter to Mr. J. Gordon Brown, of *The Globe,*
enclosing cuttings of my contributions to various weekly
publications and urging my desire to join the staff of a
daily newspaper. The answer came next morning: "I
believe you can do newspaper work. Come and see me.
I think good will come of it." I ask myself if any other
letter that I have received gave me greater pleasure or
cast such radiance upon the future. But there was to be
no immediate result. I saw Mr. Brown a few hours
later. He was courteous and considerate, sympathetic
and interested. But I was told that there was no
vacancy on the staff at the moment and that I must wait

until a vacancy should occur. He assured me that I
would be remembered, but suggested that I should not
be discouraged by delay nor hesitate to apply again.
The gloom of that night wholly eclipsed the radiance
of the morning. But I had done my best and there was
a promise.

Three or four months afterwards I wrote again to
Mr. Brown and again was asked to call at *The Globe*
office. This time Mr. Brown gave me a note to the city
editor with the definite instruction that I should go on
the staff of reporters. But the raw youth from the
country was rejected. The rejection was curiously em-
phatic and determined. Of Mr. Brown's good faith I
never have had any doubt, and I have always thought
his word should have prevailed. But the city editor, if
not discourteous, was coldly unsympathetic. It may
be that I made an unfavourable personal impression,
or that, as so often happens, the staff was encumbered
with juniors, who, whatever their natural adaptability
to newspaper work, sorely tax the patience and vigilance of city editors until actual experience is acquired.
At any rate the city editor was adamant. He insisted
that there was no vacancy, that Mr. Brown did not
understand, and that I must accept rejection without
appeal. But, standing firmly upon Mr. Brown's order,
I would not be repulsed. Finally the city editor descended to the floor below where the chief editor's
offices were situated in the old King Street building,
and returned with the message that I could not be
accepted. Against this decision I made a vain appeal.
Mr. Brown explained that the city editor was unwilling
to put me on the staff, that he was assured no more
reporters were needed, and that I would enter into an

unsympathetic atmosphere if under such circumstances he forced me upon an unwilling subordinate. I had no alternative but to submit, although I did not doubt that I could establish myself in the city editor's confidence if he would give me the foothold which I was so eager to secure.

In later years I often saw Mr. Gordon Brown in the streets of Toronto, but I never had opportunity to speak to him again. Sometimes I regret that I did not seek the opportunity, for he was gracious and considerate to a young man who had no credentials, no influential connections and little beyond his confidence in himself to excuse his persistence or justify the attention which he received. I came to know many journalists who were on the staff of *The Globe* under Gordon Brown and never one but spoke of him with regard and respect, never one who doubted his qualifications for the position which he held, never one but regretted that *The Globe* should have passed out of the hands of the Browns and a tradition broken in which there was so much of honour and dignity, of effort and achievement. What the Walters were to *The Times* the Browns were to *The Globe,* and to reverence these ancient dynasties is not to suggest that the great journals which they founded are less influential under their successors or less stable pillars of the commonwealth.

Ten years after my second failure to secure a place on *The Globe,* by decree of the Imp of Destiny, I had the chair in which Mr. Gordon Brown sat during our two interviews. Stranger is the fact that the city editor who defeated my aspirations ten years before applied to me for a position on the paper after I had become its editor. He had not passed out of my memory, although

I had never cherished any resentment. It was clear, however, that he did not recognize me nor was there any reason that he should. What had been of moment to me was to him only an incident in the day's work. We had passed each other often on the street as strangers. When he came to the office I did not reveal the fact that we had met before. If at the time I could have considered his application favourably I should have disclosed the circumstances of our previous meeting. But since I could not there was nothing to do but maintain silence. He did not renew the application, nor did he re-enter journalism. We ceased to be strangers, however, and if he reads this chapter he may remember and we will come together if only to lament the ruthless extension of the dry area which debars descendants of Scotsmen from any full expression of neighbourly feeling.

Failing with *The Globe,* I turned to *The London Advertiser.* I wrote a frank letter to Mr. John Cameron stating my circumstances and declaring my determination to enter journalism. In the meantime I had done some editorial writing for *The Tiverton Watchman* and *The Kincardine Reporter.* A few of these powerful utterances I submitted for Mr. Cameron's edification and instruction. No one, I am certain, ever spoke with greater authority than I did in the editorial pages of *The Watchman* and *The Reporter,* but in reply Mr. Cameron repressed his admiration to a degree that was surprising, if not disturbing. I must have sought advice as to the qualifications necessary for reporting and how best to secure connection with a daily newspaper. Mr. Cameron was explicit and epigrammatic. He wrote that when the statesmen at Washington were re-estab-

lishing the finances after the Civil War, Horace
Greeley declared that the best way to resume specie pay-
ments was to resume. The implication was that the
best way to begin newspaper work was to begin. He
added that it was desirable to learn typesetting and to
have experience in proofreading. When I pressed for
more definite information and for a position on *The
Advertiser,* Mr. Cameron in another letter offered me
$3.00 a week for the first year and $4.00 a week for the
second on condition that I would learn to set type and
be content with an occasional opportunity to do reporting. The offer held no immediate prospect of afflu-
ence and since I was twenty-five years of age was not
alluring. After long hesitation, however, I accepted.
I am not certain that I would have done so if I had
known that I would be required to sign a contract. But
when I reached London in October, 1881, Mr. Cameron produced an agreement in the exact language of
his proposal and I signed with reluctance and a reservation. I had no thought that I would fulfil the contract,
although I did not contemplate any deliberate or dishonourable repudiation. I reasoned that if I had any
natural talent for journalism I would soon be released
from typesetting, while if I had not Mr. Cameron
would not try to keep me at wages on which I could
not exist. I had saved nothing and had to depend altogether upon my weekly earnings. Once Hon. A. S.
Hardy and I were comparing early experiences, not in
any spirit of self-commiseration or with any thought
that we had suffered as other men had not, and I told
him that for three months in London I had drawn only
$3.00 a week and paid $2.75 for board and lodging. He
threw his head back and with a shout of laughter said,

EARLY DAYS IN JOURNALISM

"What in h—— did you do with the other quarter?"

For three weeks I stood at "the case" with submission but not with enthusiasm. For my position was that of an apprentice with the wages of an apprentice. Day by day I handed Mr. Cameron notes and paragraphs on local and general subjects. Sometimes they were printed; more often they were not. At the end of three weeks I was asked to report a lecture by Hon. S. H. Blake before the Young Men's Christian Association. That was my first actual assignment, and I rejoiced in the opportunity. In the morning, for then as now *The Advertiser* had morning and evening editions, my report appeared very much as it was written. On the next afternoon I was called from "the case" to report a lecture delivered in one of the churches by an American temperance orator whose name I do not recall. A few days afterwards I was asked by Mr. L. K. Cameron, then city editor of *The Advertiser,* and later King's Printer for Ontario, if I would be willing to set type only in the afternoons and in the forenoons "cover" London East, where a system of county police bureaux and the oil refineries were the chief sources of news. Two or three weeks afterwards my career as a printer terminated. I was made proofreader for the evening edition, and a regular reporter for the morning edition. There was an incipient rebellion in the composing-room over the eccentricities of the apprentice's proofreading, but the revolt was not general nor very acute. I knew nothing about proofreading and for a few weeks the printers had a legitimate grievance.

Once before I had set out to be a printer, not so much from choice as from necessity. As a boy I worked for two weeks in the office of *The Exeter Times.* But I did not like typesetting, while for the hand press I had even less affection. So one day I was reported "missing." When I was editor of *The Globe* Mr. W. J. White, Inspector of Immigration Agencies, called at the office. He was good enough to say that he had desired to make my acquaintance. "But," I said, "we have met before." He was positive that we had not. I asked him if he could remember a boy who entered his father's office at Exeter to learn printing but left, by the light of the moon, without notice. He could remember and declared he had often wondered what had become of him. "I know," I said; "I am the boy."

At the end of three months, as I had intended, I approached Mr. Cameron for a revision of the contract under which I had entered the office. I argued that I had been withdrawn from typesetting, which in itself was a violation of the agreement, for which I was not solely responsible, and that I must have better wages or be released. The immediate result was an advance from $3.00 to $6.00 a week. Two months later there was a further advance to $8.00, and by the end of the year I drew $10.00 or $12.00 in the weekly envelopes. For nearly two years I was a reporter on *The Advertiser*. There was nothing remarkable in my experiences. Once I was assigned to describe the live stock at the Fair, which was the great autumn festival of western Ontario. I wrote something about a pair of horses shown by a farmer from Biddulph which so pleased him that when we met next day he offered me a quarter. At a meeting of the city council an official who was somewhat active in the Conservative ward associations was made the object of a savage and I thought unjust attack. *The Advertiser* was as strongly Liberal as *The*

Free Press was Conservative and neither had mercy for opponents. But I induced *The Advertiser* to publish a defence of the Conservative official, for which he was grateful. He came to see me at the office and when he had gone I found a $5.00 bill on my desk. I have often said that I returned the quarter with indignation and the $5.00 with reluctance. The fact is that I did not misunderstand nor think my dignity grievously affronted by either incident.

In those days reporters of *The Advertiser* were not admitted to Conservative conventions, nor reporters of *The Free Press* to Liberal conventions. I was sent out to a meeting of the West Middlesex Conservative Association at Mount Brydges. As instructed, I was to "nose" among the delegates and extract information by guile and strategy. But just before the meeting opened I passed into the hall with the delegates and took my seat at the reporters' table. I was "named" within a few minutes and asked to withdraw. Mr. Alexander Johnston, of Strathroy, who was returned to the Legislature for West Middlesex in 1883, arose and suggested that no such extreme action was necessary. He argued that the convention would do nothing of which it was ashamed, and that I would probably give a fair report if I was allowed to remain. The convention agreed, I remained, and at a convention at Napier a few months later which nominated Mr. Nathaniel Currie for the House of Commons I received a vote of thanks for my "fair report" of the meeting at Mount Brydges. In all newspapers occur grievous typographical errors and mistakes and blunders in "make-up." In *The Advertiser,* while I was on the staff, we had a daily column of "Labour Notes." By unhappy accident or evil design a despatch about the birth of triplets in Mitchell appeared under that heading. There was a somewhat similar blunder in *The Ottawa Citizen* thirty years ago. The wife of a young curate gave birth to a baby and by an unfortunate transposition a line from a legal advertisement appeared at the bottom of the birth notice: "By his solicitors—and—"

If in these last few pages there is a word or a sentence that seems to reflect upon Mr. John Cameron or *The Advertiser* I have expressed myself badly. No man ever had a truer friend than I had in Mr. Cameron, relations more pleasant than I enjoyed in *The Advertiser* office or associations more lasting or more dearly cherished than those which I formed in London.

CHAPTER III

Mr. John Cameron and the Blake Wing

For half a century *The Advertiser* and *The Free Press* of London have been influential throughout Western Ontario. Neither has been over-shadowed by the newspapers of Toronto nor submissive to their authority. Mr. Josiah Blackburn, for many years editor of *The Free Press,* was a distinguished figure in Canadian journalism. He gave *The Free Press* an authority which it has retained. Although a devoted Conservative, his conception of the relation of an editor to the party leaders was that of Mr. Goldwin Smith: "A sort of literary statesman guiding his paper according to his own opinions, though in concert with his political party." No doubt like all political journalists Mr. Blackburn had occasionally to submit to the authority of the party caucus, and unfortunately for the journalist the world looks on as he turns the corner. There is a tradition in London that it was Mr. Blackburn who said when he was required by the action of the party leaders to bless where he had cursed that "it was a d— sharp curve, but he could take it." Investigation, however, has disclosed that Mr. Blackburn has no title to the gratitude of posterity for this expressive and picturesque confession of self-confidence and party fealty. In a history of the Canadian Press Association by Dr. A. H. U. Colquhoun, it is declared that the author of the telegram erroneously attributed to Mr. Blackburn was Mr. Robert Smiley of *The Hamilton Spectator.* "In 1854 *The Spectator* was attacking Hon. Robert

61

Spence, who sat for North Wentworth as a Reformer. When the Coalition was formed Spence became a colleague of John A. Macdonald, who promptly pleaded with Smiley to cease firing at a man who would next day be his associate, and Mr. Smiley wired back, 'It's a d—— sharp curve, but I think we can take it.' And he took it, thereby contributing vastly to the gaiety of nations." This rests upon the word of Mr. H. F. Gardiner, for many years editor of *The Hamilton Times,* to which he gave much distinction and authority. In 1879 Mr. Gardiner met Sir John Macdonald at the railway station in Hamilton and in conversation the Conservative leader admitted that he had telegraphed from Quebec to Mr. Smiley urging merciful treatment of Spence, and in reply had received the famous message. Mr. Gardiner reminds me that in 1854 the Great Western Railway was under construction. Hence "sharp curve" was a common expression among the people of the district.

There is, however, a reason why the phrase which should have made Mr. Smiley famous was ascribed to Mr. Blackburn. *The London Free Press* was reluctant to follow the Conservative leaders into the advocacy of Protection. In 1876 Hon. Thomas White made a Protectionist speech at London. *The Free Press* contested his teaching, but when the party became fully and irretrievably committed to Protection, Mr. Blackburn submitted. He made the curve with such gallantry and discretion that not a wheel left the track. It could not be said of Mr. Blackburn as has been said of Mr. John Redmond when he committed Nationalist Ireland, with moving fervour and eloquence, to unity with England in the Great War that he "took the curve too sharply and did not carry the train with him."

MR. CAMERON AND THE BLAKE WING

Among living journalists in Canada no man has had a fuller or richer experience than Mr. Gardiner. He learned to set type in the office of *The Canada Christian Advocate* of Hamilton, of which his father was editor. In 1871 he was reporter and night editor on *The Hamilton Standard,* directed by Mr. Jonathan Wilkinson, who afterwards published *The St. Thomas Times,* and whose descendants have followed his calling with like distinction. In 1872 Mr. Gardiner joined the staff of *The Hamilton Times,* controlled by Mr. C. E. Stewart, who also published *The Weekly Expositor* at Brantford. In the famous contest between Sir Francis Hincks and Mr. William Paterson for the representation of South Brant in the House of Commons Mr. Gardiner assisted in producing a tri-weekly campaign sheet in support of the successful Liberal candidate. In the spring of 1873 Mr. Gardiner was again in Brantford as chief press counsel for Mr. A. S. Hardy, who succeeded Hon. E. B. Wood in the Legislature. He was the first editor of *The Daily Expositor,* but when Mr. Stewart died in 1874 he was recalled from Brantford and sent to Ottawa to represent *The Hamilton Times* in the Press Gallery during the first session of Parliament under the Mackenzie Government. The only survivors of that Gallery are Mr. Gardiner and Hon. C. H. Mackintosh. Thirty-five or forty years ago Mr. Mackintosh was among the most dashing and intrepid controversialists of the Conservative party. For a time he edited *The Strathroy Despatch,* and had a passing connection with other journals in Western Ontario. From a youth he was active on the platform, vigorous in attack and fertile in political expedients. In 1874 he acquired *The Ottawa Citizen,* which under his direction was distinguished for its destructive criticism of the Mackenzie Government, its devotion to Sir John Macdonald and its eager espousal of the National Policy. For many years he was influential in Conservative councils, in the confidence of the leaders, a pathfinder in strategy and policy. For two years he was Mayor of Ottawa and for two Parliaments represented the Capital. Appointed Lieutenant-Governor of the Northwest Territories in 1893, he passed out of Government House five years later, still alert and vigorous, and still deeply concerned in the greater issues of national policy, but since, although his pen has often been busy, he has not been in the forefront of the battle. A picturesque figure with much daring and courage, Mr. Mackintosh was more influential in the public life of the country than has ever been disclosed and gave to the Conservative party services of value far greater than any recognition he has received.

But to return to Mr. Gardiner. In October, 1874, he became assistant editor of *The London Advertiser* under Mr. John Cameron. Returning to Hamilton in March, 1877, for three and a half years he was managing editor of *The Spectator*. From October, 1880, until July, 1903, he was editor of *The Times,* greatly impressing upon that journal his own vigorous personality and faithfully proclaiming an economic gospel which began with Low Tariff and Economy and ended where it began. Mr. Gardiner was a journalist before he was a politician; he was a teacher rather than a partisan. He loved to stroke the back of the under dog. He had little reverence for authority. In political controversy he was not obedient to the maxims of prudence, nor was he ever proficient in the language of comprom-

ise. If in the hour of battle he could fight well for the
candidates of the Liberal party, between elections he
was unmanageable. But he was not capricious or un-
trustworthy, nor was he unamenable to discipline save
when decent loyalty to his own convictions forbade
trimming or faltering. After thirteen years of service
as superintendent of the School for the Blind at Brantford, he has come back to Hamilton, to live among his
friends and his books, happy in old associations, surrounded with affection and respect, fresh and strong in
mind and body. There may he still have many years of
rest and peace and much of sunshine.

For twenty-five or thirty years the chief occupation
of *The London Advertiser* was to attack, and the chief
business of *The Free Press* to defend Sir John Carling.
It was all very trivial and very futile. Those old volumes reveal symptoms of madness such as still appear
in municipal contests in Toronto. No doubt there was
corruption in elections in London, but no one would
now suggest that Sir John Carling deserved all the vitu-
peration and violence to which he was subjected. Nor
would they suggest that his assailants were encased in
any panoply of virtue. Carling's chief offence was that
he was usually successful, and what title has a candidate
who will not be defeated to courtesy or justice or compassion. He was a placid, wholesome, honourable gentleman who would have been esteemed and beloved
even by those who hunted him with so much ardour
and malignity if he had kept out of politics. Even as
it was, he was trusted and respected in no ordinary degree. If not a great man, he gave the country service
of sound quality throughout a long public career. Once,
no doubt, he held the seat for London in the House of

Commons by a dubious title. There was technical justice in the judicial decision by which he profited, and
perhaps it is difficult to determine the moral validity
of a legal technicality or what latitude judges may exercise in interpreting the letter of the law instead of the
spirit. It is said that once in Council Sir John Macdonald looked long at his colleague from London and
at length remarked, "I wonder, Carling, if God ever
made a man as honest as you look." It may be that he
was not as honest as he looked, but he was honest enough
for Christian communion, reverential burial and kindly
remembrance. The press never killed a public man
who deserved to live. If this were not so Hon. George
Brown never would have reached middle life and Sir
John Macdonald would have died in infancy. I think
sometimes that if journalists would periodically examine the old files of their newspapers there would be far
more of charity and justice in political controversy.

It is doubtful, however, if any newspaper in Canada
has a more honourable history than *The Free Press* or
has been a more effective ally of the Conservative leaders. So *The Advertiser* has been a staunch champion
of the Liberal party in London and the western counties. At times wayward, it was ever valiant in the day
of battle. Like its Conservative contemporary, *The
Advertiser* has had individual flavour and distinction.
Founded by Mr. John Cameron in 1863, until 1883 it
was as much the expression of his personality as was
The Globe of the robust courage and flaming spirit of
George Brown. Associated with Mr. John Cameron
in the conduct of *The Advertiser* were three of his
brothers, of whom only one is living. Less resolute
than Mr. Brown and more distrustful of himself, Mr.

Cameron was more tractable and more submissive to authority. But it would be unjust to suggest that he had no settled opinions or was yielding when his cherished convictions were challenged. He was a prohibitionist by example long before we all became prohibitionists by compulsion. Until he withdrew from the active direction of *The Advertiser* to become editor of *The Globe,* liquor advertising was not admitted to its columns. Forty years ago when there was no such volume of advertising as newspapers now carry this involved a serious sacrifice. Nor was there much popular sympathy for what was regarded as pharisaical pretension and commercial imbecility. Two or three months after Mr. Cameron relinquished his personal control over *The Advertiser* I was detailed to write a sympathetic account of the Carling brewery. Just why I was assigned to that particular duty I have never understood. There were other members of the staff who could have pronounced a more seasoned judgment upon the quality of the product. But I had an amiable conversation with Sir John Carling and thereafter *The Advertiser* gave Carling's ale the benefit of its circulation. Mr. Cameron was favourable to woman suffrage when advocacy of the political equality of women was regarded as a feminine eccentricity. He was religious, but he hated heresy hunting and narrow denominationalism. He was loyal to British connection, but doubted the permanence of the colonial relation unless equality of citizenship throughout the Empire could be established. Restless under the domination of *The Globe,* he naturally drifted into relations with that element of the Liberal party which chafed under George Brown's ascendency.

George Brown was not jealous of equals nor contemptuous of inferiors, but he was a natural Dictator and was intolerant of carping and disaffection within the Liberal party. Those who were contumacious he would flog into submission or drive into the wilderness. If there never was an open quarrel between George Brown and Edward Blake it is certain that Mr. Blake sometimes resented the dictation of *The Globe* and its masters. Thus there were two forces, if not two factions, in the Liberal party until Mr. Blake became the Federal leader. It may be that the responsibility for this division lies upon Mr. Blake rather than upon *The Globe,* for he had the zealous and faithful support of the Liberal organ while he was Prime Minister of Ontario. I have been told by Mr. William Houston, M.A., who was on the staff of *The Globe* as far back as 1872, that George Brown exercised all his power of persuasion to get Mr. Blake to enter public life. It was the judgment of the Liberal Dictator, who was as just as he was downright, that Mr. Blake had no intellectual equal in Canada, while among British statesmen he ranked only below Gladstone and perhaps Lord John Russell. This estimate was not accepted by his brother, nor perhaps will we all agree with George Brown that Lord Palmerston was inferior to Russell in capacity and genius for government. But while Mr. Mackenzie was leader of the Liberal party, Mr. Blake was an uneasy and uncertain ally. Between the two there was constant friction and misunderstanding. If they had personal relations they were frigid and reluctant. When Mr. Mackenzie died I was sent to ask Mr. Blake if he would be a pallbearer at the funeral. He acquiesced but hesitated. There came into his face a look of memories that were not pleasant. As I turned to go he murmured, "How I was misunderstood." Whether there was discord or music in Mr. Blake's memories among Mr. Mackenzie's adherents there was a rooted conviction that Blake had not been generous or chivalrous in his treatment of the head of the Government or of the Government itself towards which his relation was so capricious and uncertain.

The truth is that Mr. Blake could lead, but he could not follow. There is reason to believe that he could have succeeded to the leadership of the Federal Liberal party upon his resignation of office in Ontario if he had permitted the Parliamentary caucus to choose between Mr. Mackenzie and himself. One reads much into a letter which Mr. Mackenzie wrote shortly before his Government was defeated: "From the first I was more willing to serve than to reign, and would even now be gladly relieved from a position, the toils of which no man can appreciate who has not had the experience. I pressed Mr. Blake in November, 1874, to take the lead, and last winter I again urged him to do so, and this summer I offered to go out altogether, or serve under him as he might deem best in the general interest." But Mr. Blake persuaded himself or deluded himself into the notion that he did not want to be leader. He was not frank with his associates nor frank with himself. He was more ambitious than Mr. Mackenzie, but his ardent and honourable craving for place and power was poorly concealed beneath an affected pretentious indifference. He was sensitive to every wind of criticism, blow it ever so softly. He was so mortally afraid he would be misunderstood that he never fully understood himself. Disabled by temperamental defects, this man of whom giants might well be afraid let his soul be harried by insects and to the gnats gave victories which belonged to the gods.

It was natural that Mr. Blake, who wanted to blaze the trail instead of Hon. George Brown, Mr. Goldwin Smith, who hated the Browns and *The Globe* as he hated Disraeli and the Jews, Mr. David Mills, who was rising to leadership in Western Ontario and was not convinced that when George Brown set his hand to the British North America Act the era of constitutional reform was closed forever, and Mr. John Cameron second in authority among the Liberal journalists of Upper Canada but not unwilling to be first, should seek a basis of alliance and co-operation. But surely there never was less promising material for conspiracy. There is no evidence that Mr. Blake had complete confidence in Mr. Goldwin Smith, while in politics the Sage of The Grange trusted no one but himself. One can imagine that at the first conclave they would adopt a resolution of mutual distrust and commiseration and disband. Mr. Cameron could have gone with the company for a day's journey, not too happily, but with the quiet fortitude of a Christian fatalist. As for Mr. Mills, he had a wise humour, a collection of stories that even Sir John Macdonald relished, much knowledge of books and of human nature, and a confidence in Mr. Blake that he gave in equal measure only to Sir Oliver Mowat. A rare company for social converse, if the mood was mellow, but difficult for any political enterprise.

If there was any intimate political understanding between Mr. Blake and Mr. Goldwin Smith it is not revealed in the speeches of the one or the writing of the other. Mr. Goldwin Smith was never happy in any political household. No man denounced party so freely and laboured so continually to organize new parties. No other man of his time wrote the English language with such beauty and simplicity, or had greater command of searching irony and biting invective. He had a genius for depreciation. He never saw a human face without warts and he painted the warts first and often in colours that never faded. His "Canada and the Canadian Question" expresses political despair with scholarly elegance and a suggestion of enjoyment. His "Political History of the United States" is as brilliant as it is destructive. He left both the Dominion and the Republic almost without a hero or a patriot. It was said when he published "Guesses at the Riddle of Existence" that having wholly lost faith in man he was beginning to lose faith in God. I doubt if he ever lost faith in either God or man, but he would be perverse and unhappy. Surely there never was a finer or serener look on a human face than when I saw him just before he died, and he said at parting, "Good-bye, when we meet again it will be in another world." He had genuine sympathy with organized labour, but to the cherished ideals and projects of Collectivists and Socialists he was resolutely opposed. No man fought more stubbornly or more continuously to prevent construction of the Canadian Pacific Railway by Government.

We are told by Baroness Macdonald that when British Columbia entered Confederation on condition that direct railway communication between the Province and Eastern Canada should be established, Sir John Macdonald desired to have the road built by the Government, but was over-ruled by his colleagues while he was engaged in negotiating the Treaty of Washington. There is reason to think that Mr. Mackenzie entered upon Government construction with reluctance and only because no satisfactory agreement with private capitalists could be effected. The Mackenzie Government and the Macdonald Government while engaged in building the railway were embarrassed by gross charges of ineptitude and corruption. Many of these charges were the emanation of partisan credulity and malice, as subsequent events established. No one was more active in these assaults than Mr. Goldwin Smith in *The Bystander* and other publications. The atmosphere of suspicion thus created throughout the country was among the chief reasons for the final decision of the Macdonald Government to reverse the policy and commit the undertaking to private capitalists. We do not know just how the negotiations with George Stephen and Donald A. Smith began. The chances are, however, that the Government was at least as eager to be relieved of the undertaking as the private capitalists were to build the railway.

Here perhaps was the only real bond of sympathy between Mr. Blake and Mr. Goldwin Smith. Neither had faith in the transcontinental railway project, Mr. Blake not only denounced Sir John Macdonald's contract with British Columbia under which the railway was to be completed within ten years from the admission of the Province to Confederation as extravagant and impossible, but was hostile to the "better terms" secured by the Mackenzie Government. He created disaffection in the Cabinet, in the Commons and in the Senate, and spread throughout the country that vague sense of insecurity which is so fatal to the spirit and unity of a political party.

MR. CAMERON AND THE BLAKE WING

Mr. Goldwin Smith was neither a Nationalist nor an Imperialist. He denounced American Imperialism as illustrated in the adventure in Cuba and the acquisition of the Phillipines, while he sought to extend the sovereignty of the Republic over Canada. As long ago as 1866 at Manchester, which begins to rival Oxford as the home of lost causes, he delivered an address in which his vision of the future of Canada is freely and boldly disclosed. "Grow," he said, "the American Federation must. Its people know that it must grow; and diplomacy will do well at once to acquiesce in the natural and inevitable course of things. But the growth will be that of peaceful expansion and attraction; not of forcible annexation, of which I believe no considerable party at the North dreams or has ever dreamed. The British North American colonies will in time, and probably at no very distant time, unite themselves politically to the group of States, of which they are already by race, position, commercial ties and the characteristics of their institutions a part. No one can stand by the side of the St. Lawrence and doubt that in the end they will do this; but they will be left to do it of their own free will." To this vision Mr. Goldwin Smith was faithful. He would not have the prophecy unfulfilled. While the British North American colonies, with high hope and eager counsel, were evolving a Commonwealth, he was making sepulchre for the new birth of Empire. It is clear that Mr. Blake was affected by his teaching, if then averse to any severance of the connection between Canada and Great Britain.

During his first years in Canada there was a disposition to forget or overlook Mr. Goldwin Smith's academic declarations in favour of political union between the United States and the British Provinces. It was believed, perhaps, that the consummation of Confederation gave adequate and final security against absorption in the Republic. He had the most intimate personal relations with the Denisons and other uncompromising British Imperialists. Even by *The Globe* he was eulogized as a distinguished scholar and publicist and his decision to settle in Toronto treated as a signal favour and distinction. There was a serious movement, in which Mr. D'Alton McCarthy was active, to have him appointed editor of *The Mail,* but, according to the tradition, Sir John Macdonald would not consent. He was the first president of the National Club established as the social home of the Canada First group, but never was in full sympathy with a movement peculiarly dedicated at its origin to Canada and British connection. Originally a faithful expression of the political faith and outlook of Colonel George T. Denison and Mr. W. A. Foster, the Canada First movement developed into the Canadian National Association, was invaded by advocates of political independence and became a refuge for doctrines upon which *The Globe* fell with characteristic ardour.

In the famous address at Aurora on October 3rd, 1874, Hon. Edward Blake, eagerly acclaimed as the mouthpiece of Canada First, advocated federation of the Empire, reform of the Senate, compulsory voting, extension of the franchise and representation of minorities in Parliament. *The Globe* treated the speech with reserve, but was not unfriendly. It said that a great Federal Parliament for the British Empire was not a novelty and was an idea that had "many attractions for a certain class of minds." Much in the abstract could be said in its favour, but its practicability was a very different affair. "The subject affords material for interesting and harmless speculation, which in the course of time may issue in some arrangement which will fuse the whole Empire more thoroughly into one united whole, and make the inhabitants of all its different parts so entirely one in sentiment and feeling and aspiration that the only country they will recognize as theirs will be the British Empire, and the only national sentiment they will deem worthy of cherishing will be one that thinks not of 'Canada first' or 'Australia first' or of 'Heligoland first' or 'Norfolk Island first,' but of the grand old British race first, and of all who love their Sovereign and all who swear by the 'old flag' as first and last and midst as well." *The Globe,* however, deprecated "tinkering" with the Constitution, and argued that the Senate as constituted assured reconsideration and amendment of measures adopted by the Commons and effectively prevented hasty and injurious legislation. It was the part of wisdom to hasten slowly, since nations, institutions and sentiments grow slowly. Changes in due time would be needed, and when needed would be effected. It argued that an elected Senate would produce conflict with the Commons, and that any second House elected for a longer period than the Commons would reduce the authority of the popular Chamber. "In the interests of the people of Ontario, who struggled for fifteen years to secure representation by population, and who are enjoying the full fruits of their labours at the present moment, we enter our protest against any change which will weaken the power of the popular Chamber in which they possess their fair share of influence and authority."

75

The London Advertiser accepted "the Aurora platform" without substantial reservation. It was especially whole-hearted in support of Blake's protest against early construction of the Canadian Pacific Railway in British Columbia. It was strongly in favour of his demand for reorganization of the second Chamber. Indeed in its columns Mr. David Mills was advocating an elective Senate. There are sentences in Mr. Blake's attack upon British Columbia and the Transcontinental Railway project which constitute an instructive warning against rash political prophecy. He emphasized "the insanity of the bargain thrust upon you by your late rulers." He believed that it would cost $36,000,-000 to build the British Columbia section, and doubted "if that section can be kept open after it is built." At best we could only find "the least impracticable route through that inhospitable country, that sea of mountains." He affirmed, "If under all the circumstances the British Columbians were to say, 'You must go on and finish the railway according to the terms or take the alternative of releasing us from the Confederation,' I would—take the alternative." Finally, he declared, "I am confident that a bushel of wheat will never go to England over an all-rail route from Saskatchewan to the seaboard."

In the speech at Aurora the more extreme Conservative newspapers saw only conflict between Mr. Blake and George Brown, and between Mr. Blake and the Mackenzie Government, which was negotiating "better terms" with British Columbia and proceeding with the construction of the Transcontinental Railway. According to *The Toronto Mail* Mr. Blake in urging reform of the Senate, to which, it must be remembered,

George Brown had just been appointed, was "in great hostility to Mr. Brown." If it were not that Mr. Blake had "removed himself from the list of Reform leaders" it would have to be said that "the Grit party had at last issued an ultimatum which means nothing if it is not a declaration that the sooner the British Columbians take themselves out of the Confederation the better." It declared that "Mr. Blake has virtually severed himself from the Grit party." Furthermore, "The foreshadowed exodus of a great body of intelligent men from the Grit organization, led by one of the boldest and bitterest spirits among them may well cause a shaking in the secret councils of the faithful at this juncture." It might be said "in respect of the crib that Brown built that the Aurora pronunciamento is the beginning of the end." *The Toronto Sun* said that for "this outspoken disloyalty there can be only one fate in store for him, and that is to blackletter him in *The Globe* as a traitor, and to read him out of the party as a renegade." *The London Free Press* denounced the Aurora platform as impracticable and absurd. But *The Montreal Gazette,* in an editorial of great moderation and dignity, said "that Mr. Blake is momentarily out of harmony with his party friends is quite possible. That they are very decidedly out of humour with him is proved by the kind of criticism which has been bestowed upon his Aurora speech—one organ declaring that the Reform party cannot consent to follow him in his principles and another dismissing him with the statement that his utterances were quite 'harmless.' "

Generally, however, Mr. Blake's address at Aurora was treated with consideration and respect. There was clear evidence that he was at variance with the Mackenzie Government, but the Liberal newspapers were discreet and conciliatory. So many of the Conservative journals discussed the Aurora proposals with such breadth and restraint as *The Montreal Gazette* displayed. It is not possible to follow the controversy in its various phases without sincere respect for the press of Canada forty-five years ago. But Mr. Blake could not escape association with Mr. Goldwin Smith and the Canadian National movement. Mr. Goldwin Smith was the first president of the National Club, and naturally was regarded as an authoritative interpreter of the Canada First movement. He rejected federation of the Empire, and proclaimed the ultimate inevitable separation of Canada from Great Britain. In answer to strong and sustained attack by *The Globe* he explained that he looked to gradual emancipation as the natural end of the colonial system. "Gradual emancipation," he said, "means nothing more than the gradual concession to the colonies of powers of self-government. This process has already been carried far. Should it be carried farther and ultimately consummated, as I frankly avow my belief it must, the mode of proceeding will be the same as it has always been. Each step will be an Act of Parliament passed with the full consent of the Crown. As to the filial tie between Canada and England I hope it will endure forever." He said he could club with Imperial federationists, but could not agree with them in opinion. This was in direct conflict with the teaching at Aurora. Nor was Mr. Blake's utterance at Aurora his only declaration in favour of federation of the Empire. He had said at Montreal in 1873 that he desired "the intimate union of the British Empire." He believed that Canada must have a greater

78

voice in "the disposal of her interests," but that voice need not be acquired by disruption. "We looked to a brighter future, to the reorganization of the Empire on another basis, which would open to us a wider and higher destiny as a member of the great British Empire."

But if Mr. Blake and Mr. Goldwin Smith divided over federation, it is impossible to doubt that they were animated by a common hostility to Hon. George Brown and *The Globe*. Through Mr. Cameron, of *The London Advertiser,* they found a common medium of expression and action. In 1875, *The Liberal,* with Mr. Cameron as editor and Mr. W. F. Maclean as Ottawa correspondent, was established at Toronto. Behind *The Liberal* were Mr. Blake, Mr. Goldwin Smith, Mr. David Mills and Mr. Thomas Moss, who represented West Toronto in the House of Commons. But the days of *The Liberal* were few and full of trouble. Its resources were inadequate for a contest with *The Globe,* while as an agency of division in the Liberal party its motives were distrusted and its constituency restricted. In its pages there was brilliant writing and a flavour of independence as refreshing as a summer shower. But it was only a summer shower, for in a few months *The Liberal* disappeared, Mr. Blake re-entered the Mackenzie Government, Mr. Moss became Chief Justice of Ontario, and *The Globe's* ascendency was re-established if it ever was seriously threatened.

The failure of *The Liberal,* inevitable from the outset, laid a burden of debt upon the backs of the Camerons. When Mr. Blake withdrew from the movement of which *The Liberal* was the mouthpiece, Mr. Goldwin Smith said that he "left him to the tiger." But it was the Camerons rather than Mr. Goldwin Smith who were devoured. It is understood that before they embarked upon the adventure in Toronto *The London Advertiser* was yielding a satisfactory revenue to its owners. But for years they did not recover from their losses in *The Liberal,* if indeed they ever recovered. There is no evidence, however, that Mr. Blake or Mr. Goldwin Smith were unfaithful to any obligation or understanding. I never heard Mr. John Cameron reproach either or suggest that he was misled or deserted. Moreover, it is certain that their personal relations were not disturbed. After Mr. Cameron became editor of *The Globe* he had intimate social and personal intercourse with The Grange, while there is no doubt that Mr. Blake was influential in the movement to seat Mr. Cameron in the chair of the Browns. I was told often that when Hon. George Brown died it was discovered that *The Globe's* finances were in disorder and the annual deficits heavier than was suspected. There was nothing dishonourable in George Brown's system of finance, but his statements were arbitrary and his optimistic estimates not always according to actual results. As a consequence the directors attempted to exercise authority for which there was no warrant in the Brown tradition. Friction developed between the board and Mr. Gordon Brown, and in degree as he became intractable the directors became determined. But I am bound to believe from many facts which came to my knowledge that political differences were a vital factor in Mr. Brown's deposition. He was not willing to be only a speaking-tube for the political leaders. He held that the function of a public journal was to discuss public questions with reasonable freedom and independence as a loyal ally, but not as the subservient creature of the party caucus. *The Globe* had marched in front with the word of command for the party which it had created, and Mr. Gordon Brown would not lower the flag and step to music which was not of its making. Faced with the alternative of submission or withdrawal he left the field humiliated but not dishonoured. It was perhaps inevitable when Mr. Blake became leader of the Liberal party that this should follow. It was as natural that Mr. Cameron should be Mr. Gordon Brown's successor. So far as I can learn there was no intimacy between Mr. Blake and Mr. Gordon Brown. There was intimacy between Mr. Blake and Mr. Cameron. It was necessary to have complete mutual confidence between the leader and the chief Liberal journal if the party was to be strong and united. The differences between Mr. Blake and Mr. Mackenzie, between Mr. Blake and *The Globe,* had long consequences.

Hon. David Mills succeeded Mr. Cameron as editor of *The London Advertiser.* But at most he was the chief editorial writer. He exercised no authority over the staff and had only a perfunctory interest in the news columns. According to my recollection he rarely if ever gave a suggestion to the reporters or concerned himself about the treatment of the despatches. But we liked to have him in the office, and in his bearing towards us there was a gracious friendliness. For a long time Mr. Mills had contributed to the editorial columns. But he was not a journalist nor was he ever an easy or luminous writer. There was a curious heaviness in his sentences, and he travelled far before the argument was completed. Mr. Mills was a philosopher, learned by the books, and "apt to teach." In his writing he did not fully reveal himself. He was best revealed in social converse and among his constituents. It was my privilege to attend the convention at Florence which nominated Mr. Mills in 1882, and to report other meetings in Bothwell which he addressed. He was like a father among his children, confidential, companionable, wise and tolerant. Between the member and his constituents there was such mutual confidence and affection as distinguishes a happy household. One felt, too, that he was invincibly loyal to his convictions and would not compromise with truth for any man's grace or favour. I can think of no man in public life who had more courage than Hon. David Mills, who was more scrupulous in argument, more just in praise or censure, more resolutely faithful to himself on the platform and in Parliament. "Praise is comely for the upright." More than once these qualities distressed associates and comforted opponents. Between Mr. Mills and Sir John Macdonald there was a firm and enduring friendship. It was often suggested unworthily that the Conservative leader flattered Mr. Mills in order to discover the designs of the Liberal party. The truth was that they had much in common. Both had read widely and thought beyond most of their contemporaries. Each had a fund of stories which could be wisely exchanged only in very confidential intercourse. The country knew how human was Sir John Macdonald; it did not know that Mr. Mills was just as human and just as companionable. Joseph Howe said in the House of Commons in 1870: "I will pass over the philosophical declamation of my honourable friend from Bothwell, but I may say of him in passing that I am not aware he ever says an ill-natured thing if he can help it."

Mr. Mills, as has been said, had confidence in Mr. Blake that never was shaken. To Sir Wilfrid Laurier he gave only a perfunctory allegiance. There is no doubt that he aspired to the leadership of the Liberal party when Mr. Blake resigned and never was convinced that a wiser choice was made. Mr. Mills was defeated in Bothwell in 1896, and chiefly because in obedience to his interpretation of the constitution, he would not deny that the Roman Catholic minority of Manitoba had ground of appeal to the Federal Parliament. Losing the votes of Catholics because the Liberal party opposed remedial legislation, and the support of extreme Protestants because he would not deny validity in the position of the minority, he was beaten when his party came into office after eighteen years of Opposition. No man had fought its battle with greater ardour, courage and ability, and the blow was severe. He was deeply stricken, too, by his exclusion from the first Laurier Cabinet. It is doubtful if he ever recovered his natural buoyancy and serenity. As leader of the Senate he was not happy. On the Supreme Court bench he was in an alien atmosphere. He fought a long and gallant battle and was sorely wounded in the hour of victory. What humiliations and tragedies mark the paths of public men! How grudging is public gratitude until it is cut into the sonorous phrases of an epitaph!

I was amazed to receive a letter written under the assumption that I had advised Sir Wilfrid Laurier to exclude Mr. Mills from the Government. My advice was not sought, nor was it offered. If I had so advised

I would have been guilty of ingratitude and presumption. I fear, however, that Mr. Mills never was convinced that I was not among those who had "conspired" against him. It was the fashion to think that the editor of *The Globe* was busy behind the curtain with decisions and movements of which he had no knowledge and for which he had no responsibility. With Mr. Mills as editor *The Advertiser* laboured somewhat heavily. Even Mr. Archie Bremner's daring and incisive paragraphs hardly relieved the sobriety of the editorial columns. At his best, Mr. Bremner was as brilliant and pungent as Mr. J. R. Cameron of *The Hamilton Spectator,* but Cameron was more spontaneous and more prolific. For many months my copy passed through Mr. Bremner's hands and I have often said that he never made an erasion or a correction that did not improve the style and the sense of what I had written. For a young reporter that was a great concession.

Few Canadian journalists have had a gift of humour equal to that which Mr. J. R. Cameron possessed. Few had a career so picturesque and adventurous. He was a printer's devil at Seaforth, and a compositor on *The Sarnia Canadian.* At twenty years of age he went to Arkansas and saw service during the Civil War. Returning to Sarnia at the close of the war he joined a company of volunteers organized during the Fenian Raid, but which was not called for active service. He was a reporter on *The Detroit Free Press* when rebellion broke out at Red River. Again he enlisted at Sarnia and became quartermaster-sergeant in the first battalion of Ontario Volunteers under Lord Wolseley, which made the long journey through the wilderness to Fort Garry. He assisted Mr. W. F. Luxton, with whom probably he had made acquaintance at Seaforth, in establishing *The Manitoba Free Press,* destined to become one of the great newspapers of Canada. When twenty-five years of age he was elected to the Winnipeg Council. For a year he was a reporter on *The Minneapolis Tribune.* But he had not yet found the soil in which he was to take root. He came back to Canada and had a short connection with *The Stratford Herald, The Guelph Herald* and *The Ottawa Citizen.* Finally, in 1894, he joined the staff of *The Hamilton Spectator,* of which he became chief editor and in whose service he remained until his death in 1907.

Mr. Cameron's honourable connection with the Red River Expedition, was often made the subject of gibe and banter by his contemporaries. Once in *The Toronto Evening Telegram,* Mr. J. R. Robinson, between whom and Mr. Cameron there was a happy vendetta for years, said "only a typographical error could have caused *The London Advertiser* to refer to Colonel John Robson Cameron as A.D.C. to Sir Garnet Wolseley. The historic fact is that Colonel John Robson Cameron was A.D.C. to Sir Garnet Wolseley's horse." Mr. J. P. Downey says that in his boyhood he thought Mr. Cameron "the funniest man alive." It is Mr. Downey's impression that he hardly wrote a serious editorial or a serious paragraph until he joined *The Spectator.* As editor of *The Spectator,* however, he had marked distinction among his contemporaries. He was clear and persuasive. Very often his leading articles were singularly moderate and dispassionate. He could be very partisan and even ferocious, but he could also carry on a long debate with a contem-

porary in admirable temper, quoting fairly, reasoning
clearly and seeking judgment upon the facts as tested
and established by reason and experience. But to the
last his paragraphs were the salt of *The Spectator,* and
never was he so happy, boisterous, delightful and insolent as when the Hamilton baseball nine defeated the
Torontos in the old Canadian League contests of twenty-five or thirty years ago.

Between Mr. Cameron and Mr. Alexander Pirie, of
The Dundas Banner, there was constant interchange of
badinage. *The Spectator* described Dundas as situated
on the g. g. c.—the god-given canal. It said that "A.
Pirie, at the gate of Eden, stood disconsolate." When
The Buffalo Express said that "Canada doesn't know
enough to come in out of the Reign Britannia," Cameron retorted, "Canada knows enough to keep out of the
Hail! Columbia." When a grieving Conservative
newspaper protested that it was a shame to bring in
Sir John Macdonald's nose when Hugh John Macdonald's qualifications for public life were under consideration *The Spectator* said, "Shame! It's more than a
shame. 'Snoutrage!" Charging *The Ottawa Journal*
with cribbing from *The Citizen,* Cameron ended the
protest with "Three shears for *The Journal!*" Mr. J.
Gordon Mowat, perhaps better known as "Moses
Oates," for many years connected with *The Globe* and
various periodicals, acquired some celebrity as a wea-
ther prophet. Once he predicted a dry, warm summer,
but in contempt of the prophet the summer was cold,
wet and disagreeable. Towards autumn an Indian
named Moses Oates was arrested and lodged in jail at
Brantford. *The Spectator* had this paragraph, "Moses
Oates, who is confined in Brantford gaol charged with a

heinous offence, wishes us to announce that he is not the Moses Oates who predicted a dry, warm summer." Devoted altogether to his profession, Mr. Cameron has left only memories of an attractive personality and the simple records of a laborious and faithful workman. But Mr. Mills, Mr. Bremner and Mr. Cameron passed through the obituary column long ago, while only the old and the garrulous write Reminiscences. If Mr. Mills did not give vivacity to *The Advertiser,* he gave it authority throughout Canada almost equal to that which *The Globe* exercised, and a steadiness and consistency for which the chief organ of the Liberal party was not so distinguished throughout quarrels and tumults which were fast coming upon the country.

CHAPTER IV.

CHURCH AND STATE IN ONTARIO

It is a pity that the old Legislative Buildings on Front Street were destroyed. In that squat, straggling, irregular structure a "State's decrees" were moulded. There sat the Legislative Assembly of Upper Canada, the Parliament of the united Provinces, and the infant Legislature of Ontario. But we have silenced the whispers of a nation in the roar of traffic. Without thought or emotion we razed buildings that would have carried inspiration and the sense of romance to many generations. In Canada we are only learning to cherish the landmarks and at best learning slowly.

A remote posterity will rejoice over the incomparable achievement of Mr. John Ross Robertson in collecting the invaluable gallery of portraits which adorn the Public Library of Toronto, and be very grateful for the priceless volumes of local history which he has produced. To search so deeply and attain such accuracy requires infinite labour and patience with sympathy and enthusiasm beyond common understanding. Because he has gone down to the foundations there will be authenticity and authority in many books that will be fashioned out of the material which he accumulated and in which perhaps the sources will not always be disclosed. But may it not be said that "one built up a wall and lo, others daubed it with untempered mortar." It is nothing even if while Mr. Robertson was engaged in these laborious investigations presumptuous municipal statesmen and temerarious contemporaries occasionally got out of hand, forgot the habit of reverence and blasphemed the Dynasty.

During the session of 1884 I first looked down at the Legislature of Ontario from the Press Gallery. At the close of 1882 Mr. John Cameron became editor of *The Globe* and in August, 1883, he offered me a place on the staff. Two hours after the proposal reached me at London I had secured a release from *The Advertiser,* collected my belongings and taken the train for Bruce County, where I had a short holiday before going to Toronto. I chose Bruce for a holiday for reasons which were continuously persuasive until I was married two years later. As the years pass I am ever more deeply convinced that in going northward I travelled wisely. On September 9th, 1883, I came to Toronto and next morning was "inducted" in *The Globe* office. For a few weeks I was Mr. Cameron's private secretary, but the duties were not congenial nor was the performance satisfactory. This fact established alike to the satisfaction of Mr. Cameron and myself, I was made assistant night editor with a "roving commission" to go through the exchanges and supply editorial comment.

A third of a century ago the debates of the Legislature excited greater popular interest than they do to-day and were far more fully reported. We had not emerged from the era of constitutional construction. We were only upon the threshold of the era of commercial and industrial expansion. It is the fashion to deplore the decadence of parliaments and to shrug shoulders at the inferior stature of statesmen as compared with the leaders in industry, finance and transportation. It is not certain, however, that the legislature has sunk to such low estate as its detractors profess to believe, while it was inevitable that the genius and energy of bold and adventurous spirits should become absorbed in problems of industrial and national organization. For fifteen or twenty years we had a supreme constitutional problem. It was necessary to establish a working political relation between Upper and Lower Canada through a federal union or the wider project of Confederation. With federation of the older Provinces achieved, extension of Canadian sovereignty over the Western Territories became the urgent object and obligation of statesmen. But the nation was not established when the constitution was fashioned, and a common federal authority created. We had only a paper scaffolding, resting upon an uncertain foundation and open to wind and rain. We had to stay the structure with a national system of banking, of commerce and of manufacture. In all this Parliament could direct but could not execute. It was necessary therefore, that other forces should appear, reinforcing statesmen, devising material machinery, giving strength and cohesion to the constitutional structure. It is a mistake to think that patriotism may be displayed and public duty discharged only within the walls of parliament and in the councils of cabinets.

In every country in seasons of political crisis there is general and instinctive concentration upon problems of government. Under settled conditions the prestige and authority of parliaments seem to decline There is diversion to other interests and activities. I recall a conversation with a public man of South Africa. Before the war between Great Britain and the Dutch Republics, there was general mourning over

the meanness and pettiness of South African politics. During the war and the era of constitutional reconstruction there was a striking revival of public spirit.
All the country had of sound moral, economic and political material was available for the public service. It
was so in Canada at Confederation. It was so during
the Great War in Europe. Who doubts that it
will be so during the difficult period of social
and industrial restoration? When the problems
of government are supreme and the demand for
Parliamentary service urgent all other interests sink
into subordination. But we confuse values when we
think that oratory is the only test of greatness and parliamentary service the only test of patriotism. Too
often fluency in expression is associated with futility in
execution. But it is still true, I think, that a great
speech is the finest of all human performances. So that
country is most secure against decadence, corruption
and civic lethargy where a seat in Parliament is the first
distinction to which a citizen can aspire.

In the Legislature thirty-five years ago there was a
Cabinet perhaps as strong in personal distinction, in
debating talent and in administrative genius as any that
has held office in Canada, whether federal or Provincial, since Confederation. There was a less impressive
Opposition. But there is a general disposition in
Canada to reverence men in office and to regard those
who sit to the left of the Speaker as pretentious mediocrities. There was, however, nothing mediocre about
either of the leaders in the Assembly when I first had a
seat in the Press Gallery. Sir Oliver Mowat, who was
Prime Minister, had sat in two Cabinets before Confederation, was a delegate to the Quebec Conference

which fashioned the federal constitution and for eight years was Vice-Chancellor of Upper Canada. It is curious that Hon. Edward Blake, who induced Sir Oliver Mowat to accept the leadership of the Liberal party in Ontario, also chose Sir Wilfrid Laurier as his successor in the leadership of the federal Liberal party. While it was Mr. Blake's fortune to spend long years out of office he nominated successors who were not easily removed from office.

Sir Oliver Mowat was a consummate politician with a genius for reconciling duty and opportunity. Crafty and longsighted, he was never in outward conflict with the Christian verities. No man ever was more cautious or bolder if the occasion required decision and action. He looked out from behind his glasses with engaging simplicity and candour, while the mind was busy with devices to confuse and confound the besieging forces. No one could seem to be more trusting and yet no one was more nimble and alert. Prime Minister for more than twenty years, one feels that he would have died in office if he had not been persuaded to join hands with Sir Wilfrid Laurier in 1896. It is certain that he would not have sanctioned the gross electoral practices which at last so tarnished the lustre of Liberal administration in Ontario. Greater integrity of character than Hon. A. S. Hardy he had not, but his authority was so absolute that the agencies which corrupted constituencies under his successors would not have been bold enough to engage in the desperate enterprises through which the Province was defamed and the Liberal party dishonoured.

There was deliberate, continuous method in the system of government which Sir Oliver Mowat devised.

But the system was not rooted in corruption in the constituencies or in the administrative departments. In respect of administration alone the watchword "Twenty years of honest Government" was not open to serious challenge. When the era of virtue was extended to "thirty years of honest Government" it was not so easy to assent without dubiety and misgiving. But substantially we have had honest government in Ontario, wise handling of the public resources and thrifty expenditure of public money whether under Liberal or Conservative Administrations. If there is a dubious chapter it is concerned with the ineffectual struggle to carry the ascendency of a party into the second generation.

But there was guile and strategy in the system which Sir Oliver Mowat devised and reduced to an exact science. He created patronage, organized patronage and trusted to patronage. In establishing central control over the liquor traffic he enlisted an army of officials in the service of the Government. Never was an army more faithful to the High Command. For the most part these officials were active agents of the Government in every electoral contest. The liquor regulations were tempered to the behaviour of license-holders. An adequate display of zeal for the Government was a fair guarantee of security when licenses were renewed. Inactivity was tolerated. Open rebellion was often punished. There has been no greater comedy in Canadian politics than the manœuvres between the federal and provincial authorities to evade responsibility for prohibitory legislation. Generally the object was not to establish jurisdiction but to evade and confuse. There was mortal apprehension lest the Imperial Privy Council should discover that definite and complete authority was vested in either the Provinces or the Dominion. There was as desperate apprehension that under evasive plebiscites the popular majority for prohibition would be decisive enough to require actual legislation.

It will be remembered that in 1898, when a plebiscite was taken by the Laurier Government, Quebec gave an overwhelming majority against Prohibition. Moreover, many days elapsed before the returns from Quebec were complete. Gradually, but steadily, the figures increased the adverse majority, bringing relief to the Government and distress to the prohibitionists. No evidence ever was produced that there was dishonest voting or interference with the ballot boxes. Probably the feeling in Quebec was expressed as fairly as was that of the other Provinces. But there was suspicion, and suspicion was strengthened by the delayed returns. In a facetious moment, before the returns were complete, *The Globe* said, "They still seem to be voting against prohibition in Quebec." This was resented. I had an immediate intimation from Ottawa that the French Ministers were annoyed by the paragraph and the implication which it was thought to carry. I explained with abject docility that I was "only joking," but discovered that it was beyond the power of a finite mind to interpret a *Globe* joke to an angry Frenchman.

There never was a more happy soul in Parliament than Dr. Landerkin of South Grey. But few knew how shrewd he was or how deeply he was instructed in the idiosyncrasies of his parliamentary associates. Sir Wilfrid Laurier knew and the knowledge was of infinite advantage to the leader. Dr. Landerkin was a sort of super-whip, advising wisely in many a difficult situation, pouring oil into joints that might be stiffening against discipline, softening moroseness into cheerfulness and reducing "contingent belligerency" to serviceable docility. He knew when only persuasion could prevail and when admonition and rebuke were required. Fortunate is the political leader that hath Landerkins in his quiver. In South Grey there was a German element that was opposed to prohibitory legislation. To alienate this element was dangerous. As dangerous was any frontal attack upon temperate measures. Dr. Landerkin therefore was often in distress over proposals to amend the Scott Act or establish complete Prohibition until, as he used to say, he got his feet upon the solid rock of plebiscite and could face any storm from any direction.

Plebiscites and referendums were refuges for Governments rather than concessions to prohibitionists. There could be no better evidence of the genius of Sir Oliver Mowat than the fact that for so long he had a generous support from the liquor interest and a still more generous support from Prohibitionists. The Mowat Government was pledged to go as far towards Prohibition as the Constitution would permit, but it was by the action of a Conservative Government in Manitoba that the measure of provincial jurisdiction over the liquor traffic was finally determined. Still, neither the Conservative Government of Manitoba nor the Liberal Government of Ontario established Prohibition.

Under Sir Oliver Mowat there was also an extension of patronage over the minor courts and a rigid exercise of patronage in appointments to the Provincial institutions. For nearly a generation no Conservative was admitted to the public service in Ontario. Although fitness in appointments was seldom disregarded the Civil Service was an essential portion of the organized political machinery of the Mowat Administration. Sir Oliver Mowat was neither unctuous nor hyprocritical. He bluntly defended patronage and its uses. To the Young Men's Liberal Club of Toronto in 1894 he said: "The Conservative Opposition urges the change to local appointment with reference to the Reform Government of the Province, but do not want it with reference to the Conservative Government of the Dominion. While our opponents pretend in Provincial politics to object to patronage as giving a Government too much power, some Reformers would favour its being withdrawn from the Provincial Government because it appears to them to be a source of weakness rather than a source of strength, inasmuch as several friends are disappointed whenever an appointment is made. I cannot say that patronage is on the whole a weakness; but it is the prestige which belongs to the right of patronage that gives to it its chief advantage to the party in power. For this purpose it is valuable, notwithstanding its disadvantages in some other respects. The prestige of the Dominion as compared with the Provinces is already quite great enough for the interests of the Province; and as the possession of patronage gives a certain prestige the Province should not be deprived of that prestige while the local prestige of the Dominion is left untouched. The Dominion Government now appoints our governors and our judges; claims and exercises power to appropriate our railways and our public works; vetoes any of our legislation which happens to be distasteful to its friends; and has a larger exclusive legislative jurisdiction than the Congress of the United States has. It is important to Provincial interests that while this constitution lasts, nothing should be done to lessen the prestige of the Provincial Government, the representative of Provincial jurisdiction and authority."

Whatever were the advantages of patronage, and they were not inconsiderable, it is certain that the Mowat Government profited greatly by its alliance with the Roman Catholic hierarchy. It is not suggested that there were evil motives behind this alliance or that there was any vital betrayal of the public interest. That there was an alliance is beyond challenge. That element of the population which George Brown alienated by distrust and violence Mowat regained and retained by conciliation and concession. In those days, "the Catholic vote" was the obsession of politicians. It was the strong fortress of Sir John Macdonald. It was the fortress which Hon. Edward Blake besieged but could not take. But Mr. Blake did not begin the siege until Mr. Sandfield Macdonald was defeated. In the Provincial contest of 1871 the Orange Association was not very friendly to the Scottish Roman Catholic leader of the Government, who had opposed Separate Schools, but was not persuaded that the murder of Thomas Scott and the capture of Louis Riel were legitimate issues in Provincial politics. As a boy I saw Riel hanged in effigy, but I had no comprehension of the political significance of the incident. Once in South Ontario, where Sir Oliver Mowat had many electoral triumphs, the cry was "Mowat and the Queen, or Morrison and the Pope." But notwithstanding his association with George Brown and the deft exploitation of racial and

7

sectarian prejudices against Sandfield Macdonald, Archbishop Lynch and Sir Oliver Mowat effected a concordat which was maintained for a quarter of a century.

The Archbishop, a bold and far-sighted ecclesiastic, skilfully enlarged the privileges of his people, and achieved his objects through a sagacious covenanting Protestant. But it is hard to believe that Protestantism was outraged or the Constitution subjected to violence. An essential condition of the compact of union was that separate schools should be maintained for Catholics in Ontario and for Protestants in Quebec. It was not suggested that the Separate School Acts should never be amended or that legislation which would minister to the convenience of Catholics should be withheld. It was not such a flagrant offence that municipal assessors in communities where separate schools were established should return Catholics as supporters of these schools or that the State should collect the taxes for separate as for public school boards. There was not much to be said for dual machinery which could only burden Catholics and excite a sense of injustice. Nor was there any serious grievance in diverting to separate schools a proportion of the taxes of public companies if there was fair division according to the relative holdings of Catholics and Protestants. The obligation of the State to separate schools did not cease at Confederation. It could not have been intended that a right guaranteed by the constitution should be grudgingly maintained or a principle conceded in the letter impaired in the practice.

The fierce attack upon the "Ross Bible" was compounded of partisan rancour and sectarian venom. Its

spirit was fairly expressed by the pious Protestant trus-
tee who declared that he would have the whole d——
Bible or nothing. The volume of Scriptural selections
prepared for the public schools, skulking in history as
the "Ross Bible," was a comprehensive concept of moral
and religious teaching, the product of a reverent spirit,
finely designed and skilfully executed, and commend-
able in content and object. But it was thrust out of
sight as something irreverent and blasphemous. One
feels that the effect was to accentuate division in education and to produce nothing fruitful in faith or morals.

The decision to establish bilingual schools in French
communities was as fiercely opposed as the separate
school amendments. It is true that such schools had
existed before Confederation in French and German
settlements but under the Mowat Government there
was definite recognition and deliberate extension of the
system. As an inevitable result of the Government's
action and the attack of the Opposition, the French
constituencies turned towards Liberal candidates. It
may be that there was political design in this legislation
as in the concessions to the Irish Catholic element, but
none of these measures have been repealed by Conservative Governments, while the attitude of Sir James
Whitney towards the French and Irish Catholic minorities was not very different from that of Sir Oliver
Mowat. There still is controversy over bilingual
schools, but the demand is for adequate recognition of
English and not for prohibition of French teaching.

During this period of sectarian tension and fury
the Protestant Protective Association appeared. A
secret movement, imported from the United States, its
literature was peculiarly intolerant and its methods

difficult to penetrate. The Association demanded not only that Roman Catholics should be excluded from the public service but that they should be denied private employment. It was alleged that by direction of Hon. C. F. Fraser a cross had been painted in the ceiling of the new legislative chamber and that Roman emissaries were swarming in the public departments. Looking through the newspapers of that period it is amazing to discover what fantastic reports were circulated and believed. Nor does censure fall only upon the Opposition and the agencies which were striking at the Mowat Government. It is true that under Sir Oliver Mowat there was a very liberal admission of Roman Catholics to the public service and that there was the atmosphere of bargaining in the relations between the Church and the leaders of the Liberal party. It was found that legislation favourable to Roman Catholics was rewarded by organized political support and measures which result from a compact naturally excite suspicion and distrust. But, as I have said, much of the legislation which was so strongly attacked was not unreasonable nor objectionable. At least the masses of Protestants could not be excited, and fortunately would not give countenance to the illiberal teaching of the Protestant Protective Association. The "extreme wing" damaged Sir William Meredith; the excesses of the attack strengthened the defence. The alliance between the Catholic Bishops and Liberal Ministers was palpable and provocative, but the offences against the public school system were not grave enough to separate Presbyterian Liberals from a Presbyterian Prime Minister whose Protestantism was beyond suspicion and whose political genius was not inferior to that of Sir John Macdonald.

CHURCH AND STATE IN ONTARIO

If the federal Conservative leader could command the common support of the Bleus of Quebec and the Orange Lodges of Ontario the Provincial Liberal leader could unite the Palace and the General Assembly. And both had qualities which greatly redeemed their patent political manœuvres.

In the long struggle between Sir John Macdonald and Sir Oliver Mowat over the legislative authority of the Province and the determination of its boundaries, the Provincial Premier never sustained a decisive defeat. No doubt he relied upon the advice of Hon. Edward Blake and the industry of Hon. David Mills, but one feels that he was not dependent upon either nor persuaded by either against his own judgment. His mind was clear, his temper reliant, his industry adequate and his resource equal to any emergency.

As a speaker Sir Oliver Mowat was dull, halting, and laborious. But he never spoke upon any subject, even at the close of a long debate in which every argument seemed to be exhausted, without reinforcing the position by new facts and fresh reasoning. In the Cabinet there were two, if not three, better speakers than himself but none of these could make a deeper impression upon the Legislature. He persuaded not by fluency or eloquence but by simplicity and solidity. He lacked the relief of humour, but he had a keen insight into the vanities and frailties of his fellows. He could redistribute constituencies with Christian humility and partisan ingenuity. He could take the fruits and know not the tree thereof. He was not a Radical, nor a Liberal, nor even a Whig. He was a Tory in social instinct and in political practice and outlook. He had honest reverence for established forms and institutions in Church and State. He had the innate quality of a gentleman. He was offended by looseness of tongue or coarseness of fibre. He kept his hand upon "the people" lest they should get out of control. He never believed that the voice of democracy was necessarily the voice of God. He neglected the University of Toronto, not because he had a low conception of the value and dignity of higher education but because he suspected political danger in generous appropriations. Primarily an economist even in his attitude towards elementary education, he expressed the economical and conservative instincts of the people. One feels that he was like an employer who is content with a solvent concern even though by raising wages and scrapping decrepit machinery he could increase both output and profits. But he would not have waste or extravagance. He was a devoted British patriot of the school of Brown and Mackenzie. Throughout the Province there were thousands of "Mowat Conservatives" whose support he had in every political contest, as there was an influential, independent element which believed with Principal Grant of Queen's University that, "Ontario could not afford to dismiss Sir Oliver Mowat." He conserved the natural resources of the Province, respected the essential moralities in the exercise of power, and resisted the influences which are ever ready to prey upon Governments for personal advantage.

Moreover, he was his own "boss." Of Prime Ministers there are two kinds. One conducts, the other is "personally conducted." In so many Cabinets there is one particular Minister who stands between the leader and the people. This type of politician is forever busy with intrigue and patronage. He nestles in the bosom of "the Chief." He seems to love him with a love passing that of women. He becomes the source of favours and honours. He persuades the leader that he is the saviour of the party and the party that he is the door of access to the leader. His instruments are flattery and corruption. He increases in substance but by methods that are seldom fully disclosed. He is an eternal danger and an intolerable affliction. In proportion as he is powerful the meaner elements of a party prevail in administration and policy. But Sir Oliver Mowat never had a master nor ever was misled by adulation.

Perhaps Sir Oliver Mowat trusted no other man as fully as he trusted Hon. T. B. Pardee. Between these two there was affection as well as confidence. But affection flowered for Mr. Pardee as naturally and spontaneously as flowers open in the spring. He was of commanding stature, and had much natural dignity of bearing. His features were rugged but attractive. In his eyes there was the look of a man who knew the world and found the knowledge pleasant. In early manhood he had sought adventure and fortune in the gold fields of California and Australia. Through such experiences men come to know human values. If they survive they become wise and tolerant. Until his death Mr. Pardee looked at the world with young eyes. If the schools refine it is true also that the rough experiences of life often give serenity and dignity. There was a rare sense of felicity in companionship with Mr. Pardee. When the Creator makes such men he must feel very pleasantly towards his creatures. The Press Gallery was always attentive and interested when Mr. Pardee was "passing his estimates" or manœuvring a contentious measure through its various stages. He was bland, conciliatory, accommodating. He could disarm the most fretful and suspicious critic. Very often he would divide his opponents, and draw timely and valuable support from the Opposition. It would be found that in the conduct of his department he had conciliated some Conservative member or shrewdly abated the grievances of some Conservative constituency. Naturally, therefore, gratitude was expressed and the unity of the attack impaired. In a volume of Reminiscences Mr. Justin McCarthy describes the perplexity of the Court and Government when Garibaldi visited England. Although he had no official status there was a passionate popular demand for official recognition of the Italian patriot. As a way out of a difficult situation Lord Palmerston suggested that Garibaldi should marry the Duchess of Sutherland. It was objected that the Duchess had a husband, but Palmerston argued that Gladstone could explain the husband away. There was nothing that Mr. Pardee could not explain away and that without such elaborate verbiage and exhaustive reasoning as often distinguished Mr. Gladstone's defences. Wise, able, faithful and lovable, Mr. Pardee served Ontario well, not perhaps without the guile which was required in an era of rigid devotion to party but with fine simplicity and simple personal integrity. One looks in vain in the streets of Sarnia for monuments to Alexander Mackenzie and T. B. Pardee.

Of different temper was Mr. C. F. Fraser. Eager, aggressive and defiant, he challenged his adversaries to combat, and pressed the battle to the gates and beyond. He could fall but he could not retreat. He could not withhold the blow even if to strike was to lose the field.

Often he was so merciless in attack as to damage the cause for which he contended. He hated all meddling and mothering legislation. He would have fought a Committee of One Hundred or a Committee of One Thousand in defence of the freedom of choice and freedom of action which he believed were the inalienable privileges of British citizenship. For waste and extravagance he had no toleration. He would burn with anger against any evidence of plotting by supporters of the Government to secure illegitimate subsidies or establish a doubtful interest in timber or mineral resources. Nor could his anger be appeased until the designs of the despoilers were abandoned or defeated. It was the boast of a campaign that the Parliament Buildings in Queen's Park were erected without "extras." In the fact we may rejoice if it is conceded that the buildings should not have been erected in the Park with or without extras. But what was a park against "economy." It is doubtful if the Legislature has had any other debater as fluent, lucid and powerful as Mr. C. F. Fraser. For vigour in attack, for resource in defence and for instant appreciation of the true significance of a complex situation he ranks in my mind above any other man that I have known in the Legislature or the House of Commons. At his side I would put Dr. George M. Grant in the Presbyterian General Assembly. Grant, however, was more adroit and more persuasive; less eager and vehement. Besides Grant seldom struck to wound and never was carried into oratorical excesses. Fraser did not care if he drew blood. He had no compassion for a writhing enemy. For years his health was not good and he was often worn and weary. He fanned the flame of life too rashly and too fiercely. Burning more energy than he could spare he exhausted the supply, the spirit faltered and the darkness came too soon. But he could not have lived otherwise, and how brilliant was the life while it lasted. A Scotch Roman Catholic, Mr. Fraser was the spokesman of his Church in the Legislature. But he never cringed to authority, and while a faithful Churchman he never was merely the instructed counsel of any group or interest. When I was assigned to service in the Press Gallery I was warned that Mr. Fraser was of uncertain and autocratic temper and that at his hands I must expect command and rebuff. But he treated me with unvarying courtesy and kindness. There was no member of the Government from whom I sought advice more freely or who gave me more of confidence and friendship. Once when I was attacked for something that I had written it was Mr. Fraser who sprang to my defence with instant and fervent protest. I think of him as a man of rare gifts and acute perception, who, if he had sat in the House of Commons would have been among its great figures and its decisive forces.

Curiously enough when Mr. Fraser was a witness before the Royal Commission which investigated the mysterious and perhaps somewhat legendary machinations of "the Brawling Brood of Bribers"—his own description of that shadowy association of inept strategists—he was embarrassed and confused by Mr. D'Alton McCarthy. Nor did Mr. Hardy pass through the ordeal of cross-examination to greater advantage. Both were easily provoked and Mr. McCarthy displayed genius in provocation. I have often wondered how Mr. McCarthy would have borne a cross-examination by Mr. Fraser. It is as easy for a camel to pass through the eye of a needle as for a man of eager temper and strong impulses to be a good witness under a skilful counsel. In any encounter on the platform or in parliament Mr. Fraser and Mr. McCarthy probably would have carried the scars of equal and honourable combat.

For Hon. A. S. Hardy and Hon George W. Ross, both members of the Mowat Government when I was in the Press Gallery, there will be another chapter. Sir John Macdonald, in a moment of fretful exasperation, described Sir Oliver Mowat as "the Little Tyrant" and scoffed at his Pardees and Hardys and Lardys and Dardys, but they frustrated all his devices and held the citadel against all the forces that he could command. Moreover, through long years the Mowat Cabinet was singularly harmonious and cohesive. Mr. J. Israel Tarte once said that in Council members of the Laurier Government "fought like blazes." That seems to be the chronic condition of governments. It would be hard for the people to have confidence in cabinets if they knew how seldom ministers have a common confidence in themselves. One thinks of the injunction of the Prophet Jeremiah, "Take ye heed every one of his neighbour, and trust ye not in any brother; for every brother will utterly supplant, and every neighbour will walk with slanders."

During the four or five sessions that I was in the Press Gallery, Sir William Meredith was leader of the Opposition. Among his supporters were Hon. Alex. Morris, Mr. David Creighton, Mr. E. F. Clarke, Mr. A. F. Wood and Mr. H. E. Clarke. Of these Mr. Creighton was very serviceable and Mr. E. F. Clarke effective in debate but absorbed in the affairs of Toronto. Mr. Morris was among the prophets of Confederation, but age had put its hand upon him and his face was turned towards the past. Mr. H. E. Clarke and Mr. Wood spoke often, generally without extreme party bias and with knowledge of the subjects they discussed. These had useful and industrious associates, and there was Mr. Metcalfe, of Kingston, eccentric and daring, grossly personal in assaults upon ministers, but so boisterously happy and exuberant that even his victims enjoyed his performances. I heard Sir James Whitney's first speeches in the House, singularly calm and judicial as compared with his later manner, but clearly revealing distinct individuality, simplicity of character and resolute integrity. It cannot be suggested that there was talent or experience to the left of the Speaker equal to that on the treasury benches, but under Sir William Meredith the Opposition was an effective Parliamentary instrument.

The Conservative leader was industrious, vigilant and aggressive. No measure was too insignificant to receive his attention. Generally his criticism of details was sympathetic and constructive. He thought it his duty even to amend and improve measures to which he was opposed. For the actual letter of much of the legislation enacted he was as responsible as the Government. One could not doubt his sincerity and integrity or withhold admiration for his zeal and assiduity in the public interest. His mind was more liberal than that of Sir Oliver Mowat; his outlook more sympathetic and confident. He forced manhood suffrage upon the Government. He was suspicious of capital and corporations. He had a close relation to organized labour. He was a zealous advocate of legislation to compensate workmen for accidents. He was with courageous con·

sistency a champion of public rights against private interests. Those who remember his teaching in the Legislature will reflect that many of his causes have triumphed, though later reformers wear the laurel, and perhaps he was not uninfluential in shaping the legislative programme of the Whitney Administration.

Sir William Meredith, perhaps through the exigency of political circumstances and the obligation of loyalty to Sir John Macdonald, was counted against Ontario in the long struggle over the Boundary Award. He was drawn into the vexatious constitutional contests between the Mowat Government and the Conservative Government at Ottawa and too often fought and lost upon ground which was not of his own choosing. Whether or not it was desirable in the national interest that he should maintain the alliance with Sir John Macdonald it is certain that the association was sometimes gravely prejudicial to his political prospects in his own Province. In his struggle with the Roman Catholic Bishops he failed to secure Protestant support in any degree equivalent to the French and Irish support which he lost. Moreover, while the Catholic votters polled for Sir Oliver Mowat in the Province they gave generous support to Sir John Macdonald in federal elections.

There was nothing illiberal in Sir William Meredith's conception of the Roman Catholic Church as a religious institution, but it was inevitable under all the circumstances that he should suspect and denounce ecclesiastical interference in political contests. It may be that he was not always judicious or judicial in his references to the heirarchy but there was provocation and under provocation he was not patient or apologetic.

REMINISCENCES

Among those behind him in the constituencies were not a few who cried in their hearts, "a barred door to Popery and no Peace with Rome." But who can confine the bounds or control the spirit of controversies which touch racial and sectarian feeling? They are hateful altogether but the world is free, or as free as it is, because through the ages courageous spirits have resisted obscurantism and absolutism and made "the bounds of freedom wider yet." One cannot think that the educational measures of the Mowat Government affecting Roman Catholics were so dangerous or so reactionary as they were represented to be, but the anger of the Conservative leaders of Ontario over the alliance between the Bishops and the Government was natural, and, as has been said, such controversies inevitably develop suspicion, rancour and all uncharitableness. Still Ontario has had no truer public servant than Sir William Meredith and it is impossible to doubt that if he had become Prime Minister he would have maintained high standards of probity and efficiency in the public departments, guarded the resources of the Province with austere integrity, and incorporated the spirit of social justice in legislation and administration.

If there is no humour in this chapter it is because there was no humour in the Legislature. Like all Canadian Parliaments the Legislative Assembly of Ontario was trying in its gravity and tragic in its profundity. Two incidents, however, I recall. Once Mr. G. W. Badgerow, who represented East York, was called to speak in a debate on the Budget a day before he should have spoken according to the order of debate arranged by the Whips. In his first sentences he explained that he was not fully prepared and was only speaking to fill a hiatus. The correspondent of *The Toronto News* remarked that he filled the hiatus but emptied the House. This was not exactly true, but could a human correspondent neglect such an opportunity. Once Mr. Tooley, a venerable and respected Conservative who represented East Middlesex fell asleep and gently slid from his chair to the floor. Mr. Tooley opened his eyes, seemed to be wholly unimpressed by the incident, arose slowly and deliberately reseated himself, and as Mr. John Lewis said in *The Globe,* "gravely resumed his legislative duties." I think also of one other incident in the Legislature which, like the story that Abraham Lincoln told Henry Ward Beecher, will not bear telling.

Of my own work in the Press Gallery I say nothing. It was petty and trivial and partisan. A glance at my daily contribution in the old files of *The Globe* was enough. It was of the atmosphere of the Legislature and in those days one worshipped his political idols; blasphemed the enemy and rejoiced. Nor do I hesitate at the confession that very often I was in complete sympathy with Sir William Meredith's legislative proposals, as I was attracted by his personality and deeply impressed by his power in debate and his wisdom in counsel when measures outside the realm of party controversy were under consideration. When Sir William ascended the Bench he wrote me a letter, as unexpected as it was welcome, in which he said that never under my editorship had *The Globe* treated him unfairly or ungenerously or misrepresented his position on any public question. Moreover, when *The Globe* building was burned in 1895 he gave me the files of *The Globe, The Mail* and *The Empire* from the time that he had entered public life to replace those which had been destroyed. Still, I think just as badly of the stuff I wrote in the Press Gallery of the Legislature more than thirty years ago.

CHAPTER V

THE PRESS AND THE PRESS GALLERY

In 1886, after prorogation of the Legislature, I was sent to Ottawa. But during the few weeks that I was in the Press Gallery towards the close of the Parliamentary session I wrote only occasional letters to *The Globe,* with a few editorials and editorial paragraphs. The immediate object, as Mr. Cameron explained, was that I should have opportunity to study Parliament in session and to establish with the Liberal leaders at Ottawa such a working relation as I had secured with the leaders of the party in the Legislature. A year later I entered the Press Gallery as *The Globe's* special Parliamentary correspondent. It was an honour to belong to that Gallery, although I would be sorry to suggest a comparison unfavourable to any other group of journalists which have represented or which now represent the press of Canada in the House of Commons. The traditions of the Press Gallery are singularly honourable and have been worthily maintained. No greater distinction comes to a Canadian journalist than to be chosen to represent an influential newspaper at Ottawa. I look back to my years in the Gallery as the most happy and interesting of my life, as desirable and enviable through association with the Gallery itself as through any intimate relation with political leaders or any necessary identification with the strategy of parties.

There began an instant friendship with Dr. A. H. U. Colquhoun, which for more than thirty years has been firmly rooted and deeply cherished. In that

113

friendship there has been not only enduring pleasure, but continuous advantage. No man has greater knowledge of the sources of Canadian history, the constitutional evolution of the Empire, the complex influences which make this a hard country to govern, the underlying forces which in seasons of crisis restore the balance of sanity and authority. Between Dr. Colquhoun and myself in the consideration of public questions there has been as much of conflict as of concord, as much of difference as of agreement, but we could always so temper contention with mercy that personal relations were unaffected. I know that this should not be said until Dr. Colquhoun is dead, but I may not be here, and the word of tribute may be neglected.

Mr. R. S. White, once member of the Commons for Cardwell, for many years Collector of Customs at Montreal, and now again writing for *The Montreal Gazette,* was perhaps the most authoritative and distinguished member of the Gallery in the eighties. If he had less natural genius for a public career than his father, Hon. Thomas White, he was as great a journalist. In handling the intricate and mysterious questions of money, exchange and finance he has had no equal among journalists in Canada save Mr. Edward Farrer. He did his work with amazing ease and celerity. The product was always lucid and finished. He spoke with the authority of knowledge and with remarkable freedom from prejudice or partisanship. If he was never uncertain in his political attitude he reasoned with such moderation and discretion that the effect was persuasive and powerful. When Mr. White was a candidate in Cardwell I ventured in *The Globe* not only to extol his personal qualities, but to suggest that he had exceptional qualifications for Parliamentary service. I was made to understand that there were Liberals in Cardwell who were not grateful for my rash candour. The editorial was distributed as a campaign leaflet by the Conservative committee. I had, however, no thought of disloyalty to the Opposition candidate, nor did I suggest that Mr. White should be elected. I never could think that a political contest was a personal quarrel or that political differences should affect personal relations. It is curious that public men who habitually compliment opponents resent generous references by friendly newspapers to the candidates or achievements of the party to which they are opposed. In this attitude there is a suggestion that the press is subordinate to the political leaders and may not be gracious without admonition nor generous without rebuke.

I met Mr. White in the lobby while the bells were ringing for the division on Sir Richard Cartwright's resolution which committed the Liberal party in 1888 to unrestricted reciprocity. He intimated that we would know in a few minutes if the ranks of either party would be broken and suggested an exchange of confidences. When I agreed he declared that not a single Conservative would vote with the Opposition. I had to tell him that the Opposition was less fortunate since Mr. James Livingstone, of South Waterloo, would go with the Government. But what was anticipated did not happen. Mr. Livingstone, who had resisted all persuasion to support Sir Richard Cartwright's resolution, intended also to oppose the Government's amendment. When the amendment was carried, however, the Opposition agreed with surprising alacrity to have the main motion defeated on the same division. Thus Mr.

Livingstone had no opportunity to vote on the Cartwright resolution, and failing a personal explanation was registered in its support. While displeased at the manœuvre by which he had been entrapped, he agreed to keep silence for the time, and I doubt if his true position ever was disclosed. Mr. White understood and I was so confident he would reveal nothing that I never even spoke to him again on the subject.

One of my close friends in the Gallery was Mr. C. H. Cahan, who represented *The Halifax Herald,* was afterwards leader of the Conservative party in Nova Scotia, and finally turned to business with financial results far more satisfactory than accrue from journalism or politics. But he cannot altogether eschew politics, for he was a Unionist candidate in Quebec in the last general election. In the Gallery, too, was Dr. S. D. Scott, whom I first met at Halifax thirty-five years ago. Not less distinguished among Eastern journalists than Hon. J. V. Ellis, he has won equal distinction in British Columbia, where for many years now he has interpreted the East to the West and counseled wisely in social and educational movements. In much of Dr. Scott's writing there is an ironic pungency, which is very searching, a furtive satire not always detected, but which strikes with mortal effect at insincerity or pretension. I know of no writer in Canada who has a keener scent for cant or humbug or who can be so penetrating when he seems to be merely casual and uninterested. One wonders if the Conservative leaders have understood how influential for a generation has been Dr. Scott's advocacy of the causes for which they contended or how arduous and unselfish has been his devotion to the principles which his judgment and conscience have approved.

One thinks also of Mr. George Ham, happy and companionable, fertile in devices to make life joyous, beloved by ministers, doorkeepers and pages, all alike the prey of a tongue that spared nothing, but never a shaft that would wound or a gibe with the flavour of malice. Was there ever a man with a greater capacity for friendship and fellowship, or one who received of what he gave so freely in fuller measure? Mr. W. B. Scarth represented Winnipeg when the Manitoba Government undertook to charter a railway from the American boundary in defiance of the provision in the original contract with the Canadian Pacific Railway Company which protected the road for twenty years against competition. During the debate on a motion against disallowance of the Provincial legislation Mr. Scarth received numerous despatches from influential citizens of Winnipeg demanding that he oppose disallowance and therefore oppose the Government. All the despatches were submitted to Mr. Ham by the embarrassed member, as faithful a Conservative as was Mr. Ham himself. They had many anxious consultations as to the wise course to pursue. But I wonder if Mr. Scarth ever discovered that these despatches were written in the press room by Mr. Ham himself and delivered by a messenger who was a partner in the conspiracy.

Mr. T. P. Gorman, editor of *The Ottawa Free Press,* and for a time *The Globe's* correspondent at the capital, had not much humour, but he was often caustic and incisive. During the debate on the Fisheries Treaty of 1888 a member who spoke often and at great length on many subjects was trying the Gallery beyond endurance when Gorman muttered: "Why doesn't the d—— fool sit down? The treaty doesn't affect him. He is more than three miles wide at the mouth." This recalls the remark of a Hansard reporter when Mr. Blake was making a speech of four or five hours' duration on the Canadian Pacific Railway. The colleague by whom he was relieved at the reporters' table, in order to be certain that the report would be complete and continuous, whispered, "Where is he at?" The answer came with energy and emphasis, "He is on the south branch of the Saskatchewan, running down grade and going like h——."

In those days there was fierce rivalry between the morning newspapers of Toronto. The Gallery correspondents as distinguished from the shorthand writers were Mr. Fred Cook for *The Empire*, Mr. A. F. Wallis for *The Mail*, and Mr. James Maclean for *The World*, while I represented *The Globe*. *The Empire* was the official organ of the Government, and even without the advantage which this relation gave to Mr. Cook, he was a dangerous antagonist. *The Mail* was passing through a period of "splendid isolation," regarded with deep suspicion by the Government and comforted by the furtive affection of the Liberal leaders. I cannot think that Canada has ever had a greater newspaper than was *The Mail* during this period of separation from the Conservative party, nor was there ever a correspondent in the Gallery of greater industry, sounder judgment and wider, truer knowledge of public questions than Arthur Wallis. He had, too, a shrewd, bantering humour, as penetrating as it was disturbing. By a few provocative sentences he could and often did excite a furious controversy in the press room, and then quietly withdraw into himself, as if he had no interest in the contention which he had excited. Curiously enough, his humour was seldom revealed in his correspondence or editorials, nor indeed can I think that his writing expressed his personality. Moreover, he so loved obscurity that his distinction among Canadian journalists has not, perhaps, been fully recognized. "Jim" Maclean was a brother of Mr. W. F. Maclean, M.P., a brilliant member of a family which has done at least as much as any other to give originality and virility to Canadian journalism.

Among other influential members of the Gallery was Mr. Molyneux St. John, *of The Montreal Herald*. Unobtrusive, agreeable, and lovable, without aggressive quality in private intercourse, and with the tastes of an English gentleman, he was by no means a political neutral nor a non-combatant in party controversy. He had the full confidence of the Liberal leaders, although it was also necessary to maintain a working relation with Hon. Peter Mitchell, who controlled *The Herald,* never neglected his own quarrels and was not always amenable to leader or caucus. It was a question whether Mr. St. John or myself would become editor of *The Globe* when Mr. John Cameron resigned. If Mr. St. John had been appointed he had the assurance that we would be loyal working comrades. We had, too, Mr. R. L. Richardson, of *The Winnipeg Tribune*, aflame with buoyant spirit and radical conviction, contemptuous of precedent and authority, and burning with the evangelical fervour which has not been exhausted. I think also of Mr. George Johnson, statistical and reminiscent; Mr. J. L. Payne, a perennial contributor to the humour of the Gallery, who had many a "scoop" at my expense when we were reporters in Lon-

119

don; Mr. James Johnson of *The Citizen,* Mr. Marc.
Sauvelle of *La Presse,* Mr. T. P. Owens, Mr. W. A.
Harkin, Mr. A. C. Campbell, Mr. John Lewis, and
Mr. Horace Wallis, Mr. Robert McLeod, who has
made the Gallery his eternal home, "Mack," who was
the friend of us all; Mr. Roden Kingsmill, Mr. John
Garvin and Mr. W. J. Healy, all three young, eager
and brilliant; Captain Chambers, a soldier, but not yet
a colonel or a censor, and Mr. Alexander Pirie, for one
session only. Later there came "Pica" Kribs, devoted
to "the party," belligerent when his idols were defamed,
but so abounding in human kindness that his partisan
ferocity had the flavour of comedy. During the "scandal session" of 1891, although I was then editor of *The
Globe,* I went down to Ottawa for a few weeks to stimulate the "tumult and the shouting" by a series of special
despatches. My first despatch began with the words,
"Chaos has come." In *The Empire* Mr. Kribs insisted
that this was a personal notice of my arrival at the capital, and "Chaos" I was in his correspondence for some
time afterwards. During those weeks Great Britain
was convulsed by the baccarat scandal through which
the future King Edward had a season of unpleasant
notoriety. One night I got a telegram from Mr. Farrer,
who was writing *The Globe's* editorials: "I am attacking the Prince of Wales to-morrow. Come home at
once or you will not have a friend left." These, perhaps, are trivial recollections, but such incidents relieved the asperities of conflict as they recall associations
that were very pleasant, but, alas are very remote.

It is not easy now to realize the handicaps against
which an Opposition correspondent had to contend at
Ottawa thirty years ago. It was difficult, if not impos-

sible, to secure information from the public departments. All appointments and statements of policy were reserved for the party organs. Very often the correspondents of friendly journals had access to blue books and returns before they were submitted to Parliament. Thus their despatches would be in the telegraph office before less favoured rivals could examine the reports. Once I made a personal appeal to Sir George Foster for equal treatment. There was much public interest in the negotiations at Washington which resulted in the Fisheries Treaty of 1888, and I was anxious to have the report in advance of its presentation to Parliament or as soon as it was laid upon the table. I called upon the Minister at his house and pleaded for consideration. My argument, as I remember, was that I represented an important newspaper, that the report was of exceptional public interest, that I had no other desire than to interpret its contents and conclusions fairly and intelligently, that there was no advantage to the Government in a system which discriminated against Liberal correspondents, and that the press, regardless of party, should have equal access to public documents and the public departments. The Minister suggested, with smiling courtesy, that my request was unusual, but that possibly my position was not unreasonable nor my argument unconvincing. I did not get the report before it was laid on the table, nor did I expect that degree of consideration, but I did get a copy shortly after it was presented, and so far as I ever knew I was treated as fairly as the Conservative correspondents. When Sir Wilfrid Laurier came into office in 1896 I advised against the perpetuation of a system which was essentially petty in spirit and vexatious in practice, which recognized a party interest in public information, and which I believed was of no advantage to the Government and of positive disadvantage to the country. Under the Laurier Government all newspapers were accorded equal treatment, and the example was followed by Sir James Whitney when the Conservative leaders obtained office in Ontario.

In those old days there were practically no social relations between Conservatives and Liberals at the capital. It is said that Sir John Macdonald rarely if ever invited a Liberal to his table. Only at Rideau Hall was there any common social intercourse between Ministerialists and Oppositionists. Mr. Alonzo Wright, "the King of the Gatineau," had a soul which would not be confined within the narrow walls of party, and once a year he gave a dinner at his house in the country at which unity and concord prevailed and where there was as much eating as men could survive and wines royal in quality but restricted in quantity to the exercise of a gracious and decorous hospitality. Few followed his example. The unbelievers were rejected. To be out of office was to be out of the world, or as far out of the world as the official element could drive the army of the aliens. In this there is no sense of grievance, for I was unknown, a working journalist, as uninterested in the social life of the capital as in the lost tribes of Israel.

Sir Charles Tupper first attacked the walls of partition. He came back from London, where he was High Commissioner for Canada, to assist in the general election of 1887, as he came again to support Sir John Macdonald in his last contest. Sir Charles Tupper's private secretary was Mr. C. C. Chipman, afterwards Hudson's

Bay Commissioner at Winnipeg, who, with knowledge of British practice, insisted that statements and documents affecting the Department of Finance should be furnished simultaneously to representatives alike of Liberal and Conservative newspapers. In this he was supported by Sir Charles Tupper, who may indeed have been responsible for the new regulation, since we had many evidences that he was anxious to extend decent consideration to Opposition correspondents. Probably he was affected by his London experiences, and possibly the representations which I made through Mr. Chipman, with whom I had friendly relations, may have had some effect. It is certain that I took full advantage of the connection which I was able to establish with the Department of Finance, and that in my despatches to *The Globe* such information as I obtained was not distorted or interlarded with partisan comment. It may even be that the Minister of Finance was treated with greater leniency than his colleagues, who kept the door closed against Liberal correspondents. From Sir Charles Tupper I had the only invitation to dinner that I ever received from a Conservative Minister while I was a member of the Press Gallery. The thing was so amazing that I hesitated to accept without authority from the office. I telegraphed to *The Globe* and was assured that acceptance would not be treated as a betrayal of the Opposition.

I had a working relation with a Conservative member through which I was able occasionally to forecast ministerial policy and even to announce impending Cabinet changes in advance of the official organs. We entered into no compact, but he was not neglected. In my despatches he was the subject of many friendly re-

ferences and often I was censured at Liberal headquarters over my apparent infatuation for this particular
member. But if I got, I had to give. Neither of us
committed any venal offence, and there was mutual
advantage in the understanding. So far as I know the
relation never was suspected, nor will there now be any
fuller confession. Sir Hibbert Tupper was among the
first to follow the example of his father in mellowing
social relations between the parties and in reasonable
treatment of Opposition newspapers. I have never
thought that it was a political advantage to the younger
Tupper to be the son of his father. That, I think, was
the common judgment of the Press Gallery, and no man
of any considerable length of service in Parliament
ever imposes upon the Gallery or gets less than justice
in the press room. Its estimate of public men is not
greatly coloured by partisanship nor affected even by
advocacy of unpopular causes. Any man to whom the
Gallery yields its final favour has in his bosom the roots
of sincerity and integrity and may safely challenge the
judgment of posterity. In this the Gallery may not
agree, but I have always thought that if there had been
no disruption under Sir Mackenzie Bowell, and if Sir
Charles Tupper had not succeeded to an estate in
Chancery, Sir Hibbert would have been leader of the
Conservative party.

Hon. N. Clarke Wallace, too, during my term of
service in the Gallery, would not tolerate any ostracism
of Liberal correspondents. He was chairman of the
committee which investigated trade combinations, and
when the report was ready insisted that the Liberal
newspapers should have copies as early as their Conservative contemporaries. But Mr. Wallace was essen-

tially fair-minded, resolute and courageous. No man could be more generous in every private relation or more uncompromising in political conflict. A man of fundamental convictions, he hated the meretricious pretension and fawning subservience which distinguish the politician from the statesman. There was more of quality in Mr. Wallace than his opponents recognized, and greater capacity perhaps than the country has ever understood. I had many an angry controversy with Liberal politicians because I held to this estimate of Mr. Wallace against every persuasion and protest. In *The Globe* my regard for Mr. Wallace was often expressed, and at many meetings of the Committee on Discipline I was reproached and condemned. But when Mr. Wallace resigned office and became an ally of the Opposition in the long Parliamentary struggle over the Remedial Bill, designed to re-establish separate schools in Manitoba, the Liberal group discovered virtues in Mr. Wallace which they had not suspected, or at least had not acknowledged. One of my first appearances on a political platform was at a joint meeting where Mr. Wallace was the chief Conservative speaker, and I was saved only by his mercy from abject discomfiture and humiliation.

From the first I had an inveterate distaste for the slander and scandal of politics. No doubt I offended often, but in the offending I was not happy. Nothing is more fatuous than the notion that a newspaper may not correct an error or express regret for misrepresentation or misjudgment. Early in the session of 1887, when I had been only a few days in the Gallery, a severe attack was made on Mr. J. C. Patterson, of Essex, over an alleged transaction, which I need not explain. Mr.

Patterson, who was not in the House when he was indicted, next day made a statement which I thought was a complete and conclusive refutation of the charges. When the House rose I sought out Sir Richard Cartwright, explained that in my despatch to *The Globe* I had joined in the attack on Mr. Patterson, that I thought he had been badly treated, and that I desired to say so without reserve or equivocation. Sir Richard suggested that a confession was unnecessary and would be awkward, because if I acquitted Mr. Patterson I would indirectly censure the Liberal members who were responsible for the charges. He admitted, however, that the charges were clearly disproved and at length agreed that I might explain and withdraw any censure that my despatch had expressed. A few days afterwards I had a letter from Mr. Patterson, in which he declared that my action was without precedent in his political experience.

I had more serious trouble over a friendly reference to Sir Mackenzie Bowell. Shortly after *The Globe* in which this reference appeared was distributed in the buildings I entered the Liberal headquarters, unconscious of offence, but was instantly assailed by a group of Liberal members in language that was neither complimentary nor restrained. In degree as I was humble and apologetic the violence increased. My chief assailant was a Liberal member from Central Ontario, who declared that for years the Liberals of Hastings had fought Bowell, that he deserved neither consideration nor compassion, that any word said in his praise in *The Globe* was treason to the Liberal party, and that I had come to Ottawa, a stranger, without political experience or knowledge of Bowell's character, and with feeble amiability or arrogant self-confidence had commended a ruthless enemy in the columns of the chief party organ. When it became apparent that humility would not avail, I grew as violent as my accusers. I think, too, that I revealed a talent in invective for which they were not prepared. Before they had fully recovered from their surprise, or admiration for my picturesque vocabulary, I left the room and did not appear again in "No. 6" until three of the members who had joined in the attack came to me in the lobby with a formal apology. They even admitted that what I had said about Bowell was true enough, although they could not fully agree that it was desirable to have friendly references in *The Globe* to any member of the Government. The member who had been most severe in reprobation of my evil conduct became one of the best friends I ever had, and thereafter I believe I had the complete confidence and good-will of the Liberal Parliamentary party. Of this regard and good-will I had so many manifestations that those years at Ottawa are the portion of my life that I would be most willing to live over again.

I think of one Sabbath day on which I was engaged from ten o'clock in the morning until midnight preparing for publication the private letters which led to Mr. J. C. Rykert's expulsion from Parliament. I know who gave me the letters and how they were obtained. But I was responsible only for the despatch to *The Globe,* and its preparation was not a pleasant duty. Ever afterwards I refused to handle private letters. More than once I declined to print such letters when they were brought to *The Globe* by disloyal officials or secured by other doubtful methods. More than once I prevented publication of statements that could only hurt private reputations and serve no public object. In the Press Gallery there was a remarkable consideration for men's private faults and follies. Of what all men knew only the Press seemed to be ignorant. Moreover, so much of what was common gossip at Ottawa was sheer, wanton slander that we were reluctant to believe even when the truth was as manifest as the daylight. Whether it be admitted or not, there is a practice of reticence and a standard of honour among journalists not less lofty than that which prevails in the legal and medical professions. Once from the platform a public man of high reputation and distinction made a savage attack upon the private character of a Conservative leader. All that he said was sent to *The Globe,* and by my order every word was suppressed. The next day the man who had made the attack came to my house to express his gratitude. He said, "I behaved like a common blackguard, and I shall never forget that you saved me from public obloquy, if not from self-contempt."

Once I entered into a conspiracy with a reporter to discover evidence that would prevent publication of a discreditable story affecting a Conservative Minister which very powerful influences had determined should appear in *The Globe.* A doubtful action, perhaps, for the story was true enough, but I am unrepentant. I have related these incidents, because this is a chapter for journalists, because I know that if I could compare my experience with that of other editors and correspondents I would find that they had done likewise, and because I am not certain that the public understands how much of restraint and reticence is commonly practised by the profession to which we belong.

THE PRESS AND THE PRESS GALLERY

In thirty years there have been revolutionary changes in journalism in Canada. The staffs of the morning newspapers have ceased to be the aristocrats of the profession. The evening newspapers have equal authority and equal circulation. They have as complete news services; they have as much individuality and distinction. But when I was in the Press Gallery *The Montreal Star* alone among afternoon journals compared favourably with the morning newspapers. There is a common notion that party feeling has been less acute and party warfare less implacable, but I doubt if this was true either in the press or in Parliament until the Union Government was organized. As it was in Canada so it was in Great Britain. We have, however, passed out of the era of corporate domination in the press and in politics. It may be that the day of deliverance was long in coming, but that it has come is beyond dispute. A generation ago it required courage for a newspaper to attack a great railway or a group of capitalists. Now it requires even greater courage to defend corporate and financial interests even when these are assailed by mercenaries and demagogues who mouth duty and patriotism, but practise personal or political black-mail. The last condition is better than the first, but neither is ideal.

It is often said that the press declines in prestige and authority. There may be loss of prestige with the few, but there is increase of authority with the many. A century ago the newspaper was read chiefly by the educated and governing classes. These in great degree did their own thinking. They had knowledge of the facts of history and the science of government. They could reject misinformation and penetrate fallacious and mis-

129

chievous reasoning. Now, however, the newspaper enters every household. It thinks for those who do not think for themselves. It reaches the multitude who are not instructed in social, economic or political science, who have meagre knowledge of the experiences of other generations, who have faith in the omnipotence of statutes and the power of governments over natural laws and inevitable human tendencies.

In proportion as we widen the franchise we enlarge the body of uninstructed voters. There are those who seem to think that the child of the twentieth century is born with the inherited wisdom of the ages. The truth is that man still lives only three-score years and ten, and few of us are much wiser than the fathers were a thousand years ago. How many of us believed that the nations would learn war no more? We scoffed at Armageddon, and stoned the Prophets of Preparation. But human nature was unchanged. Autocrats and despots still lusted for dominion. Blood was still the price of freedom. War came, and all the genius of man was devoted to the science of destruction. The press chiefly inspires a democracy to exertion, endurance and sacrifice for the preservation of its ideals and institutions. Where there is no free press there cannot be a free people. In such a world who can measure the responsibility of the journalist?

It has been said that a constitutional statesman must have the powers of a first-rate man and the creed of a second-rate man. In journalism the creed is the first consideration. Moreover, a single mind must dominate a public journal if it is to speak with the consistency which inspires confidence and gives authority. It is often said that a Delane, a Greeley, a Russell, or a Dana are impossible conceptions for the twentieth century. If so, the press must become devitalized. For a press that is unequal to wise and strong leadership is a menace to the Commonwealth. A fellow journalist once declared that one man must "spit blood" to give vitality and power to a great newspaper. It is a mistake to think that a newspaper's opinions are expressed only in its editorial columns. There is individuality and unity in every public journal. The balance inclines towards good or evil. There cannot be neutrality in motive or effect. The editorial page colours the special despatches. Even if no editorial opinions were expressed, the news columns would advocate a cause or a party, reveal the convictions or betray the prejudices of the responsible editors.

The printer with his "composing stick" has gone the way of the rural shoemaker, the village blacksmith and the household weaver. Many of the old printers survive, but often they are lonely and pathetic figures, mourning for the independence which the type-setting machine has destroyed. No craftsman had greater mastery over himself than the printer. No one was less at the mercy of employers. No one could tramp more gaily from town to town, from coast to coast, with his tools in his hand and his skill in his fingers. He was like the minstrel who had only his violin and his companion who had only her song. His successor sits at a machine which belongs to the company and feels the dependence which is inseparable from the necessity for capital.

The modern printing press, a miracle of inventive genius, and of amazing productive capacity, costs from $50,000 to $60,000. A battery of type-casting machines costs a like amount. The motor has replaced the delivery wagon, increasing the outlay and driving rival newspapers into fiercer competition. Half a century ago there were few great cities in the United States and Canada. Now there are many with a total population of 500,000, and not a few with from 1,000,000 to 5,000,-000 people within the civic area. As population expands rentals and taxes increase, cost of building, plant, delivery and general organization rises, and the investment necessary to establish, publish and circulate a daily newspaper becomes enormous as compared with the outlay and revenue required under more primitive conditions.

Thirty years ago a metropolitan newspaper could be established with $100,000 or $150,000. To-day in a community of 500,000 the publishers are fortunate who achieve success with $1,000,000. This means that the professional journalist, whatever his genius or industry or self-denial, cannot hope to own a daily journal. It may be that few men are wise enough or good enough to be a law unto themselves. God has made no more offensive creature than the editorial bully. Nevertheless, the editors who have best served their generation have had the complete control of their newspapers which ownership confers, and it is hard to believe that with less absolute authority they would have been as useful or as powerful. But there is no evidence that the independence of the press has been affected by the necessity for great capital or that there is any greater element of dependence in the relation of the journalist to the newspaper for which he is responsible before the public. Nor is the freedom of the press greatly affected by its relation to advertisers. There are communities

132

in which a material percentage of the gross advertising revenue is provided by a few great commercial houses. But these have no natural monopoly. They succeed chiefly through efficiency in service and volume of business. In many households no newspaper is acceptable which does not carry departmental store advertising. Town and county are alike interested. In the counties readers order by mail, in the towns they purchase direct. This advertising is generally trustworthy and often attractive and pungent. In many publications there is nothing of better quality. The pages of newspapers devoted to store advertising are as interesting as the news pages. Failure to secure this patronage is equivalent to sentence of death to many journals. It is a question if they could not better afford to give free space to such advertising than to be without it. The journal which loses revenue by heroic posturing ceases to exist. It is easy to practise virtue at the expense of other people. In all human relations there is occasional submission to inexorable circumstances, and as long as newspapers depend chiefly upon advertising there will be occasional consideration for the sources of supply. But few of those who censure make as great sacrifices for the public welfare or show equal disregard for private convenience and private interest.

The war has greatly affected newspapers in every belligerent country. It has been necessary to reduce size and increase prices. In many cities the price on the street has been raised from one cent to two cents a copy, and there has been a proportionate increase to mail subscribers. Generally, so far as can be ascertained, the loss in circulation has not exceeded twenty or twenty-five per cent. It is not desirable, either from the standpoint of the publisher or the public, that circulation should be reduced, but there will be compensation if the dependence of newspapers upon advertisers is relieved. There will be relief also for advertisers from the increasing charges to which they have been subjected. Fewer newspapers may enter some households, but those that are taken will be read more thoroughly. There is no danger that the volume of advertising will decline. As an agent of publicity the newspaper has established its supremacy. For classes of advertising, the magazines, the trade journals and the weekly publications are as valuable as the daily papers. Moreover, newspapers, magazines and periodicals are giving increased returns to advertisers because both the quality and the reliability of copy has improved. Newspapers also begin to recognize that they are not solely responsible for the success of charitable, benevolent and patriotic movements. Even political committees discover that they have no squatters' rights in the advertising columns. The press is bound to assist legitimate social, commercial and political movements, but the whole cost of advocacy cannot fairly be imposed upon publishers. Those who demand free space in a newspaper as an inalienable right do not expect to have offices provided and furnished at the expense of landlords.

These considerations begin to prevail with publishers and to be understood by the public. For the conditions which have existed newspapers have had a degree of responsibility. They have hesitated to confess that they are commercial enterprises, selling news and space as a farmer sells his wheat or a manufacturer his product. They are responsible for the character of the advertising they accept, for the opinions they express, and for the material which they admit into the news columns, but they have no obligation to private or even to public interests which does not rest in equal degree upon other citizens. This is not a sordid view of journalism. It does not suggest neglect of duty or sacrifice of character for revenue. It does ignore cant and pretension. It does separate the journalist from the Pharisee. No institution can have a life worth living unless it is solvent. Nothing affects the character of a newspaper more vitally than the shifts and compromises inseparable from an empty treasury. It is fortunate, therefore, that publishers have come to recognize the value of space, that prices to subscribers have been increased, and that even governments, political parties, and social, commercial, municipal, and national organizations realize that they can best advance their interests by liberal expenditures for advertising. With increase in the variety and volume of advertising, there is less dependence upon any single class of advertisers. There is also a better guarantee of quality and reliability. The final reliance of a newspaper is upon popular suffrage, upon the public opinion which in degree it may create, but which it must express if it is to have large circulation and adequate financial support. There may still be Greeleys and Danas and Delanes and Russells, as there will be many a Jap Miller, who, according to James Whitcomb Riley,

Helt the banner up'ards from a-trailin' in the dust,
And cut loose on monopolies and cuss'd and cuss'd and cuss'd.

CHAPTER VI

BLAKE AND THOMPSON IN PARLIAMENT

Of those who gave distinction to the House of Commons thirty years ago how few survive. It is long since Sir John Macdonald whispered, as he passed out of the Chamber for the last time, "It is late, Bowell, goodnight." Even Bowell, upon whom the years fell so gently, has joined the leader he followed with such trust and ardour. Hon. Edward Blake and Sir Charles Tupper, often described by Sir Richard Cartwright, with a snap of the jaws, as "Master Blake" and "Master Tupper," have vanished. More often, however, Sir Richard called the robust Nova Scotian "Mine ancient friend Sir Charles Tupper, Bart." And "Bart" came out with a bark. We think of Blake with a sense of loss, of Tupper with a sense of possession. Cartwright loved neither, and Blake had at least as much love for Tupper as he had for Cartwright. But this is not the time for that story.

Behind the Conservative leader was Sir John Thompson, who in a single session, and indeed in a single speech, established an ascendency in the Commons which he held until his death. He had, too, a moral as well as an intellectual ascendency. As much as any other man of his time he strove to give dignity and decency to the public life of Canada. I like to think that as editor of *The Globe* I protested over and over again against the common insinuation that he was more loyal to his church than to his country, and that his faith was a disqualification for public service. I said in *The Globe,* when he became Prime Minister, "With the fact that Sir John Thompson is a Roman Catholic we have nothing to do. It would be a poor tribute to the liberality and intelligence of the Canadian people if it were laid down that a Roman Catholic may not equally with a Protestant aspire to the highest office within their gift. Any attempt to arouse sectarian prejudice over his appointment will not make for the dignity of Canadian politics or the welfare of the country."

It is strange that one so gifted and naturally so generous as Rev. Doctor Douglas, of Montreal, should not only have nurtured this suspicion but boldly proclaimed his distrust. He described Thompson as "a clerical creation" and "a lay Jesuit in the Government." On his brow there was "the brand of pervert." "He was enthroned in order to manipulate with Jesuit art the affairs of this country." There was nothing in the political career of Sir John Thompson to suggest that his patriotism was tainted by his religious connection. But it is true that a Roman Catholic in the English-speaking countries rarely becomes the leader of a political party. When was a Catholic Prime Minister of England? No Catholic has held the office of President of the United States. By contrast Canada is singularly and resolutely tolerant. Is the fact that Canada is more Catholic than Great Britain or the United States the true explanation? Sir Henri Joly was Premier of Quebec, but if he was Protestant he was also French. Hon. John Sandfield Macdonald was Premier of United Canada and Premier of Ontario, and probably his Catholicism was no greater disqualification in the English-speaking Province than was the Protestantism of

137

Joly in the French Province. It is doubtful if Hon. C. F. Fraser, notwithstanding his ability and integrity, could have become Premier of Ontario. No doubt men of meagre capacity sometimes attain office because they are Roman Catholics, but as certainly Catholics reach the first places less easily because of the church to which they belong. Probably the explanation lies in the aspiration of the Papacy to temporal power, the old conflicts between civil and ecclasiastical authority, and the assumption of elements in the church to supremacy in civil affairs.

No man ever attained high office more absolutely and unequivocally by sheer force of character and ability than did Sir John Thompson. It is doubtful if he ever spoke a single word or took a conscious step to secure the leadership of the Conservative party. There is reason to think that he would have become leader of the party upon the death of Sir John Macdonald if the judgment of his colleagues had prevailed. But, not convinced that the feeling of the Parliamentary caucus was the common feeling of Conservatives in the constituencies, he strongly advised against any doubtful experiment. Sir John Abbott therefore was appointed, with full knowledge that he would be comparatively inactive and uninfluential and that Thompson as leader of the House of Commons would be the mouthpiece of the party and the actual dictator of strategy and policy. From the first, it was manifest that Sir John Thompson was the logical and inevitable leader. During the few months that he was Premier Sir John Abbott never addressed a public meeting or exercised the actual function of leadership. This was not because he was unequal to the position. For he could be wise in council and bold in action, and had qualities which inspired regard and confidence. But he knew that he had not long to live and was looking beyond the jangle of political conflict into the long silence. There was no seer to foretell that his successor would so quickly follow upon the journey which each of us takes alone and knoweth not the hour of his going.

It is to the honour of the Conservative party, in which the Orange element is so powerful, that there was general acquiescence in the elevation of Sir John Thompson. But there was not complete acquiescence. Mr. D'Alton McCarthy believed that he should have succeeded Sir John Macdonald. He so expressed himself in language which Thompson could not misunderstand. He held that neither by the length nor by the nature of his services, nor by natural identification with the masses of the Conservative party was Thompson entitled to the leadership. Even if the title were clearer, there were forces in the party which would not submit. Inevitably, whatever the prospect of the moment, these influences would express themselves and disaster would follow. He did not object to Thompson as a Minister, but as leader he was objectionable in the party interest and in the public interest. Nor was Mr. McCarthy's attitude presumptuous or unreasonable. For many years he was among the active and trusted advisers of Sir John Macdonald. In debates which involved legal and constitutional issues, in the bitter contests over provincial rights as represented by the Liberal Government of Ontario, and in many stern party battles in the Committee on Privileges and Elections, McCarthy was chief counsel for the Conservative party and the Federal authority. No one was more active in founding *The Empire* when Sir John Macdonald and the Conservatives of Ontario required an organ. Moreover, McCarthy was a Protestant and the natural spokesman for formidable forces among the Conservatives of Ontario and the other English Provinces. He could not fail to be conscious that he was reduced to an inferior position in the party and in Parliament by Sir John Thompson's phenomenal ascension to influence and natural assumption of many of the functions which he had discharged. Whether or not he resented the reduction to lower rank in the Conservative army, and like many other great men was carried by personal feeling into new courses, it is certain that he became estranged from Sir John Macdonald and made mischief for the Government. Leading the agitation for disallowance of the Jesuit Estates Act of Quebec, supporting the abolition of separate schools by the Liberal Government of Manitoba, and challenging the legal status of the French language in the Western Territories, he excited intense feeling in the country and precipitated stormy and bitter debates in Parliament. Whether or not he was actuated in any degree by personal feeling, there is no doubt that he was faithful to his convictions in opposing extension of dual language and racial and religious privileges. It is understood that when the motion for disallowance of the Jesuit Estates Act came before Parliament Mr. McCarthy was so incautious as to declare that he had pledges of support from many of the Conservative members from Ontario. The statement was carried to Sir John Macdonald, who made a personal appeal to every Conservative upon whom Mr. McCarthy relied, with the result that only seven ministerialists voted for disallowance. This interference by the Prime Minister, natural as it was and necessary as it was to the credit and dignity of the Government, McCarthy never could overlook, although it is believed his displeasure did not then extend to Sir Charles Tupper.

During my first years in the Press Gallery Sir John Thompson was the most powerful debater in the Conservative Parliamentary party, as Hon. Edward Blake was the most impressive and convincing speaker among the Liberals. Sir John Macdonald had greater authority than either, but his ascendency was the growth of years; the long result of a rare personality and a great prestige. Neither in Blake nor in Thompson was there any impelling spontaneity or magnetism. Blake was often heavy and sometimes monotonous. Thompson was always cold, sober, self-contained and distant. In his pilgrimages throughout the country Thompson was described by irreverent blasphemers as "the ice-wagon"; Blake could be very lonely and remote. Once I saw the Liberal leader mooning in solemn abstraction over the exchanges in the reading-room when a colleague on the Liberal front benches, who had returned from dinner with "a quart of wine visibly concealed about his person," if I may borrow language which Mr. Alfred Boultbee applied to a clubmate, lurched against him, brought his hand down with tremendous force upon the bowed shoulders, and gurgled, "Come—come 'long, you—you—old hulk, and have some fun." The hulk put his hand affectionately across the back of his unsteady associate and shook with laughter. One could not know from the frosty exterior how intimate and companionable Blake could be in rare moments of self-revelation. But so often he was among the glaciers.

So often he seemed to be like Goldsmith's Traveller, "remote, unfriended, melancholy." I recall a meeting which Mr. Blake addressed at Kincardine in 1882 during a bye-election for the Legislature. In early manhood he had appeared in South Bruce as a candidate for the Commons. It may be that he was softened and inspired by memories of that triumphant contest. He had set the riding aflame by his moving, sonorous oratory, the energy of his deliverance, the revelation of his eager intellectual virility. For a generation the Liberals of Bruce recalled that contest with such enthusiasm and reverence as Scottish Liberals remember Gladstone and Midlothian. As he grew older Mr. Blake became too anxious about the letter of the message and sacrificed spontaniety in dependence upon manuscript. But at Kincardine in 1882 he delivered an address remarkable for its humour, its flavour of neighbourliness, its simple human quality, and moment by moment one could feel respect deepening into sympathy and softening into affection. I heard Mr. Blake many, many times in Parliament and on the platform, and often perhaps he displayed greater power, but never as it has seemed to me was he so close to his kind and so disencumbered of his greatness. For whatever one may think of certain aspects of Mr. Blake's character and career, he was as great a man as ever was born in Canada if the mind is the test and the standard. At his side stands Sir John Thompson. The test here also is sheer intellectual power, capacity to reason, instinct to understand.

It is the common notion that Sir John Thompson was unemotional, unaffected by praise, impervious to attack. But I am told by those who sat at his side in Parliament that he boiled within under adverse criticism and muttered protests and imprecations that would have required rigid censorship in any religious publication. In a memorable attack upon Sir Richard Cartwright he amazed Parliament by the fervour and violence of his denunciation. He declared that Cartwright would rather abuse his country and defame it than eat his breakfast. He thanked God that nature broke the mould in which he was made when she cast him. He put all his passion and contempt into the savage sentence, "As a member of the bar I have sometimes spurned the fee of a blatant scoundrel who denounced everybody else in the world, and was himself the most truculent savage of them all." Upon that speech could have been pronounced the verdict of the Nevada jury, "If it please the court we, the jury, find that the prisoner is not guilty of strikin' with intent to kill, but simply to paralyze, an' he done it." It may be that in that speech only was the man fully expressed. He had schooled himself to restraint and discipline, but there was a volcano within whose forces he alone understood. It is said that in council he was companionable, unrestrained, tolerant of the asperities of associates, happy in their foibles and eccentricities. But in Parliament and on the platform he was austere, if not cold, and even when he was gracious there was more of dignity than of cordiality. Many shrewd but biting judgments ascribed to Thompson were current in the lobbies of Parliament. Unfortunately those I remember strike so hard at men still living that they cannot be repeated. He never was more happy than at a dinner of the Toronto Board of Trade when he discovered "the lean and hungry Cassius" in Hon. George E. Foster. Of great girth himself and with colleagues of equal girth he said, "Their youth and their robustness excited the imagination of a Toronto poet, who indited some verses to me and put into my mouth words which were put into Caesar's when he said, 'Let me have men about me that are fat, sleek-headed men, and such as sleep o' nights,' and I could make you to-night a little boast about the girth and weight of my colleagues if it were not that my friend Cassius here—the Finance Minister —breaks the record and utterly destroys the average."

Sir John Thompson, with grave reluctance, entered the Macdonald Government as Minister of Justice in 1885, when Quebec was inflamed over the fate of Riel and excited writers in Ontario were "smashing Confederation into its original fragments." Smashing Confederation is the common pastime of Canadian patriots when the party is in danger or the Constitution interferes with the designs of minorities or the prejudices of majorities. But the ship of State sails on and the waters are assuaged.

The new Minister first spoke in Parliament in direct reply to Hon. Edward Blake on a resolution declaring that Riel should not have been executed. So far as I can remember there was no general impression in the country that Thompson was of exceptional character or capacity. He had been Premier of Nova Scotia and a member of the Supreme Court of his Province, but at best he had only a Provincial reputation in law or in politics. When he sat down after his first speech in the House of Commons it was realized that a great figure had emerged from a curious obscurity. Parliament is seldom deceived. There are first speeches that dazzle with metaphor and rhetoric, but these reach the ear only. For once or twice such performances may attract,

HON. EDWARD BLAKE

FROM A SKETCH BY E. WYLY GRIER, R.C.A.

but they have no enduring quality. Soon the benches empty and the sounding phrases become the jest of the smoking-room. The House of Commons distrusts eloquence. It is seldom that a great platform orator catches its atmosphere. A long training in Provincial politics constitutes a positive disqualification for the Federal Parliament. But from the first Sir John Thompson had the manner of Parliament. From the first he commanded its interest and confidence. He was simple, lucid, persuasive and convincing. He seemed to be interested only in the logical structure of his argument. He was not so anxious to achieve a personal triumph as that he should be understood and that the cause for which he pleaded should suffer nothing by imperfect statement or intemperate advocacy. In short, he gave an impression of simplicity, sincerity and integrity, and in Parliament these are the qualities that prevail. If he did not overcome Mr. Blake in his first speech in the Commons even the Opposition admitted that the reply was adequate, that a man had appeared of vital power and resolute character, and that a great task had been done with high skill, wise discretion and profound judgment. Nor do I think that Sir John Thompson ever was humiliated or discredited in Parliament by any incident, attack or situation. Throughout the impression of austere integrity persisted. He came into Parliament in a difficult time, and found work to do that was not pleasant. But whether one recalls the expulsion of Rykert, the long, heated, acrimonious inquiry into the McGreevy charges, the international negotiations in which he was engaged, the measures of policy and legislation for which he was responsible, his integrity stands and his patriotism is

145

not impugned. He did not come to his country gift-less nor fail "to show fruit of his days."

There was a divided and somewhat sullen party behind the Liberal leader. Many of the French members who had stood with Sir John Macdonald from Confederation had been driven into revolt by the fierce current of feeling which swept over the Province when Riel was hanged in defiance of its angry and tumultuous protest. There are few more ugly incidents in Canadian history than the erection of the Regina scaffold into a political platform. There is no doubt that the half-breeds had grievances, that the Government had warning, and that by sympathetic decent consideration for the rights of the helpless and anxious settlers the revolt could have been averted. But Riel was at the foot of the gallows years before. In the Red River he had sanctioned murder and had received a full portion of mercy. In precipitating a second rebellion he was foolhardy, insolent and defiant. The man, perhaps, was on the verge of madness, but if so the calculating politicians did not discover that he was insane until he was executed. I think of a Liberal journal which declared before the death sentence was carried into effect that we had come to "a pretty pass" in Canada when a base, foul, red-handed murderer could escape the consequences of his crimes because a cowardly Government dare not order his execution. After he was hanged, this journal was just as certain that we had come to "a pretty pass" when a bold and chivalrous champion of his oppressed compatriots could be put to death by the Government whose neglect and ineptitude had provoked the revolt. The "curve" which Mr. Smiley took so gallantly at the request of Sir John Macdonald was nothing compared with that which was taken by Liberal politicians and Liberal newspapers when Riel was executed.

During the ferment of agitation in Quebec against the execution and the clamorous demand in Ontario for Riel's death Hon. Edward Blake was in the Old Country. Thus he was free to approve or condemn, however deeply many of his associates might be com mitted against his decision. Contending that Riel was insane and the Government responsible for the rebellion, Mr. Blake joined hands with the excited agitators of Quebec, and so far as he could prevail rallied the Liberal party against the execution. One may not impugn his sincerity, but the circumstances were singular and suspicion inevitable. It is hard to believe that Riel would have become a martyr and a patriot if he had been reprieved. It is certain the execution would have seemed to be less heinous if Quebec had been quiescent. We often get strange results when actions are measured by political exigencies. Once in the House of Commons long after the fires of this fierce controversy had smouldered into ashes, Dr. Weldon, of Albert, recalled this chapter of Mr. Blake's career in grave, cold, stern sentences of rebuke, if not of contempt. As Dr. Weldon spoke the Chamber became very quiet. Mr. Blake seemed to shrink as though a whip were laid across his shoulders. One felt as sometimes in a court-room when a great trial has ended and the Bench pronounces judgment with reluctance, but with inflexible justice. From the Liberal benches there was no protest. The Ministerialists were responsive, but there was restraint in their cheering. The common knowledge that Mr. Blake and the scholarly member for Albert had tastes in common, and that the Liberal leader thought highly of Dr. Weldon gave a curious emphasis and a startling unexpectedness to the attack. It may be that Dr. Weldon was unjust. Possibly this impressive Parliamentary incident has coloured my thinking about Mr. Blake's relation to the issues which arose out of the Northwest Rebellion and Riel's execution. But surely the Liberal party would have had its feet on firmer earth and the historian would find Mr. Blake's career less embarrassing if he had been content to leave the question of Riel's sanity to the alienists, and simply held Sir John Macdonald and his colleagues responsible for the neglect and misgovernment which, with or without Riel's malign activity, produced the rebellion, or if convinced that Riel was insane had spoken before his life was taken.

Mr. Blake was in Europe, but one may speak to Canada even from Europe. It is impossible to believe that he was ignorant of the vital facts of Riel's career, and the evidence produced at the trial at Regina, or had not definite opinions about his mental condition before he was executed. I remember how confident Liberals were that Sir John Macdonald would not dare to hang Riel and defy Quebec, and how deep was the dismay when the sentence was carried into effect. They had believed that the Conservative leader would succumb to the agitation in Quebec and that to such final and irrefutable evidence of "French domination" the English Provinces would not submit. But when Riel was hanged and feeling in the English Provinces appeased they foresaw certain defeat in the constituencies unless Quebec could be consolidated against the Government. It was not easy to detach Quebec from Sir

John Macdonald, nor easy to adjust the Liberal party to an alliance with the mutinous elements in the French Province. A political party, like an individual, develops character, firmly rooted in its traditions, convictions and sentiments. Under George Brown the Liberal party warred against Quebec. When Mr. Blake secured office in Ontario he excited Orange feeling against Sir John Macdonald over his merciful dealing with Riel after the Red River insurrection, and secured a substantial measure of Orange support in the constituencies. In the general election of 1882, in which Mr. Blake first appeared as leader of the Liberal party, there was much fervent denunciation of the "tricky Bleus," and upon many platforms the campaign vocalists sang "The traitor's hand is on thy throat, Ontario, Ontario." Now, however, circumstances seemed to require an alliance with the Bleu and the traitor. Indeed, from this time there is a clear and continuous design in Mr. Blake's course as leader of the Liberal party. He sought to detach Irish Catholics from Sir John Macdonald by aggressive advocacy of Home Rule for Ireland. In alliance with Hon. Wilfrid Laurier as leader for Quebec, he strove to secure the confidence of the French Province. He attacked the Orange Association and gave zealous support to the measures of the Mowat Government, which were so distasteful to the extreme Protestant elements. He failed because Sir John Macdonald had the enduring confidence of Irish Catholics, because Cartier was a living force in Quebec with the generation which remembered the firm and happy partnership between Cartier and the Conservative leader, because Langevin was the faithful champion of the Hierarchy, because Laurier was distrusted by the church whose faith he professed, because Chapleau could reach the soul of the French people as even Laurier could not, because Macdonald's whole career was fashioned in sincere and courageous racial and religious tolerance, and because in the Liberal party which George Brown created there were traditions and susceptibilities inimical to any effective alliance with the Roman Catholic Church and the Province of Quebec. Until Laurier appeared no Federal leader of the Liberal party was able to achieve what Mowat accomplished in Ontario. Mowat succeeded because he had in such peculiar degree the confidence of Presbyterian Liberals.

If Mr. Blake could have effected the alliances which were his deliberate objects he would have prevailed in the country, but the facts of history, the constitution of the Liberal party, and the personality of Sir John Macdonald had created conditions and established influences too great to be overcome. Moreover, when Hon. Alexander Mackenzie, Sir Richard Cartwright, Mr. Charlton, Mr. Mulock, Mr. Davies, Mr. Paterson, Mr. Scriver and other influential Liberals in Parliament could not be persuaded to condemn the Government for sending Riel to the scaffold it became difficult to consolidate the Liberal forces in the country. A party divided in Parliament is a party divided outside Parliament and disabled for cohesion and aggression in battle. Hence because of division and disunion over the execution at Regina and the firm adhesion of Protectionists to the Government, Mr. Blake failed in 1887 as he had failed in 1882, and fretful, discouraged and dispirited, he imposed his resignation upon a broken and disheartened party. It was the habit of Mr. Blake

150

to resign. If we could penetrate the secrets of Liberal caucuses between 1880 and 1887 we would discover an Opposition upon its knees in passionate pleading against the sudden decision of the leader to relinquish the command. Nor would a single incident complete the story. But the doors of caucus are so guarded that only whispers reach beyond the threshold.

It was said of a British statesman that he had not even "a feeding acquaintance with his party." This was true of Mr. Blake, and yet no one ever had more devoted adherents than he in the House of Commons. He could be petulant, inconsiderate and ungracious. He could impose laborious drudgery upon associates and absorb the material which they had accumulated through "long days of labour and nights devoid of ease" without any word of praise or gratitude. He could pass out of the Chamber without turning towards a colleague who had just spoken with power and effect in a great debate. It is said that Mr. David Thompson, who held Haldimand for the Liberal party through three or four Parliaments, upon reaching Ottawa after a serious illness was warmly greeted by Sir John Macdonald, while from Mr. Blake he had neither a handclasp nor a word of sympathy or welcome. On the day in 1890 that fire destroyed a portion of the University buildings at Toronto Mr. Blake made the first speech in Parliament that he had delivered since his resignation of the Liberal leadership. If only from the fact that he had broken a long silence the incident was of high interest and significance. But when *The Globe* reached Ottawa next day there was no report of Mr. Blake's speech nor any account of the proceedings of Parliament. So much space was devoted to the fire that the Parliamentary report had to be held over and all other matter highly condensed. Meeting Mr. Blake in the lobby, I ventured to express regret that the report of his speech had not appeared. He intimated with cold acidity that he had not discovered the fact and was at a loss to know why I should think he would be interested. There are times when language gathers within one which, owing to the proximity of the family, the presence of the stenographer or other untoward circumstances, has to be suppressed. This is serious because I have the notion that profanity which has to be muzzled is more injurious to the system than that which has free and robust utterance. I am still uncertain whether I should be proud or ashamed of the restraint which I exercised on that occasion. When I met Mr. Blake again a few days later he took me to the library and in a long conversation was confidential, gracious and almost affectionate in his references to my despatches from the Gallery and my interpretation of his own position in Parliament and potential influence upon public affairs in the freer relation which he could maintain towards parties and questions in which the exigencies and interests of parties were subordinate to national considerations.

I have been told that Mr. Blake once met a friend from Toronto in Dublin. The Canadian was effusive in his greeting, for he was lonely, and a familiar face was a gleam of sunshine. Mr. Blake responded in a few frigid sentences and passed on his way in solemn abstraction. The friend stood for a moment in dumb surprise, then stepped after Mr. Blake, and peremptorily demanded an explanation. He said in effect: "You know me well. We have been friends. I was glad to see your face. I wanted to talk with you, for you come from home, and for weeks I have been among strangers. Why do you pass me without a word as though I was unworthy of your regard or recognition?" And Mr. Blake said, with a touch of emotion: "I am sorry. I am as glad to see you as you can be to see me. I would have understood in a moment how strange my conduct must appear. If I cannot explain, I think you can understand." The friend understood, and he and Mr. Blake spent companionable hours together in Dublin. If one may say so without blatant egotism, I had more confidential relations with Mr. Blake than need be disclosed. The acquaintance began when I was in the Press Gallery and he was leader of the Liberal party. There was a closer intimacy after I became editor of *The Globe* and he was settling his future relation to the party, chafing over the adoption of "unrestricted reciprocity" with the United States as the fiscal programme, and nursing his soul in bitterness over Sir Richard Cartwright's assumption of leadership in Ontario. During his first years in the Imperial Parliament I had many letters from Mr. Blake discussing very frankly the characteristics of British statesmen, the political conditions in Great Britain and the course of events in Canada. Over and over again he expressed the desire that we could talk together, and the hope that we would have an early meeting in Canada or in England. In 1897, while this correspondence was proceeding, I visited London and met him on the street. He shook hands, made a perfunctory inquiry as to my movements, and strode away. During four or five weeks in London I neither saw nor heard from Mr. Blake again. I cannot think that I had even a momentary sense of annoyance. I believed that I had come to understand the man, and was convinced that he intended no discourtesy nor was conscious of any neglect. But there was a curious conflict between his letters and his actual conduct.

In contrast I think of the experience of a young Canadian from St. Mary's who was in London and saw across the street a man of unusual stature, with heavy shoulders and head leaning forward under a slouch hat. He thought the figure and movement were familiar, and crossing over found, as he had suspected, that the man who had attracted his attention was Hon. Edward Blake. He had the courage to introduce himself, although he had never met Mr. Blake, and save that he was a Canadian had no claim upon his famous compatriot's consideration. Instantly Mr. Blake's face shone with pleasure and his hand went out in hearty greeting. He walked with the young Canadian, took him to dinner, got him a seat in the gallery of Parliament, and treated him with such consideration and attention as he would have expected only from a close friend or a member of his own family. There is a story in Sir George Ross's volume of Reminiscences which I heard him tell more often perhaps than he knew. "I suggested to Mr. Blake," he writes, "that it might be profitable, from a party point of view, if we brought before the House some question of general public interest to show that we had some power of initiative as well. After a review of several suitable topics it was agreed that I should give notice to reopen the question of reciprocity with the United States in the form of a motion asking for correspondence between the Governments of Canada and the United States bearing upon the subject. As the question was a comprehensive one and might involve an expression of the policy of the

Liberal party, it was agreed that I should submit an outline of my speech for Mr. Blake's approval, which I did. In the course of a couple of weeks my motion was reached, and I rose to deliver myself of a speech which I had carefully prepared and which I felt confident would be a reasonably creditable presentation of my case. I spoke for about three-quarters of an hour, and was listened to with fair attention by both sides of the House. The Hon. Mr. White replied to my arguments, and with one or two short speeches the debate closed. Though not particularly impressed with my effort to instruct the House, I ventured to say to Mr. Blake a few hours afterwards: 'Well, I have done my best for reciprocity. How did you like my speech?' 'My dear boy,' he said, 'I did not hear a word of it. I slept the whole time you were speaking.' Whether to take his repose as a mark of perfect confidence in my ability to do justice to the subject or as showing a lack of interest in anything I might say was my dilemma. It was, however, the last speech about which I asked his opinion, either before or after delivery." In telling me this story as illustrating Mr. Blake's neglect of his followers, Sir George Ross added that once as he was leaving the Chamber after a speech by Mr. McQuade, of South Victoria, who was by no means among the best speakers of Parliament, he saw Sir John Macdonald with his arm about Mr. McQuade's shoulders and heard him whisper, "McQuade, you spoke like an angel, I am proud of you." In his book Sir George adds, "Whether Sir John felt sincerely proud or not I do not like to say, but I am sure McQuade did."

I have related these incidents because they explain a great man and perhaps illuminate aspects of his car-

eer. I cannot agree that he had not high qualifications
for leadership or that he was without adequate courage
for political conflict. In his nature there was a strain
of despondency. He sank easily into gloom and depression. Responsive to passing impulses, he made
decisions inconsistent with his real character and true
ambition, surrendering positions which he could not
recover, but which in honest communion with himself
he knew he should have seized or held. Still, notwithstanding his moodiness and remoteness he had the affection of many of his followers and a loyal obedience and
confidence which was not affected by successive defeats.
Hon. Alexander Mackenzie resigned the office of leader
under compulsion; Mr. Blake imposed his resignation
upon a pleading, protesting and despairing party.
There is no doubt that he was vexed by the desertion of
many Parliamentary associates upon the motion to condemn Riel's execution and was grievously wounded by
the contumacy of Mr. Mackenzie and Sir Richard
Cartwright. He was incensed, too, over utterances by
Cartwright in open conflict with his own attitude towards the tariff. It is clear that Mr. Blake sought to
disarm the Protectionists and persuade the country that
there would be no revolutionary disturbance of the industrial system under a Liberal Government. In his
address to the electors of West Durham in 1882 he
said: "I have fully recognized the fact that we are
obliged to raise yearly a great sum, made greater by the
obligations imposed upon us by this Government, and
we must continue to provide this yearly sum mainly by
import duties, laid to a large extent on goods similar to
those which can be manufactured here, and it results as
a necessary incident of our settled fiscal system that

there must be a large and, as I believe in the view of moderate Protectionists, an ample advantage to the home manufacturer. Our adversaries wish to present to you an issue as between the present tariff and absolute free trade. That is not the true issue. Free trade is, as I have repeatedly explained, for us impossible, and the issue is whether the present tariff is perfect or defective and unjust." He said again at Malvern in 1887: "No man, I care not how convinced an advocate of absolute free trade for Canada he may be, has yet suggested a practical plan whereby our great revenue needs can be met otherwise than by the continued imposition of very high duties on goods similar to those we make or can make within our own bounds or on the raw material. I invite the most ardent free trader in public life to present a plausible solution of this problem, and I contend that he is bound to do so before he talks of free trade as practicable in Canada. I have not believed it soluble in my day, and any chance of its solubility, if any chance there were, has been destroyed by the vast increase of our yearly charge, and by the other conditions which have been created. The thing is removed from the domain of practical politics."

But, as in 1882, *The Globe* would emphasize the tariff as the chief issue between the parties, so in 1887 Sir Richard Cartwright was taunted into violent denunciation of the Protectionists, and as prospective Minister of Finance in a Liberal Administration he was perhaps naturally treated by Conservative speakers and writers and by the industrial interests as the authoritative interpreter of Liberal fiscal policy. It is understood that Mr. Blake's statement at Malvern had been submitted to a Liberal conference and approved even by Cartwright, and undoubtedly there was feeling that Cartwright had not observed the compact. But Sir Richard's tongue was an unruly member. Abuse of manufacturers with him was an instinct, a duty, a recreation, and a profession. It is suspected that he was deliberately incited to provide the campaign literature which Conservatives required to offset Mr. Blake's attempt at Malvern to remove the tariff from "the domain of practical politics." The course of *The Globe* in 1882 was among the reasons for the removal of Mr. J. Gordon Brown from the editorship. The course of Sir Richard Cartwright in 1887 aggravated an incompatibility between Mr. Blake and Sir Richard into an enduring estrangement and perhaps explains incidents and events in the later history of the Liberal party as yet uninterpreted and misunderstood. When Mr. Blake resigned the leadership of the party did he not entertain a vagrant notion that he would be recalled and restored to the dignity and authority in the councils of the country which his ambition coveted despite fitful impulses of revolt and wayward denial of his dominant attributes?

CHAPTER VII.

WHEN LAURIER BECAME LEADER

As I have said elsewhere, it is not easy to penetrate the secrets of a party caucus. Of this I had conclusive evidence when Hon. Wilfrid Laurier was chosen to succeed Mr. Blake as leader of the Liberal party. I knew that the caucus was to nominate a leader and that Blake's choice was Laurier. I knew also that there were influential elements in the Opposition unwilling to accept Blake's advice, and convinced that Laurier had neither the industry nor the energy required to discharge the heavy and exacting duties of the office. Furthermore, he was of the French race and a Catholic in religion. There was much feeling that Mr. Blake had received a meagre support from Catholic voters and a keen sense of exasperation over the realignment with Sir John Macdonald of the French Conservative "bolters," whose anger over the fate of Riel did not outlast the first division in the new Parliament. But caucus set aside these grievances, and despite his own resolute protest, Mr. Laurier was elected to the office of leader. The motion which prevailed was submitted by Sir Richard Cartwright, and seconded by Hon. David Mills, both of whom doubted the wisdom of the decision since both aspired to the position. But neither slackened in devotion to the party or ever conspired against Laurier. They were slow, however, to admit that caucus had acted wisely, and for years their speeches contained no eulogy of the leader. Mr. Mills cherished the hope that Mr. Blake would return; Sir Richard did not. 159

For hours I sought to learn whether or not a successor to Mr. Blake had been appointed. But every tongue was tied and every ear closed to my appeal. No one maintained a more resolute silence than Laurier himself. He would neither deny nor admit, confirm nor affirm, agree nor disagree. Nor would he even engage in any suggestive speculation. Finally, towards midnight, when the appeal from *The Globe* for a statement became imperative, I saw Mr. Laurier and told him that with or without his consent my despatch would announce in the morning that he had been chosen to succeed Mr. Blake. He protested that I could have no knowledge that the statement would be accurate and intimated with cold civility that he did not believe I would be rash enough to send out any such message. But I was rash enough to do so, and the message was substantially if not strictly accurate. I intimated in my despatch that the appointment was temporary and conditional upon Mr. Blake's restoration to health and resumption of the leadership. *The Globe,* however, amended the despatch, erased the qualifying sentences, and declared editorially that Mr. Laurier had been appointed and that Mr. Blake's resignation was final and irrevocable. In *The Globe* office there was fuller knowledge of Mr. Blake's position than I possessed, but for some time there was no disclosure of the proceedings of caucus. The truth was that Mr. Laurier was elected leader, but could not be persuaded to accept, and insisted upon the appointment of an advisory committee to counsel and direct the Opposition during the current Parliamentary session.

Curiously enough, my action never was questioned nor the accuracy of my despatch ever denied or admitted by any member of the Liberal Parliamentary party. It became necessary to see Mr. Laurier often, but he made no reference direct or indirct to the incident. On the day that Parliament prorogued, however, he called me down from the Gallery and intimated that he had definitely accepted the leadership, and that there was no reason his decision should not be announced. But I cannot think that his judgment was settled or that he was yet persuaded that he could command the general support of the Liberal party. He was comparatively unknown in Ontario and the East, and wholly unknown in the West, while in Quebec he was distrusted by the Hierarchy and regarded with more of respect than affection by the French people.

Once a group of Liberals were discussing the political outlook in Quebec as the election of 1896 drew near and the Manitoba school question hung heavily on the horizon. Laurier said, "How can I be strong in Quebec? I am an old Rouge, I have been fighting priests and bishops all my life." Dr. Landerkin, who was of the company and in very happy temper, rose to his feet, brought down his right hand with a sweeping gesture upon his bosom and declared with impressive fervour, "I am an old Rouge, too, but I am not such a d—— fool as to fight bishops."

There was a common notion that Laurier had no iron in his constitution, and at best would be an ornamental figure, obedient to the commands of stronger men in the party. This, I believe, was the judgment of Sir Richard Cartwright. I know that this was the view of Hon. David Mills. Recalling the estimate in which he was held by so many of his Parliamentary associates one thinks of Bap.

McNabb's little red rooster of which Herndon tells in his Life of Lincoln. Beaten in the ring it mounted a wood-pile, flirted its feathers and crowed lustily. Bap., looking on in disgust, exclaimed irreverently, "Yes, you little cuss, you're great on dress parade but not worth a d——n in a fight."

Laurier had a reputation for eloquence which does not always denote strength, and a reputation for indolence which it was not thought he could overcome. If I ever had this impression it was soon dispelled. Shortly after he became leader I was his guest for a few days at his home in Arthabaskaville. During those days he talked much and I very little. In nothing that he said was there any suggestion of arrogance or boasting. But he revealed his knowledge of men and of books, his clarity and vigour of mind, his inflexibility of will and purpose. At least I thought I had discovered a man of very different quality from the amiable Laodicean whom many Liberals feared and most conservatives believed had been installed in a position to which he was unequal. In a long letter to *The Globe* I sought to convince the Liberal party that Mr. Blake's successor would be an actual and dominant leader. If there were those who doubted and derided, in the judgment of history the prophet will not be dishonoured.

It was my fortune to accompany Mr. Laurier on his first visit to Ontario after he became leader of the party. He and Madame Laurier spent a short holiday in the Muskoka Lakes with Mr. J. D. Edgar and Mrs. Edgar. At Bracebridge, Port Carling, and Parry Sound the leader delivered short addresses, and at Parry Sound he attended a Methodist camp-meeting. Later he visited Orillia, Cannington, Lindsay, Sturgeon Point,

Guelph, Mount Forest, Wingham, and St. Thomas. At St. Thomas, where he was the guest of Dr. Wilson, M.P., and Mrs. Wilson, he attended service at the Presbyterian Church, for which, by the way, he was gravely rebuked by the Conservative organs of Quebec. The preacher was Rev. J. A. Macdonald. The sermon was vigorous and eloquent. I have often thought that Dr. Macdonald is even more effective in the pulpit than on the platform. But most of his speeches are sermons, and perhaps I think of the pulpit as his natural setting. This, I believe, was the first meeting between Laurier and Dr. Macdonald, as it was my first meeting with the man who was to be my successor in a position to which I had no immediate prospect of appointment.

Mr. Laurier's only serious addresses were delivered at Cannington and Guelph. Again and again during those summer days in Muskoka and throughout his leisurely journey across the Province, Laurier insisted that a French Canadian and a Roman Catholic could not hope to secure the common allegiance of Liberals in the English Provinces. Again and again he protested that his elevation to the leadership could be no more than a temporary expedient. In his speeches he declared that he was only a tenant of the office of leader until Mr. Blake's restoration to health, and there can be no doubt that this was his hope and expectation. As a consequence he was not as aggressive nor as authoritative as could be desired. I did not think that he made a strong impression upon the meetings which he addressed. There was lack of vigour and confidence. There was no energy in his deliverance. Nor was even the attraction of personality which was his great possession fully displayed. Only at Cannington did he reveal his actual quality. An Anglican clergyman with gross discourtesy arose in the meeting and shouted that they could not learn the true way from a Roman Catholic. Laurier retorted with passionate energy, "You could—in politics," and he proceeded in sentences of stern rebuke to flog the interrupter into humiliation and silence. The rest of the speech was animated and confident, in contrast to the tame and listless spirit in which most of it was spoken. I had the impudence to tell the leader that he should engage the belligerent divine to attend and interrupt at subsequent meetings. But Laurier seldom was embarrassed by heckling. Nor was he ever overcome by organized interruption. I cannot think, however, that his reputation was enhanced by his visit to Ontario in the summer of 1888, and I am confident that he did nothing to dispel the common notion among Liberals that he was too gentle and too gentlemanly for the hard, rough, uncompromising, aggressive warfare in which a political leader must engage if he is to establish his own position, control a party in Parliament and inspire respect and devotion in the constituencies.

It is curious that the qualities of decision and resolution which Laurier possessed in such remarkable degree were those in which he was thought to be deficient. It is just as remarkable that despite his reputation for indolence when he became Prime Minister he was an example of industry in office, indefatigable in his attendance in Parliament and diligent and vigorous in the direction of the party which he recreated and over which he exercised such complete authority. No one who had knowledge of his career in Quebec before he became a national figure could have doubted his courage, but his comparative inaction in Parliament from 1878 to 1887 explains many misconceptions which prevailed in the other Provinces. He loved the Library of Parliament more than he loved the Chamber of the Commons. He browsed among books, reading and thinking leisurely but spaciously, happy in a few intimate friendships, and content apparently with the position that he had achieved. For years I was a faithful patron of one of the second-hand book-shops of Toronto. My taste was for biography and memoirs, for the books which describe great figures, great incidents, great events in French and British history, and for the old books and pamphlets which relate to the political history of Canada and the United States. I learned that if I did not order as soon as the catalogues appeared the best books would be taken by Laurier. The range of his interest was wide and catholic, but of modern fiction he read little. While he was at Washington in 1899 he read Uncle Tom's Cabin. When I asked him if he had not read the book before, he admitted that he had, but declared that he found a second reading more interesting and profitable than any of the newer novels. Once I asked him what biographies of Lincoln he had read. His answer was that he had read them all, and that he thought the best was that by John T. Morse in the Series of American Statesmen. Few books have been written about Lincoln that I have not read, but I think the little volume by Carl Schurz has the first place in my affection. Mr. Isaac Campbell, K.C., of Winnipeg, who has read much of the Lincoln literature and has a very complete Lincoln library, values highly the volumes by Morse and Ida M. Tarbell, but he has read so many books illuminating so many phases of Lincoln's character that he hesitates to admit that one or other is a favourite. I once heard Mr. Laurier and Mr. Goldwin Smith discuss treatises on French cookery with a familiarity as interesting as it was surprising. It was this Laurier who did not aspire to be leader of a political party and who seemed to have settled in a way of life which he was reluctant to forsake. But the separation from these old tastes and interests was not at all complete. He read much while he was in office. One may be certain that he read more in the greater freedom and leisure which he enjoyed after his Government was defeated. But surely there was a great reserve of ambition in Laurier which would have gone unsatisfied if he had never commanded a party and dominated a Cabinet.

It was commonly believed when Laurier became leader that he would submit to the stronger will of Sir Richard Cartwright. But if there ever was a struggle between the two the decision came quickly. I do not think there ever was any actual conflict, for Laurier prevailed without apparent effort or assertion. So all those who thought they might be Seward to Laurier were undeceived. It was said that Sir Richard imposed Commercial Union, or Unrestricted Reciprocity, upon the Liberal party. But probably Commercial Union was conceived in *The Mail* office. Although Mr. Erastus Wiman was the reputed father, one suspects that Mr. Edward Farrer instructed Wiman, and by his persuasive and trenchant writing, made the proposal attractive to the Liberal leaders. At this time *The Mail* was at variance with Sir John Macdonald, and there is reason to think that *The Globe* espoused Commercial Union because *The Mail,* by its vigorous advocacy of the new programme, was dividing *The Globe's* constituency. In those days *The Mail* was in search of a party, and the Liberal leaders were very willing to encourage its advances. There never was a complete union, but there was co-operation for mutual advantage which, as I well remember, *The Globe* regarded with disfavour and concern. Between Sir Richard Cartwright and Mr. Farrer there was a personal relation of long-standing, although not an intimate friendship, and probably Mr. Farrer persuaded Sir Richard to pronounce in favour of continental free trade before Laurier had committed himself. But Laurier was as favourable to the policy as his associate, even if he was not the first to deliver judgment. I am thinking only of the genesis of the movement and the suspicion that Sir Richard imposed his will upon the titular leader of the party and not of the wisdom or unwisdom of the proposal to which they gave mutual sanction and support.

By a speech which Laurier delivered in Toronto in 1889 he dispelled many prejudices among English-speaking Liberals outside of Quebec and finally established himself as the national leader of the party. He could not have become leader at a more inauspicious time. The alliance with Mr. Mercier in Quebec was distasteful to the Liberals of the other Provinces. Indeed, it was not unusual for a French Liberal to whisper that he was a Rouge, not a Nationalist, a disciple of Dorion and Laurier, but a reluctant follower of Mercier. More than once I heard Mercier speak in Quebec. No one except Chapleau could exercise such wonderful command over a French audience. Eager, dashing, dominant, bold and direct, he set the blood of French

Canadians leaping, and enlisted in his service all they had of emotional fervour, of racial instinct and racial prejudice. He was not scrupulous, but he had political genius and he was very competent. It was not easy for Laurier to maintain an alliance with this daring provincialist without loss of trust and prestige in the English Provinces. But Mercier was the stronger in Quebec, and any open quarrel would have destroyed the Liberal party in the French Province. There is a story, probably not authentic, that on the eve of polling in the Federal election of 1891 Mercier said to a friend, "If I were leader of the Liberal party I would have a majority of twenty in Quebec to-morrow." The friend asked why Laurier should not do as well since he had Mercier's most active and energetic support. "The reason," said Mercier, "is that Monsieur Laurier is an honest man." I have often heard Laurier say that Mercier had such influence with the French people that if he had determined to impose economical and conservative government upon Quebec he could have held the Province as easily as by the methods which he practised and which made his last days a tragedy instead of a triumph. At least Mr. Marchand did, and Sir Lomer Gouin has done what Laurier believed Mercier could have done to his own great honour and to the infinite advantage of his Province.

The Jesuit Estates Act, which produced the Equal Rights movement in Ontario, greatly embarrassed Laurier, not because there was any sound constitutional basis for the Protestant agitation, but because he could speak only with diminished authority against the tempest of sectarian feeling which swept over the country. In Parliament he opposed disallowance of the objectionable Provincial measure, as he was bound to do, and as, indeed, did the great majority of Parliament, but there was a formidable element in the Liberal party, as there was a multitude of Conservatives, who would not hear the voice of reason and against whose wrath over the appropriation of $400,000 for the Jesuit Order by a Canadian Legislature no constitution could prevail. While this flaming anger possessed the country Laurier was eager to come to Toronto in order to explain and defend his position. But the Liberal leaders of Ontario would not entertain the proposal. They insisted that he could not get a hearing, that he would meet with violence, that he would be humiliated and discredited, and would damage the party irretrievably. While I was his guest at Arthabaskaville he lamented again and again that he could not get permission to speak in Toronto, and insisted with absolute conviction that none of the untoward consequences which his associates predicted would follow. I was then President of the Young Men's Liberal Club of Toronto, and I suggested that if he was so determined to speak in Ontario I would go home and organize a meeting. It was agreed that I should make the attempt, although he doubted if I could succeed. I had his promise, however, that once the meeting was announced he would not have it cancelled no matter what objection might be offered or what pressure might be exerted to prevent his appearance at Toronto. The executive committee of the club, was easily persuaded to afford Laurier the opportunity which he desired. Without consultation with the editor of *The Globe,* any member of the Mowat Government, or any Liberal member of Parliament, I secured the Horticultural Pavilion and an nounced the meeting. There was much foreboding and head-wagging. But, as I anticipated, once the fact that he was coming was announced it was recognized that the decision could not be reversed and that all possible measures must be taken to ensure a favourable result. But there were representative Liberals, afterwards his docile if not obsequious followers, who would not attend and who were only less vigorous in condemnation of the Liberal leader than in censure of those who were responsible for the invitation which he had accepted.

I was chairman of that meeting. The hall was crowded. Every member of the Mowat Cabinet was on the platform. Many Liberal members came in from the country. The bulk of the audience was not unfriendly, but there was a hostile element which was not easily controlled. During the first hour I was not so confident that those who had predicted confusion and disaster were not of the House of Wisdom. My few introductory sentences were taken well enough, and when Laurier rose there was generous applause. But one felt instinctively that there were undercurrents of suspicion and unrest. When he mentioned *The Globe* there was satirical jeering and hissing. As I was a member of *The Globe* staff, that was not pleasant, but since its attitude towards the Jesuit Estates Act and the equal Rights movement had been so variable and vacillating I was more abashed than surprised. Once, I remember, I was stopped on the street by an acquaintance, who intimated, with stern displeasure, that he did not like *The Globe's* position on the Jesuit Estates question. I retorted angrily and in unparliamentary language that he must be d—— hard to satisfy since there was no possible position on the question that *The Globe* had not taken. The truth was that *The Globe* had first opposed disallowance of the Act, discovered later that public opinion was overwhelmingly in favour of disallowance, and finally argued that the Act should be disallowed because the Pope was mentioned in the preamble. Possibly the Pope had no business there, but since he had been there from the beginning *The Globe's* sudden anger at his presence was not convincing. Those indeed were grievous days for *The Globe* staff, and the hissing at the Pavilion meeting was only a disconcerting manifestation of the contumely to which we were continually subjected.

There was a far more disturbing demonstration when Laurier named Mr. D'Alton McCarthy and Dr. Caven, the wise, revered, acute, judicial Principal of Knox College, whose severely logical mind did not apparently perceive the illogical position of an Association which demanded disallowance by the Federal Government of an Act within the constitutional competence of a Provincial Legislature. Laurier struggled to recover control of the meeting but again and again the cheering for McCarthy and Caven was renewed. There was nothing violent or ruffianly in these demonstrations. There was perhaps a suggestion of respect for the speaker, but with this there was cold, stern, deliberate displeasure over his attitude and resolute, uncompromising allegiance to the champions of the Equal Rights movement. One could see that Laurier felt the actual physical strain of the struggle. Not only was there a hostile element in the meeting determined to express itself, but on the faces of many of those who were voiceless there were no evidences of concern or sympathy. There was not, as so often happens when a speaker is badgered and harassed, the quick and fierce rally of the defensive forces and the greater volume of counter cheering which overwhelms a body of disturbers. Laurier had not only to silence interruption, but to dispel coldness, create sympathy and compel conviction. If he did not wholly succeed, he did at least reduce the meeting to subjection and inspire respect for his courage and tenacity. There was no further disorder and as he proceeded there was frequent cheering and manifest agreement with many of his arguments. But the sentences which were applauded were those which recalled his battles for freedom against ecclesiasticism in Quebec, which asserted his devotion to the principles of British Liberalism, which pleaded for sympathy and understanding between Ontario and Quebec, and which deplored racial and religious intolerance. I think of the long roll of cheering when he quoted the great sentence, "No Italian priest shall tithe or toll in our dominions," and the fine fervour of his peroration, "When the excitement has subsided let us remember that though divided by different tenets and of different religious creeds, we all worship the same God. Let us remember that though divided by religious forms, still we all believe in Him who came to earth to bring to men peace and good-will, and if we are true to these teachings, if we are ever ready to give and to take, to make all allowance for the opinions, nay, for the prejudices of my fellow countrymen, for my part I shall never despair of the future of our young country."

The man triumphed, but the Jesuit Estates Act was still an alien and a fugitive in Toronto. The triumph was greater than appeared at the moment. There could be no better evidence of the temper of the meeting than the conduct of Sir Oliver Mowat. He had prepared a speech for the occasion, and the manuscript was in *The Globe* office. But not a sentence of that speech was delivered. Wary and cautious, as he ever was, he felt the ground step by step, never going an inch too far, nor ever reaching the point of danger. He was cheered by those who had harassed Laurier, although he did not actually challenge any argument that Laurier had advanced. He spoke for Mowat with keen, shrewd appreciation of the feeling in Ontario, and the danger of any open rupture with the Equal Rights Association. The eulogy of Laurier which he had prepared was not pronounced, and any positive support for the position of the Federal leader was withheld. Laurier at most carried only a portion of the meeting; for Mowat there was universal cheering and vast enjoyment of his smooth, deft, adroit handling of an audience which knew as well as he did himself that he was manœuvring for safety and leaving Laurier to such judgment as would be pronounced upon his own appeal and argument. At the close of the meeting Mowat whispered to me that he could not afford to make the speech which he had prepared and that I must destroy the manuscript which he had sent to *The Globe* office. As he spoke his eyes twinkled behind his glasses.

It was discovered next day that the common judgment on Laurier's speech was far more favourable than could have been expected by those who had attended the Pavilion meeting. Even Sir Oliver Mowat and many of those who had opposed the meeting admitted that Laurier had greatly enhanced his own prestige and had convinced many doubting Liberals that objectionable as the Jesuit Estates Act might be, the demand for disallowance could not be conceded. At a luncheon to Laurier at the old Reform Club on Wellington Street, Mowat spoke of the Federal leader with none of the reserve and caution which had characterized his speech at the Pavilion. When he had finished, Laurier whispered, "D—— him, why, did he not say that last night?" I have heard Laurier declare that the Pavilion meeting was the most severe ordeal of his public career, and that there were moments when he was mortally apprehensive he would have to abandon the struggle for a hearing. But he prevailed and never again in Ontario did the Liberal leader find an audience unwilling to receive his message, nor did he ever again encounter public feeling as adverse as that which was expressed at the Pavilion nearly thirty years ago.

Not only was Laurier embarrassed by the alliance with Mercier and the eruption over the Jesuit Estates Act, by the Protestant Protective Association and the movement against Catholic schools in Manitoba, but also by the agitation of which Mr. D'Alton McCarthy was the inspiration and protagonist against official recognition of the French language in the Western Territories. In the memorable debate in the House of Commons in 1890 on a motion by Mr. McCarthy to deprive French of its legal status in the Territorial Legislature there was a greater display of fervour and passion than in any other to which I have listened. Mr. McCarthy was assailed by both front benches and defended only by the faithful O'Brien, by Mr. John Charlton, whose letter expressing despair for the Liberal party under a

Catholic leader and connection with the Equal Rights movement revealed his political temper, by Mr. Alexander McNeill, whose personal devotion to McCarthy was only less intense than his devotion to the British Empire, and by a small group in Parliament responsive to Presbyterian or Orange influences. For five days McCarthy sat silent, patient, unprotesting under the persuasive, insinuating, impressive reasoning of Sir John Macdonald, the luminous, sympathetic, tolerant argu ment of Hon. Edward Blake, the cold, unfriendly logic of Sir Richard Cartwright, the angry, bitter, arrogant attack of Sir Hector Langevin, the nervous, elevated eloquence of Laurier and many other speeches from both sides of the Chamber aspersing his motives or attacking his position with all the resources of persuasion, dissuasion and denunciation they could command. I cannot remember that he ever showed a symptom of feeling or interjected a word of protest until the attack languished and he was free to reply. Then he spoke for three or four hours with superb self-control, remarkable precision of statement and complete concentration upon fundamental facts and principles. If he did not convince, he commanded attention and respect, and the whole effect upon a hostile Parliament was singularly pervasive and profound. Those I have always thought were Mr. McCarthy's great hours in the House of Commons. If he was overwhelmed in the division, he triumphed in the debate, and the triumph was accentuated by his high bearing and grave repose. The man was in his cause. He spoke for it and not for himself. At least that was the impression made even upon those who were cold and unresponsive. No one was more generous in praise than Laurier or more convinced that the effect upon the country would be still greater than the effect produced in Parliament.

There was a time when Laurier was not so far removed from Mr. McCarthy in the House of Commons and Sir William Meredith in the Legislature of Ontario. In "The Day of Sir John Macdonald," by Sir Joseph Pope, there is this passage: "About a month before Sir John Macdonald died Mr. Laurier came to his office in the House of Commons to discuss some question of adjournment. When he had gone the Chief said to me, 'Nice chap, that. If I were twenty years younger he'd be my colleague.' 'Perhaps he may be yet, sir,' I remarked. 'Too old,' said he, 'too old,' and passed into the inner room." I think I know where Laurier, if he could have disencumbered himself of obligations and conditions, would have made his alliances when he became Leader of the Liberal party. It is interesting to remember that just before his death Mr. McCarthy had agreed to accept from Sir Wilfrid Laurier the office of Minister of Justice, which he would not accept from Sir John Thompson. From the meeting at Toronto in 1889 Laurier was firmly and finally settled in the Liberal leadership. If his withdrawal ever was imminent it was because entire devotion to the public service entailed financial sacrifices too onerous for his slender resources. But when one thinks upon the questions which disturbed and divided the country thirty years ago, of Nationalism in Quebec, of Protestant agitation in Ontario, of acute division over schools and language in the West, it will be admitted that the leadership of a Federal party was a delicate and difficult undertaking for a Frenchman, a Roman Catholic and a citizen of Quebec.

CHAPTER VIII

THE OLD MAN AND HIS WAYS

Around no other name in Canadian history gathers so much of praise and detraction, of confidence and distrust, of story and legend as around that of Sir John Macdonald. Those who loved him loved greatly; those who trusted him trusted fully. But no man ever excited greater ferocity among political opponents or was the object of more continuous and relentless attack. The association of George Brown and John A. Macdonald in the Coalition Cabinet which united the Provinces was a truce but not a reconciliation. The personal relationship between the two men was unfriendly before the Coalition and more unfriendly afterwards. Both had vital elements of character, but in impulse and texture, in mental and moral attitude they were destined for conflict. This is only to recognize essential constitutional differences and not to assign moral or intellectual inferiority to either. Each was vitally ambitious and in early manhood each saw a common goal in the distance. Brown had the temper of an agitator and the outlook of a reformer. Macdonald had genius for government. The one sought to accomplish his objects by sheer driving power while the other conciliated, persuaded and prevailed. Macdonald would have said with Cavour, "If you want to be a politician, for mercy's sake do not look more than a week ahead." Brown looked towards the hills whence came his strength. One was a political evangelist, the other a shrewd, wise, patient shepherd who gathered many

12

flocks into his fold and so long as they followed him found humour in variety and harmony in contrasts. Just as Gladstone was offended by the sardonic cynicism and deliberate levity of Disraeli, so George Brown was outraged by the flippancy, audacity and dexterity of the Conservative leader. Looking backward to those days one seems to see a camp meeting with George Brown in the pulpit and "John A." making merry with the unrepentant on the outskirts of the congregation.

It was very, very hard for Liberals to laugh with Sir John Macdonald. In his jokes they saw only coarseness, buffoonery and irresponsibility. The truth is that he was seldom coarse and he laughed at himself as freely as he laughed at his political opponents. He had a humour which the people understood. They forgave much because he so frankly admitted human weaknesses and because looking into themselves so many men knew that they had like faults and frailties. And because women know men better than they know themselves and better than men ever suspect there was among women a passionate devotion to Sir John Macdonald such as no other political leader in Canada has inspired. No man of ignoble quality ever commands the devotion of women although perhaps the standards of judgment which we commonly ascribe to women are the standards which many women least respect.

Sir John Macdonald was a man with his feet on the earth and his head not so far above it. He seldom sought to climb to moral elevations where the footing might be insecure. For a time he drank freely but any whisper of censure only stimulated Conservatives to fiercer personal loyalty. He said himself that the country would rather have "John A." drunk than George

Brown sober. He warned D'Arcy McGee that "this Government can't afford two drunkards and you've got to stop." His drinking was exaggerated, as were his other faults and follies, by sleepless and insensate opponents. Very often the attack was so violent as to bring chivalrous souls to his side and actually react in his favour. Down to middle life and beyond Sir John Macdonald had periodical "sprees" and nothing that he attempted was done badly. Sometimes he was disabled for public duty. The authorities seem to agree that not only may a "spree" come unaware but that it is as uncertain in its going as in its coming. Begun in complete privacy it may develop various phases and attract more public notice than is desirable even though the performance may be original and artistic. Unlike any other pursuit every rehearsal is a performance and every presentation a surprise. The public seldom saw "John A." in liquor, but occasionally there were symptoms which even Conservatives could not mistake. Once he was to speak at a town on Lake Huron, but he was so long in sleeping off the consequences that the vessel on which he was a passenger dare not put into harbour. That was fifty years ago but not yet have local Conservatives discovered any humour in the incident or become reconciled to the graceless chaffing of their Liberal neighbours. A common story, resting upon no adequate authority, is that a shorthand writer once undertook to make a verbatim report of a speech which Sir John delivered at Kingston. When he had examined the manuscript he sent for the reporter, gravely intimated that he had read portions of it with pain and surprise, and with the mild austerity of a grieving father added, "Young man, if you ever again undertake to report the speech of a public man be sure that you keep sober."

There is an authenticated story of Macdonald in the early sixties. He was Attorney-General for Upper Canada, and lived in lodgings in Quebec. He had been absent from duty for a week; public business was delayed, and the Governor-General became impatient. He sent his aide-de-camp, young Lord Bury, to find the absent Minister. Pushing his way past the old house-keeper, Lord Bury penetrated to the bedroom where Macdonald was sitting in bed, reading a novel with a decanter of sherry on the table beside him. "Mr. Macdonald, the Governor-General told me to say to you that if you don't sober up and get back to business, he will not be answerable for the consequences." Macdonald's countenance reflected the anger he felt at the intrusion: "Are you here in your official capacity, or as a private individual." "What difference does that make?" asked Lord Bury. "Just this," snapped the statesman, "if you are here in your official capacity, you can go back to Sir Edmund Head, give him my com-pliments, and tell him to go to h——; if you are simply a private individual, you can go yourself." In after years Lord Bury often told the story but with more of affection than of censure for Sir John Macdonald.

In his time Sir Richard Cartwright was perhaps the most caustic and scholarly speaker in the Canadian Parliament. Too many of his speeches had the flavour of malice and the acid of bitterness. But every word carried its exact meaning. There was no verbiage or redundancy. The argument was direct, deliberate, compact and luminous. In his humour there was the frost of Autumn, but the radiance, too, of its piercing sunshine. Always stately and severe he relaxed nothing

of his outward austerity when he was striking at a vic-
time with biting irony or brilliant badinage. But the
irony was always corrosive and the badinage often
malicious and sometimes insolent. In social intercourse
Cartwright could be gracious and intimate. As a host
he was a simple gentleman, kindly without condescen-
sion, interesting without effort, sage without pretension.
But in political warfare he knew only the law of the
jungle. For Sir John Macdonald he had a consuming,
incurable hatred. Than his Reminiscences nothing
more sardonic and merciless ever was written. But
they reveal the author more clearly than they disclose
the qualities or establish the motives of his adversaries.
He had distinction and integrity but a brooding venge-
fulness against those who stood in the gates through
which he would pass vitiated his judgments, filled his
days with anger and made political reverses the seed
plots of sleepless animosities.

One was often amazed at Cartwright's ferocity when
he spoke of the Conservative leader. It was commonly
believed that his hatred had its origin in a personal
humiliation. He aspired to be Minister of Finance but
was set aside for Sir Francis Hincks. But when one
changes his political relation an ignoble motive is always discovered. It is hard to believe that this could
be the only reason for Cartwright's lifelong pursuit of
Macdonald. According to Sir Joseph Pope the Conservative leader never understood the bitter inveterate
animus towards himself which possessed Cartwright
and could not fully reciprocate his contempt and hatred.
Very often while I was editor of *The Globe* Cartwright
sought to have charges made against Sir John Macdonald which would have violated every tradition of

181

responsible journalism and every principle of decent controversy. Towards other opponents he was less malevolent. Indeed there was sometimes a sense of equity in his judgments. When Sir John Macdonald disappeared and the Liberal party was restored to office he became mellow and humane, gracious and tolerant. In Parliament thereafter he was persuasive and conciliatory. Deputations which came in doubt and apprehension departed with glad hearts and smiling faces. He even neglected to blaspheme the manufacturers. One feels that he could have slept in the "Red Parlour" with an easy head and a good conscience if Sir John Macdonald's picture had not hung upon the wall. But even the new Cartwright cherished the old grudge. When a sum was put in the estimates for a statue to Sir John on Parliament Hill he was determined to offer an amendment requiring that the facts of the "Pacific scandal" should be inscribed upon the monument. For days his Parliamentary associates pleaded and reasoned that he would injure only himself and the Liberal party if he should actually submit such a resolution. But it was long before he would yield and he yielded at last to the persuasion of friends who were brought to Ottawa to reinforce the appeals and protests of the Parliamentary party. The madness broke out again in his Reminiscenses. His final bequest to posterity was his hatred of Sir John Macdonald.

Nothing that Cartwright ever said in Parliament better displays the quality of his humour than his reference to Mr. J. E. Collins's biography of the Conservative leader. Facing Sir John in the House of Commons he said: "That work was couched in chaste and elegant language, and no doubt it will be very satisfactory to the honourable gentleman's friends, because I observe from it that in all the acts of the honourable gentleman's career which evil-minded persons have misinterpreted, he has been actuated by the purest and most patriotic motives, and has even sometimes allowed his reputation to be tarnished for the general welfare of the country. It is a happy association of ideas, and what a lamented friend of mine called the 'eternal fitness of things,' that a gentleman who in his life has done justice to so many John Collinses should at last find a John Collins to do justice to him."

It will be remembered that after the Conservative party in Parliament had committed itself to Protection the leaders addressed many political demonstrations throughout the country. Referring to these demonstrations Mr. Joseph Rymal said that he was reminded of one who went to and fro on the earth many years ago, tempted the people with false promises, took the Saviour into a high mountain, showed Him the Kingdoms of the earth and declared that He should possess these and the glory of them if He would fall down and worship him. Failing to make the application Sir John, who always maintained good relations with Rymal, interrupted with the remark, "You did not finish the story about the man who went up into the high mountain." Rymal retorted, "That was not a man, that was the devil; the other tempter did not go to the top of the mountain; he went round the country holding picnics and tempting the people."

Occasionally Sir John emphasized an argument by the experience of the old squaw who had found that a little too much whiskey was just enough. He used to say that he was like a certain old nag, "a rum 'un to look at but a rare 'un to go." In a bye-election in West Toronto in 1875 necessitated by the appointment of Mr. Thomas Moss to the Bench, the Liberal candidate was Alderman John Turner and his Conservative opponent Hon. John Beverley Robinson. Speaking in behalf of the Conservative candidate Sir John said Mr. Robinson had assisted and might again assist him at Cabinet making but he was no turner. In Mr. E. B. Biggar's very complete anecdotal life of the Conservative leader he describes an incident in which Colonel Playfair of Lanark was the victim. Colonel Playfair was urging the construction of a colonization road of which he desired to be superintendent. Exasperated by repeated failures to get a decision he visited Ottawa and had Sir John called out of the Council Chamber. The Prime Minister grasped Playfair by both hands and exclaimed, "God bless my soul, Colonel Playfair, is that you? I am so glad to see you. We have just been discussing in Council a military matter that we cannot decide. Now you with your great military experience and your memories of Salamanca and Talavera will be able to solve the question. How many grains of powder would have to be put under a bull's tail to blow his horns off?" And Sir John disappeared into Council. Colonel Playfair withdrew in disgust and anger and in sad conviction that he would never receive the appointment. He was mail carrier between Perth and Playfair and the first letter he took out of the mail bag when he got home was an official notice of his appointment as superintendent. This military problem was often submitted for solution in the townships forty years ago, but I cannot recollect that it was ever connected with

THE OLD MAN AND HIS WAYS

Sir John Macdonald. Mr. Biggar has another story which I have not found or heard elsewhere. Visiting the Provincial Fair at Kingston Sir John was attracted by the performances of a troupe of female acrobats and remarked that no doubt it was the custom to show the calves first. A Scotch Liberal in Parliament he described as "Mackenzie and water." Of another member, erratic but brilliant, he said the world never would have heard if God Almighty had given him common-sense. Once Hon. Robert Watson, then the only Liberal in Parliament from West of the Lakes, urged Sir John not to allow party feeling to affect the consideration of a proposal he had submitted to Parliament. The Prime Minister put his hand upon Watson's shoulder and whispered, "You are right, Watson, you are right, it would be far better for the country if every member of the House were as free of party feeling as you and me." When he "hived the Grits" in a group of constituencies in Ontario by the redistribution of seats in 1882 he scoffed at their righteous protest and with jaunty insolence suggested that they could not hope to get on with Tories when they could not live with themselves. He said it was not men who voted for him when he was right but those who voted for him when he was wrong who had the stronger claim upon his favour and gratitude. The humour in his insolence and the laughter in his levity exasperated his opponents but delighted his adherents and predisposed to lightness and leniency many people who held their political opinions loosely.

In *The Canadian Magazine,* twenty years ago, Mr. W. F. Maclean, M.P., described Sir John Macdonald as "The Canadian Themistocles." Nothing else that anyone has written about the Conservative leader is so frank, so faithful and so penetrating. In a few rapid, comprehending sentences he reveals the man and illuminates his whole career. "Sir John," he said, "had a wonderful influence over many men. They would go through fire and water to serve him, did serve him, and got, some of them, little or no reward. But they served him because they loved him, and because with all his great powers they saw in him their own frailties. He abounded in the right kind of charity. And speaking of the love his friends and followers had for him, Mr. Pope dwells on the 'old guard' and the old loyalty to the chief. So it was, but there were dark days also, when even those who afterwards enrolled themselves in the guard, passed by on the other side. If ever there was a man in low water, it was Sir John as I saw him one day in the Winter of 1875, coming out of the House into the bitter air, dressed in a Red River sash and coat, and the old historic mink-skin cap, tottering down the hill to the eastern gateway alone, others passing him with a wide sweep. The lesson of Sir John's life is that he pulled himself out of those days and trials into higher and more solid footing. But Sir John's real 'old guard' were not the men who stood with him at Ottawa, but the greater old guard who stood and fought for him in every township, year after year, and to whom a call by name or a nod of the head was all the recompense they got and yet the recompense they most prized. Sir John has been praised for his statesmanship, and for this I, too, give him all praise. But his statesmanship was limited to two things: carrying on the government when no one else could do it, and do it so well and so continuously, and forging the country together. He originated no great principle. He appropriated, however, freely from others when an opportunity offered, or when he thought another's idea would lead to or keep him in office."

Interesting, but far less searching and fundamental, is Mr. Nicholas Flood Davin's appreciation. It has value as a contemporary judgment for it was written nearly forty years ago. Davin had often heard Disraeli, who was said to have a physical resemblance to Sir John Macdonald and in language as brilliant as ever was spoken by any man in Canada he would describe the likenesses and differences between the two leaders. "Sir John Macdonald," he said, "is a type of politician which has never failed to delight the English people—the man who, like Palmerston, can work hard, do strong things, hold his purpose, never lose sight for a moment of the honour and welfare of his country, and yet crack his joke and have his laugh, full of courage and good spirits and kindly fun. . . . Sir John Macdonald in the English House of Commons would have been equal, in my opinion, to Mr. Disraeli in finesse, in the art of forming combinations and managing men. He never could have equalled him in invective, or in epigram, or in force as an orator. Sir John Macdonald brings up his artillery with more ease. He is always human, even in his attacks. Lord Beaconsfield, as Mr. Disraeli in the House of Commons, approached his opponent like some serpentine monster, coiled himself ruthlessly round him, fascinated with his gaze, and struck out with venomed fang. But Sir John is probably the better debater of the two. His delivery is lively, natural, mercurial; Lord Beaconsfield's is labored. The power of making a statement is not the forte of the author of Endymion. Sir John Macdonald makes a luminous statement, and his reasoning faculty is at least as high as Lord Beaconsfield's. He has very little, comparatively, of the latter's *curiosa felicitas,* in coining phrases, but his humour is more spontaneous. Lord Beaconsfield has the charm which is inseparable from genius, but it may well be doubted if his power of conciliating men and fixing their affections surpasses that of the Prime Minister of the Dominion. I am sure that in sober strong sense the balance is in favour of the Canadian statesman. There is nothing viewy about Sir John Macdonald. Though a man of imagination, reason is lord every time."

From my seat in the Press Gallery for four or five Parliamentary sessions I looked across at Sir John Macdonald. I was so placed that I could sometimes see shades of expression cross his face, the defiant jerk of the head when he was angry, the shrug of contempt for a mean gibe that was meant to wound, the quick, natural, human manifestation of pleasure over a generous word from an opponent or a tribute of affection and confidence from an associate. I think he liked best to have the word of praise come from the back benches as he was most attentive to those who spoke seldom and in sweat alike of brow and brain. Few men have had such charm for his kind, or such power to inspire sacrifice and devotion. Mr. James F. Lister, of Lambton, often attacked Sir John Macdonald in language as personal and violent as was permitted under the usages of Parliament. I once asked him if he had any active dislike or actual hatred for the Conservative leader. He confessed that he was so attracted by the man's personality that he dare not trust himself in his company. I was told by a Conservative member of the Commons that he had never sought a favour for his constituency from Sir John Macdonald that was not refused and yet could hardly ever convince himself that the refusal was not a favour. I have known gray-haired Liberals who had persuaded themselves that the Conservative leader was the favourite offspring of the father of evil forever disarmed by a few quick, happy, spontaneous sentences, spoken carelessly enough, but which, as he intended they should, penetrated to the very marrow of their self-esteem. I think of a Liberal member, dull but fluent, who died in the conviction that he was among the most effective debaters in Parliament because Macdonald so insinuated in language just deft enough to conceal the motive and effect the object.

There is reason to think that few men had his complete confidence. He never had any real affection for Sir Charles Tupper. He often distrusted his judgment and his motives. It is said that he was always uneasy when Tupper was under attack and often disturbed by the rash courage of his colleague from Nova Scotia. But when there was a great battle to be fought in Parliament or in the constituencies he relied upon Tupper as a commander in jeopardy relies upon a reserve army. Whatever may have been the judgment of his contemporaries there were the roots of greatness in Tupper. He was bold, tempestuous, and audacious. In debate he was often imaginative. In action he could be unscrupulous. But he could sacrifice for a great object; he could be loyal and he was steadfast. In constructive genius he has had no equal among the public men of Canada. Thus he was the natural complement of Sir John Macdonald. For Sir John was not naturally constructive nor had he any such reserve of courage as Tupper possessed. The Conservative leader waited upon opportunity; Tupper made opportunity and by the energy of his character seized the vital position before the opposing forces could organize and occupy.

Not long before his death Tupper said a thing which faithfully illustrates his temper and method. Discussing the trade agreement with Washington negotiated by Mr. Fielding and Mr. Paterson, the situation which developed in Parliament and the defeat of the Laurier Administration, he said the facts afforded final evidence that Laurier was neither a politician nor a statesman. If he had been a politician he would have dissolved Parliament and gone to the country as soon as the agreement was negotiated, while if he had been a statesman he never would have made the agreement. Whether or not Tupper would have made the agreement it is certain that he would have taken an immediate appeal to the constituencies and probably have secured a favourable judgment before the Opposition could have adjusted itself to the situation. It may be fair to soften this hard judgment upon Laurier for which I am not responsible with a hostile estimate of Tupper. Once when Sir Charles was speaking in Parliament with characteristic vigour and vehemence a Liberal member said to his deskmate, "What a d—— liar that man Tupper is." "Yes," was the reply, "he just wastes lies." But as happens so often in these reminiscences this is a digression which perhaps even the irrelevant material brought into the story may not justify. There can be no doubt that Tupper was a valuable and powerful ally of Sir John Macdonald and that without this alliance some of the more striking achievements of Conservative Governments would neither have been conceived nor executed. 190

THE OLD MAN AND HIS WAYS

The alliance with Cartier was fortunate for Sir John Macdonald and fortunate for Canada. Without Cartier the union of the Provinces could not have been accomplished. While it is true that George Brown made greater sacrifices for Confederation than any other political leader Cartier was beset by greater political dangers and among all the statesmen who co-operated to establish the union had the most difficult personal position. We often forget that the career of Sir John Macdonald in United Canada was a preparation for the alliance with Cartier, that his infusion of liberalism into McNab toryism was a vital element in the alliance and that his wise, sagacious, deliberate cultivation of Quebec provided the necessary assurances that the movement for Confederation was not a conspiracy against French Canada. When all is said Sir John Macdonald was the only statesman in the Quebec Conference who had a personal constituency in both Upper and Lower Canada and whether or not he fashioned his career to that result federation became feasible because of the character which he had developed and the authority which he exercised.

No successor to Cartier arose in the Conservative party after Confederation. Masson was scholarly and gifted, but he was a churchman before he was a statesman. Langevin was dull but faithful; Chapleau was neither. In political practice Chapleau was of the school of Mercier and he was even more brilliant on the platform. There is, however, no more striking illustration in Canadian history of the failure of the orator in the House of Commons. In mastery of men's emotions when he spoke in French Chapleau was incomparable and invincible in Quebec. He was hardly less effective in English when he spoke to great public meetings in the other Provinces. When he came to Ontario in 1886 to defend the execution of Riel, affirm his allegiance to Sir John Macdonald, and denounce the agents of mischief in his own Province, his vibrant, moving, passionate speeches held men breathless or brought them to their feet in a tumult of cheering. He was tall and erect, his face lean but mobile, his hair gray and long and shaken by the energy of his deliverance, his gestures free and appropriate to his language, his sentences eager and rapid. He had the fire of a prophet and the unction of a deliverer. But at best he was a great performer without continuous purpose or depth of conviction. In Parliament he was comparatively futile, perhaps even unequal to Langevin, who had greater industry and no pretension. Once perhaps Chapleau was equal to himself in the Commons. In the wide, eager, hungry searching for scandal during the session of 1891 Chapleau was assailed. In defence of his reputation he held the House to silence and respect and fought at least an equal battle with his accusers. But when one remembers that Mr. Tarte was in daily association and conference with Mr. Chapleau while he was formulating the charges that were designed to destroy Langevin and McGreevy and that Chapleau and Langevin sat in the same Cabinet one feels that Tarte should have been left to his own devices or that Chapleau should have withdrawn from the Government.

According to Sir Joseph Pope there was a time when Sir John Macdonald thought of Langevin as his successor in the leadership of the Conservative party. The statement would not be accepted if the authority were not so unimpeachable. But apparently that was Sir John's judgment in 1888 when he professed to be willing to retire and when it was believed that Sir Charles Tupper would prefer to remain in England as High Commissioner. As surprising as his choice of Langevin is the statement that when Pope suggested Sir John Abbott, Macdonald declared he had not "a single qualification for the office." But in this connection there is some conflict. While the Conservative leaders were considering who should succeed Sir John Macdonald, Mr. C. H. Cahan, K.C., of Halifax, was staying with Sir John Thompson at Ottawa. There was an active movement in behalf of Mr. D'Alton McCarthy and Mr. McCarthy himself believed that he should be chosen. Thompson, convinced that he was ineligible because of his religious affiliations, was urging Abbott to take the Premiership and reorganize the Cabinet. "At the close," said Thompson, "of the last meeting of Privy Council which Sir John Macdonald attended, he seemed very weary. The other ministers were leaving hurriedly as it was late. I remained to help Sir John put on his coat. He then put his arm about my shoulder, and, looking at me in a serious way, said: 'Thompson, when I am gone, you will have to rally around Abbott; he is your only man.' I walked out with him to his carriage but nothing more was said. He seemed in deep thought. When Sir John's illness became severe he sent for me and I went to his bedside. He spoke with difficulty a few words about immediate affairs and then added: 'Thompson, some time ago I said you would have to rally round Abbott, that he was your only man. I have changed my mind now, he is too selfish.' Those were the last words Sir John spoke to me." 193

13

REMINISCENCES

In "The Day of Sir John Macdonald" there is a frank disclosure of the relations between the French ministers but nothing is revealed that was not suspected or perhaps was not of common knowledge at Ottawa. "It was no secret," Pope writes, "that the French Canadian ministers, Langevin, Caron and Chapleau, were far from showing that spirit of mutual trust and confidence which is supposed to exist among members of the same Ministry. Sir Hector Langevin, the senior of the triumvirate, had been the lieutenant of Cartier, but, in this instance, the mantle of Elijah had not fallen upon his successor. In my experience I never met a man who more nearly fulfilled Bismarck's cynical description of Lord Salisbury—'a lath painted to look like iron.' He was a good departmental officer—but he was nothing more. The moment Sir John Macdonald's support was taken away he fell. Yet Sir John stood by him against the attacks of his opponents, and generally sided with him in his differences with his colleagues. . . . When asked why he thought so much of Langevin, the reply was at once forthcoming: 'He has always been true to me.' The same thing might have been said of Sir Adolphe Caron, ever a faithful supporter, and from his youth up equally in prosperity and adversity, a close personal friend of the old chief; but Sir John thought that Caron sometimes allowed his personal feelings to obscure his judgment, or, as he expressed it, 'Caron is too much influenced by his hates—a fatal mistake in a public man, who should have no resentments.' Sir Adolphe Chapleau, with all his attractiveness and charm, Sir John never quite trusted. The relations between these three French Canadian ministers were hard to define. I frankly confess that, with all my opportunities, I could never master the intricacies of Lower-Canadian politics in those days. In the beginning it seemed to be a case of Langevin and Caron against Chapleau; later it sometimes looked as though Langevin and Chapleau were making common cause against Caron; perhaps most often it resembled a triangular duel. There was absolutely no difference between those three men in respect of public policy, but the personal jealousy and suspicion with which they regarded one another was amusing. 'Langevin,' said Sir John, 'on his way down to Quebec, cannot stop off for lunch at Montreal but Chapleau writes me that he is interfering in his district, and if he leaves his house in Quebec for a walk down John Street, Caron wires in cypher that a breach in the party is imminent.' Langevin, on his part was equally vigilant to resent the encroachments real or supposed, of his colleagues upon his domain, and altogether Sir John had no pleasant time in keeping the peace among them." The insensate jealousies among these ministers culminated in the scandals of 1891, the fall of Langevin and McGreevy, and the disruption of the Conservative party in Quebec. It was through intrigue within, not by accidental discovery or the vigilance of opponents that the revelations of the memorable "scandal session" were produced.

Sir John Macdonald was faithful to the old guard who stood with him and around him in 1873. He had affection for Sir Mackenzie Bowell. He never deserted Sir John Carling and he reposed great and continuous confidence in Hon. Frank Smith. He was grieved by the death of Hon. Thomas White, a potential Prime Minister and leader of the Conservative party. But in no man had he greater confidence than in

Hon. J. H. Pope. Among Liberals in Parliament there was a disposition to regard Pope with offensive toleration if not with open contempt. Angular, ungainly, slow of speech and awkward in gesture and manner he was not impressive in Parliament, but no one who was not wholly encrusted in his own prejudices could think him contemptible. During my first sessions in the Press Gallery I tried to understand the Liberal attitude towards John Henry Pope. I was told that he was uneducated, but that was not a thing so uncommon in a new country. It was said that his English was irregular and faulty and perhaps it was sometimes, but so was that of other men of more pretension. It was Pope who was said to have met a charge against his department with the single sentence, "There ain't nothin' to it." But I never could discover whether this was a fact or a fabrication. There is no doubt that when he was on his feet Mr. Pope floundered and hesitated and threw his arms wide in vague, uncertain, impotent gestures, but he never blundered into dangerous admissions or ever was fretted into haste or anger. Moreover, about the man there was a patriarchal simplicity and dignity which inspired liking and respect. At least, this was how I felt towards Mr. Pope when I was in the Press Gallery and when I had heard little or nothing of his wisdom in council or what Sir Joseph Pope calls "his remarkable political sagacity." In "The Day of Sir John Macdonald" there are these sentences. "Macdonald used to say that Pope could have been anything he desired had he only received a good education in his youth. He added that he had never known Pope's judgment to be at fault. In times of stress and difficulty Pope was the colleague of whom he first sought counsel and upon whose rough good sense he implicitly relied. Pope died two years before his chief, who never ceased to mourn his loss."

Sir John Macdonald was rarely at fault in those whom he trusted. The men he used were serviceable if not always brilliant. There were men of greater lustre to whom he gave little confidence and slight recognition. For this he was reproached but in many of those whom he set aside there were defects of temperament or insurrectional tendencies which time disclosed. Human as he was, he was not too susceptible to flattery. Not by adulation did men obtain his confidence and recognition. It was often said that he exalted mediocrities in order to seem great by contrast when the truth was that he would not have brilliance that was not serviceable and reliable. He wanted to govern with material that was workable and his supreme objects were to unify Canada and maintain the connection with the Empire. He distrusted Sir Alexander Galt who nourished the vision of an independent Canada. Premature advocacy of a federated Empire he discouraged. He was sensitive to the predilections of Quebec, not only because he needed the support of the French Province, but because he believed that Quebec should have co-ordinate authority in the Confederation and that unity of feeling was the essential condition of national stability. Sir John Macdonald was not a reformer, but he was more than an opportunist. He was reluctant to unsettle public opinion by revolutionary proposals. For the evangelical school of reconstructionists who would remake the world in their own image and redeem mankind by legislation he had only a complacent tolerance. He bore the trouble which they made because he respected their motives, because he seldom lost confidence in his own genius to govern and because government as he understood it was to advance or recede as public opinion required and so manage the people as to command a majority in Parliament. But the substantial consistency of Sir John Macdonald's career is good evidence that he directed while he managed and that he abandoned none of his essential convictions for office.

It is true that he adopted Protection with reluctance. As he said himself, "It's devilish hard for a free trader to make a Protectionist speech." But he became a convinced, uncompromising protectionist for Canada. If he moved slowly it was because he hesitated to break new ground and because he was very unwilling to be misunderstood in Great Britain. We were not then emancipated from the old colonial idea of restricted commercial and political sovereignty for the Dominions. We had not come to understand that commercial independence was compatible with the Imperial relation and that as a self-governing community within the Empire Canada was as free to establish protection as Great Britain was to maintain the free trade system. The colonial autonomists who insist that free trade is the necessary policy of all portions of the Empire because the United Kingdom adheres to free trade deny the natural incidence and vital principle of their own teaching. Those were days when Canada acknowledged no obligation for the common defence of the Empire and had not established equality of citizenship by the fact of common sacrifices and the acceptance of common responsibilities. Even yet we do not always distinguish between loyalty to Great Britain and loyalty to the British Empire. 198

THE OLD MAN AND HIS WAYS

Sir John Macdonald was a shameless corruptionist to those who did not follow his standard. For his direct appeal to Sir Hugh Allan there is no defence. He sanctioned bribery and misuse of public appropriations for party purposes. But in the party by which he was opposed there was a considerable admixture of pretence and hypocrisy. George Brown was as unscrupulous in elections as Sir John Macdonald. Mackenzie and Blake set their faces against corruption and to a degree they prevailed. But no one who has knowledge believes that corruption ended when the Conservative party, twenty-three years ago, entered upon its long service in Opposition. This is not said in justification of Sir John Macdonald nor in defamation of his Liberal successors in government. But history should not be perverted in order to maintain the evil pre-eminence of a great man who with all his faults loved Canada and served Canada with singular fidelity and remarkable ability. Other Canadian statesmen had great qualities which were not his in equal degree and freedom from faults which he possessed but in the sum of his service and in high fitness for the tasks of his time he was greater than any of his contemporaries. I recall that May day when Sir Hector Langevin arose in Parliament and read in halting sentences and with deep emotion the bulletin from Earnscliffe which gave the first certain intelligence of his mortal illness. Men flocked down from right and left to the centre of the Chamber, affected by an instant common grief, lifted in a moment above all rancour and contention, and no one who looked into their faces or caught their hushed voices could say from what he saw or heard who was Conservative or who Liberal, who had praised or who blamed, who had followed or who had not. I think of the gloom which lay over the country until the end came, and the universal sorrow which bound all Canadians together on June 6th, 1891, when he passed out of the turmoil of this world into whatsoever God willed for him. It was no common man who so touched a nation's heart and as time passes we see his stature more clearly and forget the way in which some things were done in gratitude for all that was achieved.

CHAPTER IX

THE CHAIR OF THE BROWNS

On June 19th, 1890, I was appointed editor of *The Globe,* but the appointment did not become effective until July 1st. During the winter and spring I had been in the Press Gallery at Ottawa. From Mr. James Somerville, member for Brant, I first heard that Mr. John Cameron was to leave *The Globe* and return to *The London Advertiser.* To my complete surprise he declared that there was a common feeling among the Liberal members from Ontario that I should succeed Mr. Cameron. I told Mr. Somerville that I was neither foolish enough nor vain enough to entertain the proposal and that I doubted if he had sounded his parliamentary associates very deeply. A few days later Mr. Somerville, Dr. Wilson, of East Elgin, and Dr. Landerkin, of South Grey, came to me with the assurance that the Ontario Liberal contingent would petition the directors of *The Globe* in favour of my appointment if I would agree to have the petition circulated. I remonstrated and dissuaded so strongly that for the time at least the proposal was abandoned. Nor was I convinced that any such action should be taken even when I discovered that Mr. Laurier was favourable to my appointment. This assurance I had from himself and I have no doubt that Mr. Robert Jaffray, President of The Globe Printing Company, had a like assurance from the Liberal leader. Indeed, I believe Mr. Jaffray had determined that I should be appointed even before I knew that Mr. Cameron was to resign. I had hardly recovered from my surprise that I could be seriously considered as a candidate for the editorship when I was ordered to report at Toronto. I asked Mr. Laurier and Sir Richard Cartwright to send messages to Mr. Cameron urging that I should not be recalled until the close of the Parliamentary session. If they did so the messages were ineffective. When I got home I learned that the Legislature, which was sitting simultaneously with the Federal Parliament, was to be dissolved as soon as the session was ended and that I was to go into the Legislative Press Gallery until prorogation and conduct *The Globe's* campaign during the general election. Mr. Cameron was still editor of *The Globe,* but he explained that I was to have complete responsibility during the contest and that nothing of which I disapproved would appear in the news or editorial columns. It was a curious position, but the private understanding between Mr. Cameron and myself was strictly observed. The few contributions to which I objected Mr. Cameron rejected, and while I did not hesitate to seek counsel from my associates when I was in doubt as to the wise course to pursue, I did exercise the authority with which I was temporarily invested. The Government was returned by a substantial majority, although "Mowat must go" was the Conservative slogan in that contest. Leaders of the party expressed general satisfaction with *The Globe's* contribution to the result. My associates in the office who knew that I had been in close association with Mr. Cameron during the campaign gave me more praise than I deserved.

Long before the election was over I understood the situation better perhaps than Mr. Cameron or the directors of *The Globe* suspected. I knew that if *The Globe* made no capital blunder in the campaign and if the Government was sustained I would succeed Mr. Cameron, and that if the Government was defeated I would not. Throughout the contest my wife expressed frequent surprise at my philosophy and unconcern. I never lost an hour's sleep nor had a moment of worry. I knew that *The Globe* was in deep water; the actual depth I did not suspect. I knew that it was low in reputation as compared with its great days, and that there would be a long and difficult climb towards the hilltop. As I have said elsewhere, members of the staff were often distressed by the disconcerting candour of unsympathetic critics. Once I drove out with Mr. Laurier to a village in Drummond. On the way he told me that we would have dinner at a hotel kept by an old Scottish Liberal. I suggested that if the landlord should discover I was connected with *The Globe* he would hint that it was not the paper it was in George Brown's day. He did not hint, but bluntly expressed his conviction in the very words that I had used. On my way to the office in Toronto one morning I turned back three blocks to find for a stranger an address for which he had been vainly searching. He was grateful and inquiring. When I told him that I was a writer for *The Globe* he shook his head and murmured sadly, "*The Globe's* not what it was in George Brown's time." Thus it was thirty years ago with the fathers who still mourned for George Brown and the great old days of rigid faith and glorious controversy. All this I knew and I did not believe that a man under thirty-four years of age, without either connections or reputation, could restore *The Globe* to its ancient ascendancy.

Hence my reluctance to succeed Mr. Cameron and undertake a task to which I believed he had proved unequal. Hence when I was asked to meet the directors I refused to be considered as a candidate for the editorship and urged that only a journalist of greater experience and established reputation could give the paper the prestige and authority which its traditions demanded and its situation required. But the experience which I had acquired in the election gave me confidence, and when I learned what other names were under consideration my indifference lessened and I told friends at Ottawa whom I had urged not to write to Mr. Jaffray in my behalf that I was a candidate for the editorship.

I did not know until two or three days before I was appointed that Mr. Edward Farrer was to leave *The Mail* and become *The Globe's* chief editorial writer. There is reason to think that Sir Richard Cartwright and other active counsellors of the Liberal party had this in mind for some time. Mr. Farrer stood foremost among Canadian journalists and was better equipped than any other writer to expound the fiscal policy to which the Liberal party had committed itself. It was true that in *The Mail* he had thundered against Rome, the Bishops, the Obscurantists, the black Militia, and the Jesuits, lay and clerical, domestic and imported, while *The Globe,* through the Mowat Government, as Conservative Oppositionists contended, was in practical political alliance with all these interests and agencies. But it was believed that Mr. Farrer could safely become an editorial writer for *The Globe* if he was not available as its official editor. When I was told that Mr. Farrer was engaged I acquiesced, but did not re-

veal the extent of my understanding. I knew that Hon.
Edward Blake, Sir Richard Cartwright and Sir Oliver
Mowat were not very favourable to my appointment.
They doubted, as I did myself, if I had the necessary
experience. But they did not agree upon any other
candidate. Sir Richard was eager to have Mr. Farrer
associated with *The Globe* and thought Mr. St. John,
of *The Montreal Herald,* had qualifications for the
editorship which I did not possess. I like to think that
Mr. Blake, Sir Richard and Sir Oliver agreed later
that I had proved my fitness for the position, although
for a time Sir Richard's confidence in my discretion
and judgment was not excessive. Indeed, he would
have had me dismissed for causes which this chapter
will explain.

The conditions prescribed for the government of
Mr. Farrer and myself were impracticable and impossible. It was provided that Mr. Farrer should be chief
editorial writer, but that I should read all editorials
before publication, and should hold such articles as I
did not approve for the judgment of a committee of the
Board of Directors. I saw at once that if I reserved an
editorial for the committee's consideration and my advice was rejected my resignation must follow. Besides,
it was impracticable to hold over for a subsequent issue
an article which must appear in the issue for which it
was written if there was to be continuous and authoritative treatment of public questions as they arose. It was
just as clear that friction would develop if I undertook
to embarrass Mr. Farrer by criticism of his editorials
or appeal to the Board of Directors. I said not a word
to Mr. Jaffray or any other director of the paper. I
believed that the real character of the understanding

would be disclosed eventually, and recognized that for the time Mr. Farrer's authority over the editorial page could not be challenged. I never reserved any article of his for the Board's consideration, nor did I ever get behind his back when I was subjected to criticism for articles for which he alone was responsible. He had a two-years' agreement, and at its termination his resignation was accepted. No two men ever had more satisfactory personal relations nor did either of us ever mention to the other the curious contract under which we were expected to divide the responsibility for editorial policy subject to an outside court of appeal. When Mr. Farrer withdrew from the paper I gave the Board my candid opinion of the abortive system of joint control, and confessed that I never had intended to submit any of his articles to the court of last resort which they had established. Indeed, during the twelve years that I was editor of *The Globe* I rarely if ever submitted an article for the Board's judgment, nor did I ever have the Board called to consider any question of editorial policy. There were moments of conflict, but they were not lasting and seldom, if ever, disturbed very happy personal relations.

Although it was announced in June that Mr. Farrer had joined the staff he did not begin writing for the paper until August. In the interval prescient contemporaries discovered great merit in articles written by Mr. John Lewis and myself. I recall a cartoon which pictured "Signor Farrer bringing up *The Globe*." But Signor Farrer was taking a holiday and less able workmen were doing their best to achieve that result. I confess that I found this irritating, and once was so feebly and fatuously unwise as to write a private letter of protest to a publication which had expressed only contempt for *The Globe* until it was understood that Mr. Farrer was writing its editorials. But my balance was soon restored, and even yet I have an itching desire to recall that letter. More than once in the months that followed I had to read praise of Mr. Farrer for articles that I had written, as in subsequent years I acquired considerable reputation from the editorials of Mr. John Lewis and Mr. John A. Ewan.

Edward Farrer belonged to the era of Confederation and the time of Sir John Macdonald. He had personal and political relations with Macdonald, and Tilley, and Tupper, and Thomas White, with Carling, and Haggart, with McCarthy and Cartwright. Among his personal friends were E. B. Wood and C. F. Fraser. He was the associate of T. C. Patteson and N. F. Davin and John Maclean and George R. Kingsmill. He put Sir John Macdonald first among Canadian statesmen. Sir Charles Tupper he disliked. He never believed that George Brown had statesmanlike quality. He fought Mackenzie and Blake. For Mackenzie as a leader he had no admiration. Mackenzie as a man he respected. Blake he ranked with Macdonald. He gave a zealous support to Sir William Meredith in Ontario, but rarely lost an opportunity to thrust at Sir Oliver Mowat. He was one of the effective writers in the Canadian Protectionist movement, although it was not easy for those who knew him well to determine what were his actual opinions on fiscal questions.

Between Mr. Farrer and Mr. Goldwin Smith there was a close friendship. Both were active in support of Sir John Macdonald during the protectionist cam-

paign of 1878, and both later advocated reciprocal free
trade with the United States. Goldwin Smith had no
genius for research. He never had the laborious, continuous patience of the historian. Mr. Farrer had these
qualities, and Goldwin Smith often sought his advice
and co-operation. It is doubtful if any clearer or
stronger writer on economic subjects ever appeared in
Canadian journalism. He was always lucid and decisive. There was no "oratory" in his writing, and yet at
times it was singularly sympathetic and elegant. He
knew many men and he was interested in many subjects.
He could fight the Roman Catholic hierarchy and yet
have friendly relations with Roman Catholic
ecclesiastics. He could be an active advocate of the
platform of one party and be intimate with leaders
in the other party. Few men knew so much of the
undercurrents in Canadian politics. Few men received
so many confidences or more scrupulously kept the confidences with which they were entrusted. He came to
The Globe from *The Mail;* from the Conservative
party to the Liberal party. He brought with him no
secrets that could help the one or discredit the other.
If he had any such secrets they were not disclosed. It
is perhaps doubtful if he had much sympathy with any
political party. He was often contemptuous of the
issues which divided politicians. For years he was the
chief editorial writer of *The Mail,* and at no time was
that newspaper more powerful. For two years he was
chief editorial writer of *The Globe* and there, as on *The
Mail,* he was influential. It was inevitable that he
should determine the character and temper of any page
to which he contributed. He could not occupy a subordinate relation. Whether it was admitted or not he

was at the head of the table. This was not because he strove to be first, but because his knowledge was so wide and his experience so great that his authority was the natural result.

It was during his connection with *The Globe* that his celebrated pamphlet, practically advocating political union with the United States, was stolen from a printing office and extracts from the book read at a great meeting in Toronto, at which the chief speakers were Sir John Macdonald and Sir Charles Tupper. Although we were together on *The Globe,* I had no knowledge of the pamphlet until the day on which the meeting was held. When I was told by a friendly Conservative journalist that it would be produced, and that an attack upon *The Globe* office was contemplated. I did not believe that any assault upon *The Globe* was intended and I opposed firmly but unavailingly a proposal to have the office guarded by police. It was so guarded, but there was no attack. One thought at the back of my mind was that an assault upon the office would give a grievance as an offset to the sensation which publication of the pamphlet was bound to create. How much it may have had to do with the defeat of the Liberal party in 1891 cannot be determined. It is hard to think that Sir John Macdonald could have been defeated in any event. But free use of the pamphlet was made by the Conservative press and Conservative speakers all over the country, and naturally it was thought that the thing did damage. Mr. Farrer rightly enough took full responsibility for what he had written. He never seemed much worried or distressed by its publication. I never heard him express any regret for writing it. The Liberal leaders knew nothing of the pamphlet until it was produced at the Toronto meeting. Even Sir Richard Cartwright was unaware of its existence.

Mr. Farrer often talked of his experiences as an immigration agent in Ireland, and on no subject was he more entertaining. But he was entertaining on all subjects. He had an amazing collection of stories. He saw humour in any and every situation. He was brilliant in conversation and he loved to talk. He was fond of sport. Before the time of baseball he was often seen at cricket matches. In later years, while he lived in Toronto, he was a devotee of the diamond. He could write on pugilism with as much authority as he wrote on finance, and he could describe with singular accuracy all the great encounters between the heroes of the ring for generations. He would talk for hours of great historical trials for murder with exact knowledge of the evidence and the pieces of testimony which brought conviction or acquittal. I never saw him more utterly absorbed than in the trial of Birchall at Woodstock, and from the first he saw that the letter to Colonel Benwell was fatal. For some time he was in Winnipeg, where he was connected with *The Sun* and *The Times,* and to both of these papers he gave distinction. It is believed that Mr. Farrer was brought back from Winnipeg to *The Mail* chiefly upon the advice of Mr. D'Alton McCarthy. Mr. C. W. Bunting, according to Mr. McCarthy's story, had asked Farrer to return, but Farrer declared that he was not willing to be a professional "sandbagger." "That," said Mr. McCarthy, "is an additional reason why the offer should be renewed. A man who will not stoop to party savagery is the man who will best serve the paper and the party." Mr.

Bunting gave Farrer satisfactory assurances that he would not be required to sandbag, tomahawk, or scalp, and he returned to Toronto. No journal to which Mr. Farrer contributed could be dull or commonplace. He was bold at times, and now and again greatly disturbed his political associates. One thinks of quotations from his pen which did service in various campaigns, and not always in behalf of the party with which he was allied. Such utterances, however, were generally in denunciation of abuses and were not dictated by any mere desire to create annoyance or friction. Behind the scenes he did much. He moved many men who perhaps hardly understood the influences to which they responded. He had perhaps more personal acquaintances than any other man in Canada, and more friends also. No one who ever worked at his side could forget his humour and his genius for comradeship, or ever cease to wonder at the ease with which he did his work, his familiarity with many books, his knowledge of the affairs of many countries, his prodigious memory and the numerous and varied channels through which he collected information on the subjects in which he was interested.

Of his early career I learned nothing. He told me once that even his wife knew nothing of his antecedents or of his history before he came to Canada. I was told by the physician who attended him during a serious illness at Winnipeg that when his life was in danger he tried, at Mrs. Farrer's request, to discover where her husband had spent his boyhood and what were his connections and pursuits before he came to Canada. The first question he put when the patient had a lucid moment was whether or not the family to which he belonged was distinguished for longevity. But with death at the door Farrer was himself. He assured the physician wearily but whimsically that generally his relations died shortly after the court rose, but occasionally one was fortunate enough to pull through until the next assizes. I can get no trace of Mr. Farrer before 1870. In the spring of that year he offered *The Lindsay Expositor* a series of sketches of leaders in the British House of Commons. The second or third article was criticized by a correspondent, and Farrer told Mr. Peter Murray, publisher of *The Expositor,* that he had no wish to engage in controversy and discontinued the contributions. It is understood that he had spent the previous winter as bookkeeper in a lumber shanty. When the season's work was over he had come to Lindsay. For a time, too, and possibly before his connection with *The Expositor* he wrote for *The Oshawa Vindicator.* Later he joined the staff of *The Daily Telegraph,* and when *The Mail* was established became one of its writers. During his connection with *The Globe* he was continuously and bitterly attacked by the Conservative newspapers. But his serenity was seldom disturbed and he never wrote a word in his own defence. There was a certain lawyer in Toronto who was often unfit to appear for his clients, and Mr. Farrer protested that this man was his counsel and that he would deal with his accusers as soon as the lawyer got sober. Once Mr. Erastus Wiman came to *The Globe* office with the manuscript of a speech in favour of Reciprocity with the United States that he was anxious to deliver in Canada. He read the speech to Mr. Jaffray, Mr. Farrer and myself, but our unanimous judgment was that he had spoken too often on the subject and that speeches in Canada by residents of the United States in favour of commercial union between the two countries were politically mischievous and damaging to the Liberal party. Wiman was so angry that he left the room without a word of farewell. We sat for some moments in a sober silence, which was finally broken by Mr. Farrer, who declared that Wiman would read the speech to the coloured porter on the Pullman between Hamilton and Buffalo and have Mr. H. P. Dwight, superintendent of the Great North-Western Telegraph Company, send it out for publication. When Mr. Farrer was short of money, as he was sometimes, and wanted to borrow, he used to tell me that he had some beautifully lithographed stock in a mine called "The Gates Ajar," which he would put up as security. He often declared that he was the last of the Baldwin Reformers, but had been absorbed by the Patrons of Industry and was not exactly certain that the absorption had not impaired his political consistency. Once when he was telling me about an Englishman he had met at Montreal he paused to remark, "You ought to see his wife; she has enough powder on her face to free Ireland." He declared that when he was in Winnipeg Van Horne brought an expert from Chicago to report on the prospect of hog raising in Manitoba, who found that if each hog could be furnished with a parlour stove and a buffalo overcoat success would be assured. He called me aside at Goldwin Smith's funeral to ask if I had heard that the Liberal platform of 1893 was a Tory forgery. He said of a mutual friend who had grown wealthy and did not conceal his opulence, that he could not give a quarter to a porter without taking $400 in bills out of his pocket.

Whimsical, happy, alert, companionable, unpretentious, scholarly, simple, profound, mysterious, and elusive, I have known no more remarkable man than Edward Farrer nor any of greater gifts or greater knowledge. Once Mr. Goldwin Smith asked me if I thought Mr. Farrer ever had a sincere conviction. I suggested that at least he was sincere in his desire to annex Canada to the United States. He said, "Oh, no, if Mr. Farrer could get Canada into the United States to-morrow he would start next day to get her out." His own opinion was that Mr. Farrer was sincere only in his dislike and distrust of the Roman Catholic hierarchy. I could not agree for I think he had a liking for the cultivated priesthood of the Church, however hostile he may have been to the tenets of ultramontanism and the absolutism of Roman Catholic teaching. But although he was nominally a Catholic when he came to die, he did not seek the consolation of the Church. A strange and great man he was who found much zest in life, but I think was often lonely. There was no window through which we could look into his soul. There was reticence which we could not penetrate; there was mystery that we could not fathom. It is said that he was educated in a Jesuit college, but I do not know. That he was a scholar was manifest. He had French and the old languages. But he walked in strange ways and it is literally true that his left hand did not always know what his right hand was doing. He had the quality of a detective and that talent was exercised for various and curious causes. I had knowledge that I do not disclose and confidences which cannot be betrayed. In his outlook for Canada he was an incurable, mischievous, dangerous pessimist. For the British

Empire he cared not at all. The story of his life would reveal remarkable connections and far-reaching influences. But no one can tell the story from the fragmentary material that remains.

When I became editor of *The Globe* it was the fashion to ignore or give little attention to Conservative meetings. The Liberal leaders always had crowded houses. Their speeches excited tremendous enthusiasm, At Conservative meetings there were empty benches and perfunctory attention. I have known *The Globe* to give eight or ten columns to a Liberal meeting at the old Pavilion and less than a column to a Conservative meeting at least as well attended and addressed by speakers of equal attraction and distinction. Moreover, there was often deliberate misrepresentation of Conservative speeches or calculated suppression of passages which were regarded as damaging to the Liberal position. I recall that two members of *The Globe* staff detailed to trail Sir John Macdonald from house to house and from place to place during one of his visits to Toronto refused to take the assignment. It is to the honour of Mr. Cameron that he respected their scruples. They were not required to resign nor affected in body or estate. From the first I resolved that reports should be accurate and that Conservative readers of *The Globe* should not require to go elsewhere for the speeches of their leaders. I recognized that it would not be judicious to discover as much enthusiasm at Conservative as at Liberal meetings, but I determined that there should be no deliberate misquotation or misrepresentation. The staff, and no better staff than that which I had on *The Globe* ever served a Canadian newspaper, gave loyal and even eager support to the policy to which I sought to give effect. But from certain of the directors there was often angry criticism and severe disapproval. Extreme Liberal partisans were bitter and contemptuous. I had to read many a savage letter and endure much misunderstanding with such equanimity as I could command. It was a long and hard battle, but I never wavered or retreated. In time the commercial and political wisdom of fair and full reports of public meetings was established and those who had blasphemed came to believe that they were responsible for the revolution. For in the columns of *The Globe* a revolution was effected and the example was influential with other public journals. After the general election of 1896 Sir Charles Tupper declared that *The Globe* had reported his speeches more fairly and more fully than any other newspaper, and other Conservative leaders supported his testimony. Not only has *The Globe* been faithful to the tradition which was established nearly thirty years ago, but few Canadian newspapers now tolerate the practices which were so common when Macdonald and Blake, Mowat and Meredith, contended for political supremacy. That, I believe, was my best contribution to Canadian journalism. I think my contemporaries will agree that I was influential in establishing the better fashion and yet not feeble or uncertain in the editorial columns in defence of the Liberal party or in attack upon the methods and policies of its opponents. For I never tried to persuade myself that *The Globe* was not the organ of the Liberal party or that its independence was not affected by its political connections.

In the third issue of *The Globe* which appeared under my editorship there are four articles which betray uneasiness over the situation in Quebec. I wrote all four with the deliberate object of dissociating *The Globe* from the extreme nationalism, or rather the extreme provincialism of Mercier, and in apprehension of disclosures of methods and practices in the government of the Province which would incidentally but inevitably affect Laurier and the Federal Liberal party. When through the investigation in the Senate corruption was exposed in Quebec at least as bold and systematic as was revealed during the "scandal session" at Ottawa, I could not be persuaded that *The Globe* should turn from denunciation of rascality under a Conservative Government to defence of rascality under a Liberal Government. But powerful influences in the Liberal party were outraged by my candour and treason. Early one morning a colleague on *The Globe* came to my house with the report that I was to be "removed from office." On the same day Mr. John Cameron came down from London with the suggestion that I should resign, as dismissal was certain if I did not forestall the fiat by immediate resignation. Both acted in complete good faith. Neither was in sympathy with the demand for my decapitation. Mr. Cameron argued that dismissal would affect all my future and that recovery would be less difficult if I evaded the stroke by a strategic withdrawal. My colleague insisted that if I were dismissed he would resign, since he had written many of the articles for which I was to suffer. I did all that I could to dissuade him from any such rash action, but he was inflexible and certainly would have gone out if I had been disturbed. But I told Mr. Cameron, as I told my loyal colleague, that I did not believe I was in danger, that whether I was or was not, nothing

was more certain than that I would not resign, and that
if my resignation was required there would have to be
a public disclosure of the motives and reasons behind
the demand. I was confident, however, that there was
no cause for alarm for *The Globe* was steadily improv-
ing its position and my relations with Mr. Jaffray and
the directors were singularly happy and satisfactory. I
said nothing to Mr. Jaffray or to any other of the directors, nor did I receive any information from any other
quarter to support the conviction of Mr. Cameron and
my associate in the office that resignation or dismissal
had been decreed. Two years later Mr. Jaffray told
me that a group of Liberal politicians, through Sir
Richard Cartwright, had demanded my dismissal on
account of my unsympathetic attitude towards the Mercier Government and inconsiderate denunciation of
evil political conditions in Quebec. He added that the
Board rejected the demand without a moment's consideration and that every precaution was taken to keep
the incident from my knowledge. I did not discover,
nor have I ever sought to discover, who beyond Sir
Richard Cartwright were concerned in the movement.

Two or three years later there was a formidable
intrigue within the Liberal party to exclude Sir Richard from Parliament. There was a common conviction
that he had so alienated the industrial and business interests that the party could not hope to succeed
in the constituencies while he was active and influential in its councils. It was designed, therefore,
to deprive Cartwright of the Liberal nomination for
South Oxford and to prevent his nomination elsewhere.
As editor of *The Globe* I was asked to join in this movement. When I declined peremptorily and emphatic-

ally to assist, or even to maintain silence if there was any serious prospect that Cartwright would not be re-nominated I was reminded of the fact, of which it was thought I was ignorant, that he had sought to have me dismissed from my position and could, therefore, have no possible claim upon my consideration or gratitude. My answer was that Sir Richard's attitude towards the editor of *The Globe* did not enter into the question. I urged that for a generation he had fought the battle of the Liberal party, often unwisely as I believed, but with self-sacrifice and devotion, and that to take his service in the day of his strength and dishonour him in his old age would be for him a mortal humiliation and for the party a shame and a disgrace. A few days before the convention in South Oxford, which he carried by a narrow majority, I made an earnest appeal in *The Globe* for his renomination which may not have been wholly without effect. Those who sought to unhorse Sir Richard shared his opinions but were embarrassed by his inveterate prejudices and violence of language. They believed that the party was more than the individual and that he was an obstacle to party success. Nor is it true that the manufacturers were behind the movement against Sir Richard. It may be that certain Liberal politicians were cultivating the protectionists, but if there was any reciprocal action it never came to my knowledge. There never was a quarrel that was more strictly domestic and it is not ungenerous to suggest that Conservatives were not eager to have Sir Richard dethroned. I once sat behind a group of Conservative members of the Commons in a railway carriage when Parliament was convulsed by the scandals of 1891 and was startled by the fierce energy of their common declaration that no matter what might be revealed they would never cast a vote to put Sir Richard Cartwright in office. Yet as I have said he mellowed in office and was more favourable to the protectionists than Fielding. I do not think he ever knew that I had knowledge of his attempt to drive me out of *The Globe* office, nor have I ever believed that Sir Wilfrid Laurier gave his consent to the demand for my dismissal. Sir Richard was grateful for *The Globe's* intervention in South Oxford and until his death he treated me with much consideration. As one goes on his journey—short at best—chances for revenge intrude, but to take revenge is to sour life to the core and make all the world unlovely.

As editor of *The Globe* I persisted for months and even for years in the agitation for a Federal Railway Commission. A Cabinet opposed finally yielded and the Commission was established. I was not the pioneer in the movement, and other forces were active and powerful. In the final decision no one was more influential than Dr. Rutherford, who has just been appointed to the Commission. I advocated reform of the Senate and reform of the civil service, but the last came slowly and the first not at all. When the Liberal party came into office in 1896 *The Globe* protested so strenuously against dismissal of Conservative office-holders save for active, offensive interference in elections that I was honoured by a vote of censure from the Young Men's Liberal Club of Toronto. When the Conservative party was restored to office in 1911 I protested as strongly against interference with Liberal officials. Returning from the Democratic Convention at Chicago in 1892 which nominated Cleveland, I began an agitation for a national convention of the Liberal party. There was protest and resistance from the official leaders of the party, but the agitation prevailed. If the platform which the Convention adopted was more honoured in the breach than in the observance nothing ever more greatly stimulated the national spirit of the Liberal party. Moreover, the party, greatly divided over the issue of Unrestricted Reciprocity with the United States, compromised its differences, and whether the country understood or not, declared against fiscal discrimination against Great Britain.

Convinced by my visit to the Western Provinces in 1895 that the agitation for the abolition of the Northwest Mounted Police was fatuous and the attitude of the Liberal party towards the Canadian Pacific Railway unwise and unnational, I modified *The Globe's* position and bore with such fortitude as I could the common insinuation that I was purchased by Van Horne and overcome by Police hospitality. *The Globe* had many articles in favour of law reform. In this agitation one of my confidential advisers was Chief Justice Armour. Before I met him letters were exchanged in a correspondence which he began. One day a huge man, in a rough gray suit, with a wide soft hat came into the office and without a word of greeting dropped heavily into a chair, brought a big stick down on the floor with unnecessary emphasis, turned keen, searching eyes upon me and rumbled, "Do you know who I am?" I guessed that he was Chief Justice Armour. "I am," he declared, "and I just wanted to look at the d—— fool who thinks he can get law reform from Mowat."

Mr. John Ewan came down from the head of the

lakes with a story about Mr. James Conmee. It was said that Conmee had a long and irreconcilable feud with a man at Port Arthur and that when he became a magistrate he had the object of his dislike confined in an out-house while he went through the Statutes to find if he had power to have him hanged. The story, of course, was exaggerated, but Mr. Ewan told it in *The Globe* and Mr. Conmee came down from Port Arthur to protest. His protest never got beyond the first few sentences. As Harry Lauder says, "I couldna keep frae laughin'," and Mr. Conmee finally joined in the laughter and we turned from law to politics. The truth was that a man named Bond at Port Arthur was believed to have violated the Act against selling liquor in the neighborhood of public works in the construction of which Conmee was interested. Conmee had Bond arrested, taken from Port Arthur to Sault Ste. Marie, and there tried before himself as a magistrate. He sentenced Bond to a term of imprisonment and ordered his property to be confiscated and destroyed. The prisoner was conveyed to jail bound with a logging chain to another offender. He was, however, discharged on a writ of Habeas Corpus and afterwards brought an action against Conmee for trespass and false imprisonment which was tried before Mr. Justice Armour. All the proceedings against Bond were held to be illegal, he recovered judgment for $1,600 and on appeal the judgment was confirmed. Conmee was a rough, aggressive, masterful personality, bold and confident alike in politics and in business, with a genius for litigation and the temper of an autocrat. But because he was a Liberal politician and *The Globe* was a Liberal organ I was able to divert his attention from a suit for libel to his political prospects in West Algoma.

I was connected with *The Globe* for nearly twenty years, and for twelve years I was its editor. During all that time I was in close association with Mr. C. W. Taylor, business manager, whose death sixteen years ago was like the loss of something out of myself. Both of us were touchy and impetuous and there were days when the bells jangled out of tune, but we were loyal to each other and quick to unite for offence or defence as circumstances required. It was hard to leave *The Globe,* and probably I shall not disclose all the motives by which I was actuated nor all the considerations which affected my judgment. At least I did not resign because I sought any recognition that was withheld or through any personal differences with the leaders of the Liberal party.

CHAPTER X

A LETTER AND A MYSTERY

It is not easy to discover the sources of the antipathy between Hon. Edward Blake and Sir Richard Cartwright. If we remember, however, that Cartwright was very loyal to Mackenzie, while Blake was an uncertain and uneasy colleague we shall probably be close to the roots of the quarrel. It was Cartwright's fortune to sustain many defeats and to wander far and often in search of a constituency. He was one of those candidates who could be elected only in the strongholds of his party. He could not draw support from among his opponents nor even attract independent voters to his standard. He was, however, always anxious to be in Parliament and possibly believed that if Blake had exercised in his behalf all the authority which a leader commands he would not have found it so difficult to secure a nomination and hold a constituency. Possibly he was more eager to be in Parliament than Blake was to have him there. At least it is certain that the two men had no love for each other and that the unhappy personal relation affected the cohesion of the Liberal party.

When Mr. Blake resigned the office of leader Sir Richard became the chief spokesman for the party in Ontario. In practice the dual leadership which prevailed in United Canada had persisted. Holton was the leader for Quebec under Mackenzie, Laurier under Blake, Langevin under Macdonald, and Monk under Borden. Gradually, however, under Thompson, Laur-

ier and Borden the single leadership developed and
after Monk disappeared from Parliament the old system ceased to have even nominal recognition. Mr. Blake
was in Europe when commercial union with the United
States, subsequently watered down to unrestricted reciprocity, was adopted as the fiscal platform of the Liberal party. In the adoption of this platform Mr. Blake
was not consulted. This neglect he resented since he
still had a seat in Parliament and had not expressed any
intention to withdraw from public life. Upon his
reappearance in Parliament after two years of rest and
travel abroad it was discovered that he was restless and
discontented. When Mr. Mulock introduced a resolution affirming, perhaps unnecessarily, the attachment of
Canada to Great Britain, Mr. Blake left the Chamber
as the bells rang for the division. "I will not vote for a
sham," he said when asked why he had retreated. I
had full knowledge of the incident and an interpretation
of his attitude which need not be emphasized. It soon
became apparent that he was not under discipline nor
in consultation with the official leaders of the party. In
the debate over the charges which necessitated Mr. J.
C. Rykert's withdrawal from Parliament he separated
himself from his Liberal associates and submitted an
amendment which they had to support, although a substantial modification of the Liberal position was involved. His ascendancy in the House was very manifest, but in degree as he was mutinous and disposed to
independent action the position of Laurier became diffi-
sult.

There were still those who would have restored
Blake to the office of leader, and there was a suspicion,
perhaps unfounded, that he was willing to be recalled.

Always sensitive to any suggestion that he desired recognition or preferment, Mr. Blake wrote to *The Globe* from Maisonrouge, Pointe au Pic, on June 30th, 1890, "My attention has been called to the fact that your recent article has given circulation among Liberals to Conservative allegations that I desire to resume the leadership of the Liberal party. I beg space to say that there is not a grain of truth in these allegations and that I am no more desirous to resume than I was to assume or to retain that post. My only wish is that the confidence and affection of Liberals of all shades may induce Mr. Laurier to hold the place which he so admirably fills." This letter is very like Blake in its complete repudiation of all interested motives and even in the delicate suggestion that his attention "was called" to the article which gave occasion for the statement. Probably at this time, and possibly at no time, had he any settled desire to replace Laurier. Had he any such notion he would have guarded even against self-discovery of the motive by which he was actuated. That was his way. He would not let his own soul express itself nor ever recognize the human impulses which were of the essence of his being. For as I have said elsewhere, Mr. Blake was essentially aspiring and ambitious and fundamentally unhappy in any subordinate relation.

If the country was slow to discover evidences of friction, the Opposition in Parliament was anxious and the Conservative front benches deeply interested in the domestic situation on the other side of the Chamber. Nothing so comforts a Parliamentary party as signs of disturbance in the opposing forces. It is seldom that the signs are misinterpreted. One party rarely fails to penetrate the secrets of the other or to discover the personal relations among opponents. But if there was suspicion there was no immediate revelation of Mr. Blake's attitude towards unrestricted reciprocity. In the first weeks of 1891 rumours of a general election pervaded the country. There is reason now to believe that Sir John Macdonald had learned that the long and bitter quarrel between the Langevin and Chapleau factions in Quebec would probably produce grave disclosures in Parliament, and he feared that the Opposition would greatly increase its supply of ammunition if the House was not dissolved before the charges against Langevin and McGreevy of corrupt dealing with public contracts could be formulated. Moreover he had knowledge of the Farrer pamphlet suggesting political union with the United States, abrogation of the bonding privilege and a blockade of canal traffic at Sault Ste. Marie as coercive measures against Canada. Doubtless he was apprehensive also that the Liberal leaders had established dubious relations with American statesmen and that money would be provided from American sources to corrupt the constituencies. So far as I could ever discover, however, no American money reached the Liberal treasury, nor would the political leaders at Washington even agree to reciprocal free trade with Canada or to any definite alliance with the Canadian Liberal party. There is no doubt that Sir Richard Cartwright sought to effect such an alliance and that Mr. Farrer made pilgrimages to Washington, but there was no ground for the suspicion that any compact was entered into affecting the political status of Canada, nor was there any understanding that commercial union should be regarded as a deliberate and conscious step towards political union. The truth was that the Liberal party had pledged itself to establish free trade with the United States, but had no assurance and could obtain no assurance that the United States would enter into any reciprocal commercial agreement with Canada even if the Canadian constituencies should return the Liberal leaders to office. But there was ground for suspicion and doubtless Sir John Macdonald feared that negotiations between the Liberal leaders and the statesmen at Washington would produce an understanding inimical to the future of Canada and sought by timely dissolution of Parliament to secure a political victory and destroy a movement which threatened the Canadian industrial fabric and the unity of the Empire.

Believing that a general election was imminent the Liberal leaders summoned a Provincial Convention of the party for February 17th and 18th, 1891, at Toronto. It is certain that Cartwright suggested the convention although the call was issued by Mr. Laurier. It is certain, too, that Mr. Blake was not consulted. This oversight, intentional or otherwise, produced momentous consequences, or at least revealed the actual relations between Blake and Cartwright. A few days after the convention was announced I received in the midnight mail a letter from Mr. Blake of ominous and startling import. As was his habit "personal" was written upon the envelope, but in that there was no comfort. I knew that it was intended for immediate publication, and I was dismayed at its contents. The letter, which was not lengthy, was a sweeping attack upon the Liberal trade policy as unwise, elusive and misleading, feeble in conception and impossible of execution, uncandid in evasion of the inevitable results, requiring assimilation of the tariffs of Canada and the United States, undistinguishable from commercial union, which should come as the precursor of political union, and involving a constitutional issue for which the people were unprepared. In the letter there was no direct counsel to the country. It was destructive and denunciatory, hopeless in temper and outlook. Mr. Blake opposed unrestricted reciprocity in language that could not be misunderstood, not as disloyal or fundamentally inimical to Canadian nationality, but as less practicable than commercial union, which he seemed to favour as a preparation for political union. I do not suggest that the letter was a deliberate declaration for annexation to the United States, but that was the impression conveyed by a first reading, and it is certain that he gave no general support to the arguments which Conservatives were urging against the Liberal fiscal proposal. They were agreed as to the impracticability of establishing unrestricted reciprocity between Canada and the United States without a common tariff and discrimination against Great Britain, but there was nothing in this letter as there was nothing in the longer letter which Mr. Blake published on the morning after the general election to support the contention of Conservative newspapers and politicians that Mr. Blake rejected unrestricted reciprocity out of concern for British trade or British connection or because of any taint of disloyalty in the commercial policy of the Liberal party. At least he was not more loyal than his old Liberal associates nor was he averse to commercial union between the United States and Canada.

Although it was midnight when I received Mr.

Blake's letter, one of the editorial writers was still at his desk, and I sought his counsel. When he had read the letter he advised, not with the discretion of a politician, but with the instinct and ardour of a journalist. "Publish it," he said, "we have the opportunity to produce one of the greatest sensations in the political history of Canada." I pointed out that if we did so the Liberal party would be overwhelmed in the election and argued that we should not take the responsibility without consultation with Mr. Jaffray and the directors. He acquiesced, perhaps with reluctance, not because he was anxious to have the letter published, but because he was apprehensive, as I was, that it had been sent to *The Mail* and that by delay *The Globe* would lose the advantage of contemporary publication. On the way home in the morning I mailed a note to Mr. Blake acknowledging receipt of the letter and suggesting that as it was marked "personal" I assumed that it was not intended for publication.

When I reached the office next day I found a letter from Mr. Blake intimating in a few frigid sentences that the letter was intended for publication and that in the general interest, in his judgment, "the sooner it was published the better." During the afternoon I laid Mr. Blake's letter before Mr. Jaffray, and he called a meeting of *The Globe* directors. I feel even now the depth of gloom which pervaded that meeting. No one doubted that the statement would be fatal to Liberal prospects in the election, but the unanimous judgment was that Mr. Blake would insist upon publication and that it must appear. For the moment I submitted, but I was not convinced that *The Globe* should be the first to reveal Mr. Blake's position to the country, nor was I persuaded that publication was inevitable. That night I had dinner with Hon. David Mills, to whom I submitted the letter and with whom I collaborated in preparing an editorial to accompany its publication. Returning to the office I had the letter and the editorial put into type, but when I got the proofs into my hands I resolved to risk another day's delay and to make a personal appeal to Mr. Blake to maintain silence until Mr. Laurier could be consulted. I collected the type and the galley proofs, locked them in a cabinet in my room, and sent the paper to press without the disturbing letter and the feeble, inconsequential editorial which Mr. Mills and I had produced.

When I called upon Mr. Blake next day I found that he had sent for Mr. Jaffray, that he was aware of the decision of the Board and my contumacy, and had been assured that there would be no further attempt to suppress his statement. Mr. Blake also told me that he had sent the letter to Mr. D. Burk Simpson, president of the West Durham Reform Association, and he suggested that if it did not appear in *The Globe* it would appear in *The Mail* as a despatch from Bowmanville. I tried to give reasons why he should see Mr. Laurier before publishing such a destructive statement in face of a general election, but he retorted angrily that Laurier and Cartwright had not thought it necessary to consult him before calling a convention of the Liberals of Ontario, and declared that if the convention were not abandoned he would appear before the delegates and expose the impracticable and impossible trade policy which they sought to impose upon the party. Mr. Jaffray induced Mr. S. H. Blake, K.C., to appeal to his brother for withdrawal of the letter, but he was as unsuccessful as was Sir Oliver Mowat, who also saw Mr. Blake and advised its suppression. When it seemed to be settled beyond all question that neither persuasion nor remonstrance could turn Mr. Blake from his purpose *The Globe* directors met again and again agreed, with the approval of Sir Oliver Mowat, that the letter must be published. I did not oppose the decision for I could not see that there was any alternative. In the meantime Mr. W. T. R. Preston, organizer of the Liberal party, had heard of the letter and entered a very vigorous protest against its publication. I gave Mr. Preston no promise, although as the hours passed I drifted steadily towards the definite conviction that the Board's instructions would be again disregarded. At one o'clock in the morning I called Mr. Jaffray out of bed and reported that the letter would not appear, and that I believed I had a compromise to suggest which Mr. Blake would not reject. Mr. Jaffray remonstrated mildly at the other end of the telephone, but I knew that he was more surprised than angry and that whatever the political consequences of my action the judgment of the Board would be tempered with mercy.

In a note which I arranged to have delivered to Mr. Blake early next morning I explained that I was wholly responsible for the further delay in publication, suggested that I should go down to Quebec and place the facts before Mr. Laurier, and urged that he should not make any public statement until I could report the result of my interview and present any proposal which Laurier might submit to avert an open rupture, the disastrous consequences to the party and the embittered personal relations which must be the result of the course of action upon which he had determined. To this Mr. Blake finally agreed. I telegraphed to Mr. Laurier at Montreal an urgent appeal for an immediate interview. I did not feel that I could consult Mr. Laurier or Sir Richard Cartwright without Mr. Blake's consent, but even if I had thought otherwise both were out of the country. On January 29th Mr. Laurier was to speak at a dinner of the New York Board of Trade, which was interrupted by the sudden death of Mr. Windom, Secretary of the Treasury in the Harrison Cabinet, while on January 30th Sir Richard Cartwright spoke at Boston. As I had hoped, Mr. Laurier got my despatch at Montreal on the way home from New York. His answer was: "I will be in Toronto in the morning." I saw Laurier shortly after his interview with Blake, but much of what was said cannot be disclosed. Blake agreed to defer any public statement until after the general election on condition that the Provincial Liberal Convention which had been called was not held. Cartwright bitterly resented the condition which Blake imposed, but the alternative was submission or disruption. I have always believed that Blake never fully understood, or at least would not admit even to himself, how vitally his dislike of Cartwright affected his action at this time, even if he did not cherish the expectation that Laurier would be set aside for himself as Hartington was set aside for Gladstone at a momentous hour in the history of the British Liberal party. I have wondered, too, if Sir Oliver Mowat was very anxious to suppress Mr. Blake's letter. He disliked unrestricted reciprocity and was inflexibly opposed to commercial union. But he was acute enough to see that Blake's letter would compel the Liberal party to reconsider the whole fiscal issue and he had no apprehension of any serious or definite movement towards political union with the United States. There was an eruption of annexation sentiment more formidable than he foresaw, but the masses of the party were not affected nor did any of the leaders give actual support to the agitation.

During the negotiations with Mr. Blake for the suppression of his letter, Mr. Farrer was in Washington. There is no doubt that he was trying to induce Mr. James G. Blaine, Secretary of State, to give public assurances that unrestricted reciprocity would be established if the Liberal party succeeded in the election. He was greatly embarrassed by the announcement from Ottawa when Parliament was dissolved that the United States Government had agreed to consider a renewal of the Reciprocity Treaty of 1854, with the modifications required by the altered circumstances of both countries. Sir John Thompson declared that the answer of Mr. Blaine "on behalf of his Government" to the representations of the Government of Canada "was an overture to Reciprocity." Mr. Farrer did not obtain from Blaine such a statement as he desired, but he did persuade the American Secretary of State to address a letter to Congressman Baker, of Rochester, in which he said: "There are no negotiations whatever on foot for a Reciprocity Treaty with Canada, and you may be assured no such scheme for reciprocity with the Dominion confined to natural products will be entertained by this Government." Of Mr. Farrer's activity at Washington Mr. Blake had no knowledge, nor had Mr. Laurier any direct responsibility for his movements. Sir Richard Cartwright had full knowledge and, as I have said, had himself gone to Washington in the endeavour to effect an understanding with the United States Government, but beyond the letter to Mr. Baker, which was not indefensible under the circumstances, neither Mr. Blaine nor any of his colleagues entered into any compromising alliance with the Liberal leaders of Canada. There can be no doubt that Mr. Blaine was favourable to political union between the two countries and that he had confidential relations with Mr. Farrer, but he did not engage in any intrigue against the Macdonald Government or give moral or material support to the Opposition in the general election in which free trade with the United States was the supreme issue between the Canadian parties. On the other hand, the McKinley tariff and other measures of legislation and administration at Washington during this period were designed to affect the political destiny of Canada.

In Sir Richard Cartwright's volume of Reminiscences there is this reference to Mr. Blake's letter: "The election at the last was rather hurried, and the writs were issued at a moment when both Sir Wilfrid Laurier and myself were absent from Ontario. The instant it was known that they were about to issue, Mr. Blake prepared to publish a letter condemning our policy and had it actually in type in a paper in his old riding. This was discovered by a staunch friend of ours who had influence enough with the publisher to defer the publication of the letter till he had time to communicate with certain of our supporters in Toronto, who brought such pressure to bear upon Mr. Blake that he finally, though with a very bad grace, suspended its publication till after the election. My own opinion of his conduct was such that I never spoke to him nor held any communication with him from that day, and I prefer to state the facts without further comment. The results are another matter." In references to Mr. Blake or Sir John Macdonald it was difficult for Sir Richard to be just and impossible for him to be generous. There is no reason to think that Blake took deliberate advantage of the absence of Laurier and Cartwright from the country. He could not have thought that *The Globe* would refuse to publish his letter or that Mr. Burk Simpson would block its publication at Bowmanville. Moreover, there was *The Mail* in the full flower of independence, and other journals which would have been eager to give him a hearing. But from the first Mr. Simpson seems to have resolved that the letter should not go to the public. It is understood that it was not in type at Bowmanville, nor ever left Mr. Simpson's possession. He had a more difficult task than mine, but he was skilful enough and resolute enough to control a convention of Mr. Blake's own constituents. There was read to the convention a letter from Blake expressing gratitude for long and faithful support which deeply affected the delegates, but they had no knowledge of the reasons for his refusal to be re-nominated nor any suspicion that Mr. Simpson had persuaded Mr. Blake not to appear at the convention chiefly by insisting upon a rigid observance of the compact with Laurier that he would not speak until after the election. In *The Globe* office the printers, proofreaders and reporters necessarily had knowledge of the letter, and although there were many Conservatives among them, the fact that *The Globe* had received such a communication or that it was put into type was not revealed.

236

A LETTER AND A MYSTERY

This I have always regarded as a striking illustration of the high code of honour which prevails among printers and journalists. Nor did I exact any pledge of silence or suggest directly or indirectly that there was any obligation upon printers, reporters or editors to respect the secrets of the office in which they were employed.

The letter which Mr. Blake published on the morning after the election appeared simultaneously in many Canadian journals and in *The London Times*. The Ottawa correspondent of *The Times* was Mr. Fred. Cook, who was also correspondent of *The Toronto Empire,* then the chief organ of the Conservative party. Mr. Cook was also Reuter's agent at Ottawa. Rumour was busy with the paper which Mr. Blake was understood to have written in explanation of his attitude towards unrestricted reciprocity and his reasons for not seeking re-election in West Durham. Naturally Mr. Cook was anxious to obtain a copy. He suggested to Reuter by cable that he should be instructed to see Mr. Blake and explain how deeply Great Britain was interested in his attitude and how much Reuter would appreciate a copy of his statement. Armed with this message, Mr. Cook came to Toronto and saw Mr. Blake at his home. Mr. Blake expressed surprise that the Reuter Agency should be interested, but explained that while he was honoured by the request, his first duty was to his own country and that the letter must be published in Canada as early as in Great Britain. He would not promise that Reuter should have first publication, but assured Mr. Cook that he should have a copy of the statement as soon as any other newspaper or agency. A few days later Cook had a letter from Blake dated at Toronto, February 22nd, 1891. "Referring," he said, "to the request made through you by Reuter for a copy of my paper, which, as I informed you, is not to be made public till after the election, I have looked at it in view of what you told me and I see that even eliminating the personal paragraphs, it is much longer than ordinary cable limits would allow. I intend to-morrow to mail a copy to a friend in London, England, and if you desire, I will request my friend to let Reuter have it for the press as soon as it reaches London, not earlier than 5th March. Should you not so desire, my friend will place it in other hands. If you wish me to give this direction wire me to-morrow giving me Reuter's London address. I write this in fulfilment of the spirit of my promise that your people should have the paper as early as any on the other side of the Atlantic. But I need hardly repeat to you that I have no personal wishes on the subject."

Mr. Cook was apprehensive of delay on the ocean and suggested that Mr. Blake should let him have a copy of the letter in confidence on the day preceding that set for publication. On February 25th Mr. Blake wrote that he would mail a copy to Mr. Cook "by the morning mail of March 5th if you wish, so that you can have it in Ottawa that evening in case of any mishap in London. This, however, I can do only on your undertaking to keep the document absolutely secret on this side of the water." The letter reached London a day or two before polling in Canada. Early on the morning of election-day Mr. Cook received a cable message from Reuter's Agency to that effect and expressing gratitude for his foresight and vigilance. An hour or so later Mr. E. F. Jarvis, at that time Mr. Blake's parliamentary private secretary and now Assistant Deputy

A LETTER AND A MYSTERY

Minister of Militia and Defence, called at Mr. Cook's house, as instructed by Mr. Blake, with a copy of the letter in a sealed envelope. Cook showed Jarvis the message from Reuter and suggested that as he did not require the copy it was probably better that it should not be left in his hands. He refused the envelope because he was anxious not to leave himself open to suspicion of bad faith if there should be premature publication. *The Times* gave the statement in full, and a summary furnished by Reuter appeared in many other newspapers in Great Britain. For securing this letter in advance of other news agencies and for an early copy of Sir John Macdonald's last appeal to the Canadian people, the Reuter Agency gave Mr. Cook $500. One of the grievances among Liberals was that Mr. Blake had transmitted his letter to London through the correspondent of the chief Conservative organ. This was not done, but even if Mr. Cook had been chosen as the direct medium of communication with Reuter it is certain that he would have scrupulously observed the confidence reposed in his honour and discretion, notwithstanding his intimate relations with Sir John Macdonald and the Conservative leaders.

The letter which Mr. Blake published on March 6th, 1891, was not the letter he sent to *The Globe* and Mr. Burk Simpson. The original statement, much shorter, but similar in argument and conclusion, has never been published. The manifesto of March 6th argued that Great Britain would never reimpose protectionist duties in favour of colonial producers while unrestricted free trade with the United States secured for a long term of years would, even though accompanied by higher duties against the rest of the world than he for one admired, give Canada in practice the great blessing of a measure of free trade much larger than we enjoyed or could otherwise attain. "Direct taxation, even in its most promising form, a succession tax, was out of the question, and therefore of the financial problem presented by unrestricted reciprocity he had seen no solution which would leave us without a great deficit." Any feasible plan of unrestricted reciprocity involved differential duties and the substantial assimilation in their leading features of the tariffs of the two countries. The absence of agreement would give to each country power to disturb at will the industrial system of the other and unrestricted reciprocity, without an agreed assimilation of duties, was an unsubstantial dream. Unrestricted reciprocity, therefore, in its redeeming features was difficult to distinguish from commercial union. Hence "Commercial union, establishing a common tariff, abolishing international custom houses and dividing the total duties between the two countries in agreed proportions, would be the more available, perhaps the only available plan." The tendency in Canada of unrestricted free trade with the United States and high duties against the United Kingdom would be toward political union, and the more successful the plan the stronger the tendency, both by reason of the community of interests, the intermingling of population, the more intimate business and social connections and the trade and fiscal relations amounting to dependency which it would create with the States, and of the greater isolation and divergency from Britain which it would produce, and also and especially through inconveniences experienced in the maintenance and apprehensions entertained as to the termination of

the treaty. Therefore, Mr. Blake contended, "Whatever you or I may think on that head, whether we like
or dislike, believe or disbelieve in political union, must
we not agree that the subject is one of great moment,
towards the practical settlement of which we should
take no serious step without reflection or in ignorance
of what we are doing. Assuming that absolute free
trade, best described as commercial union, may and
ought to come, I believe that it can and should come
only as an incident, or at any rate as a well understood
precursor of political union, for which indeed we
should be able to make better terms before than after
the surrender of our commercial independence. Then
so believing—believing that the decision of the trade
question involves that of the constitutional issue for
which you are unprepared and with which you do not
even conceive yourselves to be dealing—how can I properly recommend you now to decide on commercial
union."

The Globe interpreted Mr. Blake's manifesto as a
declaration in favour of political union between the
United States and Canada. It pointed out that during
the election campaign the Conservative press had continuously asserted that he had withdrawn from public
life because he felt that unrestricted trade with the
United States was a disloyal policy, while his letter
showed that he was for absolute free trade on the distinct understanding that it should terminate in political
union without which it could not be carried out or even
so much as be obtained. "Mr. Blake," *The Globe* said,
"alone is responsible for these opinions and for the far-
reaching conclusion to which they lead. The Tory
press which alleged that he was not willing to go as

far as his party made a crucial mistake—his party is not willing to go as far as he. It is confident with all respect for him that unrestricted trade can be got without any sacrifice of political autonomy and worked without any very serious inconvenience to the revenue. It refuses pointblank to move in the direction of political union and is convinced, moreover, that it would not be necessary to do so in order to secure the boon which it has set out to obtain. Such is the view of all those Liberals whom *The Globe,* in the present hurly-burly, has been able to consult. Speaking for itself, this journal feels bound to say with all the emphasis at its command that Mr. Blake's main proposition, if we may so term it, is wholly distasteful. The country is in a bad plight, but a rough hand was laid on the Government's shoulder yesterday, and there is still a chance for recovery, provided the people assert themselves before it is too late. We prefer to take that chance rather than to share with Mr. Blake the responsibility of advocating political union which, as he knows, would be for Canada a revolution of tremendous magnitude, and for Britain perhaps the beginning of the end of her glorious Empire. At the same time we would not be Liberals if we challenged his right or that of any other Canadian to discuss the subject of our national future from the continental standpoint. What effect the pronouncement of so distinguished a man may have upon current politics remains to be seen. The present régime is fast breaking up and the confusion visible on all hands will be increased by this weighty deliverance. It will be the duty of the Liberal leaders, we should imagine, to define their position without delay, for, coming on the heels of yesterday's elections, Mr. Blake's utterance cannot fail to produce a feeling of profound anxiety throughout the Dominion. *The Globe* has championed British connection for fifty years and means to continue on that line until loyalty to Britain becomes treason to Canada. Things have not reached that fateful pass yet and we pray they never may."

Naturally there was a fierce outcry in the Conservative newspapers over *The Globe's* interpretation of Mr. Blake's statement. Many Liberal journals read the letter only as an exposure of the impracticability of unrestricted reciprocity and a frank intimation to the country that political union was the inevitable, ultimate outcome of the policy to which the Liberal party under Laurier and Cartwright was committed. Many messages came to Mr. Blake in urgent appeal for a more definite explanation of his position and an unequivocal repudiation of *The Globe's* conclusion. For four or five days he was silent, but on March 11th he wrote from Ottawa: "The contradictory inferences to which a sentence in my Durham letter, detached from its context, has in several quarters unexpectedly given rise, conquers my reluctance to trespass again so soon upon your columns, and I crave space to say that I think political union with the United States, though becoming our probable, is by no means our ideal, or as yet our inevitable future." But no word of reproof ever came to *The Globe,* nor in many intimate conversations that I had with Mr. Blake before he left Canada for London to take the seat for Longford in the Imperial Parliament did he ever refer to the subject. When the National Liberal Convention of 1893, responsive to powerful influences within the party, so recast its fiscal policy as to escape the implication of intention to discriminate against Great Britain, Mr. Blake in a public statement expressed satisfaction and declared that the revised platform was in consonance with the views which he had entertained and expressed. So I leave the mystery of the West Durham manifesto to the future, which may or may not afford a final and complete revelation. In the bye-elections of 1892 Blake's letter was the chief reliance of the Conservative Government and was infinitely damaging to the candidates of the Liberal party. Thereafter the door was closed forever to any prospect of reunion or co-operation between Blake and the leaders of the Canadian party which he had done so much to create and so much to divide and destroy.

CHAPTER XI

RACE AND RELIGION IN CANADA

In 1896 the Manitoba school question was the chief issue between the parties. The Conservatives, under Sir Charles Tupper, were committed to the restoration of separate schools in Manitoba which a Provincial Liberal Government had abolished. The Liberal party under Mr. Laurier opposed coercion of Manitoba, but in all the Liberal leader's speeches there is no direct denial of the constitutional soundness of the position of his opponents. He was wonderfully dexterous, but neither uncandid nor dishonest. Substantially he contended that compulsion was impracticable and that greater concessions could be secured for the Roman Catholic minority of Manitoba by compromise and conciliation than by any legislation however ingeniously devised which must be imposed upon the recalcitrant Province by Federal authority. Whatever impression his guarded language may have created in the English-speaking communities, he never suggested that he would not apply Federal pressure if the Province should refuse adequate concessions, nor did he ever admit that the grievances of the minority were insignificant or that the Provincial legislation was not a substantial violation of the spirit of the Constitution. He was attacked with such violence by the Bishops of Quebec that a multitude of Orange Protestants flocked to his support. In the Quebec parishes, however, the lower clergy and the masses of his compatriots were persuaded that he would secure greater concessions for

245

the minority of Manitoba than the Remedial Bill would ensure. As the controversy developed all other considerations in Quebec became secondary to the sentiment of racial loyalty to a French Canadian who had become leader of a national party and would become Prime Minister if his own Province and his own people adhered to his standard. There is nothing more remarkable in Canadian political history than the private canvass of Quebec for Laurier in 1896 and the skill, ardour and courage of his candidates in creating an organization and a sentiment, despite powerful adverse influences, which were irresistible on the day of polling. Under an English leader the Liberal party would have been defeated and without Quebec Laurier would not have triumphed.

It has to be said for Laurier that he did not try to keep the school question open for any partisan object. The issue was as embarrassing to the Liberal as to the Conservative party. If Sir Donald Smith had succeeded in effecting a settlement between the Liberal Government at Winnipeg and the Conservative Government at Ottawa Laurier would have rejoiced. He would have supported the settlement as a happy release from a difficult situation. Of this Sir Donald Smith was convinced or he probably would not have attempted to compose the differences between the two Governments. It is not certain that the Provincial Ministers were so willing to sacrifice the political advantages of a dispute by which they had profited in successive elections. Nor was Mr. D'Alton McCarthy anxious for an understanding between the Governments. There is reason to think that his responsibility for the abolition of separate schools in Manitoba was neither indirect nor remote. By his opposition to separate schools and official recognition of the French language he had created the nucleus of a party and he did not favor concessions in Manitoba which would impair his strength in the country and destroy an issue upon which he relied to embarrass the Conservative Government. He was opposed also for the higher reason that any concessions in his judgment would recognize the principle of separation in education, and he was greatly concerned to have only a common public school system established throughout Western Canada. He had closer relations with the Liberal Government of Manitoba than had the official Liberal leaders at Ottawa. When Hon. Joseph Martin determined to abolish separate schools in the Western Province neither Mr. Laurier nor Sir Oliver Mowat were consulted. They would not have approved if they had been consulted. Mr. McCarthy not only was consulted but probably directed, and there is no doubt that Mr. Edward Farrer had knowledge of what was contemplated. *The Mail* down to the amalgamation with *The Empire* in 1895 was behind Mr. McCarthy. It was the steady champion of all movements in which he was concerned, and it is curious that Mr. McCarthy, Mr. Farrer and Mr. Goldwin Smith, united against the Roman Catholic hierarchy, created conditions in the country which finally destroyed the unity of the Conservative party and gave victory to the Liberals under a Roman Catholic leader.

But among Liberals there was grave perplexity and foreboding for some time after the final judgment of the Imperial Privy Council in the Manitoba school cases. It was believed that the judgment of the

Supreme Court affirming the constitutionality of the
Provincial school legislation would be sustained. There
was consternation, therefore, when the Privy Council
decided that the Manitoba school regulations affected
prejudicially the privileges of the Catholic minority
and that if adequate concessions were refused by the
Provincial authority the Federal Government could
constitutionally give such relief as justice to the minority and fair observance of the Constitution required. It
is doubtful if Conservative Ministers were grateful for
the judgment. It is certain that Laurier was reluctant
to move out of Torres Vedras. *The Globe* had steadily
and firmly opposed interference with Manitoba. Now,
however, an influential element in the Liberal party
demanded that it should reverse its position and support remedial legislation. I was even provided with
an editorial in which "the curve" was taken with infinite
casuistry and temerity. But I resisted the appeal with
such argument as I could command, took counsel with
Mr. Jaffray, and on the morning on which it was desired that the retreat should begin *The Globe* restated
its original position so resolutely and unequivocally that
there was no further attempt to control its utterances,
although there was much grieving and cursing over its
precipitancy and implacability. At the time there were
references in many newspapers to a dispute between the
directors and the editor over the Manitoba school question so acute that I threatened to resign if *The Globe's*
position was reversed. But there was no such quarrel
nor any reason that I should offer my resignation. The
course which *The Globe* pursued the party followed, at
first perhaps with misgiving, but finally with conviction
and confidence. If *The Globe* had hesitated or tempor-

ized confusion would have descended upon the Liberal party and ultimately the paper would have been repudiated or the party committed to a dubious and equivocal position on the chief issue before the country.

It is believed that Mr. J. Israel Tarte saw more quickly and more clearly than most of his parliamentary associates that if the Opposition could be united against the Remedial Bill the Conservative party would be disrupted in the English Provinces. With characteristic ardour and courage, he laboured to impress Liberal members from Quebec with the certain prospect of office for Laurier if they would boldly challenge the influences against which they would have to contend in the French constituencies. They hesitated, for they knew that the Hierarchy were behind the bill and would exert all their authority in behalf of members who gave the support required, and against those who opposed or obstructed its passage through Parliament. But courage was never lacking in the old Rouge element of Quebec. They may sometimes have fought rashly and sometimes unwisely, but they were ever gallant and resolute. In many a battle they tasted defeat, but they seldom capitulated nor ever left the field dishonoured. Between the Rouges of Quebec and the Liberal party of Upper Canada which George Brown created there was a natural alliance, and their common efforts and achievements constitute brilliant chapters in Canadian history.

If Mr. Laurier hesitated to oppose the Remedial Bill it was because he knew, as few men did, the strength of the forces which would unite in its support and the character of the contest in which he must engage. He was, too, a French-Canadian and a Roman Catholic and naturally reluctant to seem to oppose the church and the race to which he belonged. For the school legislation of Manitoba affected French Catholics chiefly and was more peculiarly the concern of the French than of the Irish ecclesiastics. In the election, however, a far greater proportion of Irish than of French Catholics supported the Remedial Bill through the candidates of the Government. But however Laurier may have hesitated, he finally determined to maintain the doctrine of Provincial Rights, which was a cardinal principle of the Liberal party, although, as I have said, he never admitted that there was not a constitutional right of Federal intervention on behalf of the religious minority of Manitoba. He moved the "six months hoist" of the Remedial Bill and sanctioned, if he did not direct, the obstruction which prevented adoption of the measure before the legal life of Parliament expired.

There was a moment of intense concern when Laurier rose to move his motion, for Mr. Clarke Wallace rose simultaneously, and if he had been recognized by the Speaker, would have offered the motion which Laurier intended to submit. A motion by Laurier to reject the bill the French Liberals had agreed to support. A like proposal from Wallace they would not and could not support. They would have stood before Quebec as the allies of the Grand Master of the Orange Association, and a situation difficult enough for French Liberals would have become intolerable and impossible. Nor is it conceivable that the Opposition by any subsequent device or manoeuvre could have escaped the consequences of such association with the Orange leader if they opposed the Bill in Parliament or in the country. Fortunately for the Liberal party, Hon. Peter White, then Speaker of the Commons, recognized Mr. Laurier, and for Mr. Wallace there was no alternative but to support the motion which expressed the attitude of the Opposition. It was natural that the Speaker should recognize the leader of the Opposition against any private member, however eminent, but there is reason also to think that Mr. Peter White disliked the Remedial Bill and believed that if Mr. Wallace offered the motion for its rejection, the Liberal parliamentary party would be divided and a majority for the measure assured. Mr. Wallace, who had resigned from the Government over the decision to restore Separate schools in Manitoba, was not aggrieved by the Speaker's action. He was among the most vigorous and effective obstructionists in Parliament and was very influential during the general election in solidifying the extremer Protestant element against the Government. But if he co-operated with the Liberal party, he entered into no actual alliance with Mr. Laurier, and unlike Mr. D'Alton McCarthy when a settlement with Manitoba was effected by the Laurier Administration, he re-established an independent connection with the Conservative party. It is curious that Orangemen, who are commonly regarded as the "backbone" of the Conservative party, should have so often assisted the Liberal party to obtain office. A great body of Orangemen, angry over the murder of Thomas Scott at Fort Garry and dissatisfied with the behaviour of John Sandfield Macdonald, voted for Liberal candidates in Ontario in 1871 and gave Mr. Blake a victory which he probably could not have won without Orange support. Sir John Macdonald was greatly weakened in

1872 by the defection of Orangemen who believed that Riel was treated with excessive consideration and that there was feeble and indecisive handling of the Red River insurrection. In 1896 the revolt among Orangemen gave many constituencies to the Liberal party. Indeed, it is doubtful if Laurier could have carried the country without the support of an element which Liberals have seldom conciliated and generally distrusted and contemned.

I never doubted that the Liberal party would triumph in 1896, although the result in Ontario was less decisive and in Quebec more decisive than I expected. I remember that a few days before polling *The Globe* received a message from Quebec that at most only two or three Conservative candidates would be elected in the Quebec district. We thought the estimate so exaggerated and extreme that the despatch was not published. But the prophet was not discredited by the result. The tremendous energy and amazing endurance of Sir Charles Tupper vitally affected the situation in Ontario. He revived the spirit and restored the courage of the Conservative party and steadied a multitude of waverers. In all his strenuous life he never was more powerful or aggressive, more effective or more destructive, than in the campaign of 1896, although he fought upon an issue which was not of his making and with a party broken by mutiny and dissension. I have often wondered how Sir John Thompson would have handled the Manitoba school question if he had lived, or how Sir Charles Tupper would have framed the issue if he had been recalled from England before the Remedial Bill was introduced. While Tupper was reorganizing the Cabinet, it was

reported that Mr. B. B. Osler, K.C., had been offered
the position of Minister of Justice. But when the reor-
ganization was completed and the Cabinet announced,
Mr. Osler's name did not appear. I had not expected
that he would enter the Cabinet, for he was opposed to
Federal interference with the school legislation of
Manitoba. If, however, he had accepted Sir Charles
Tupper's proposal the bill would have been abandoned.
On his return from Ottawa after his interview with
Tupper he asked by telephone if he could see me at *The
Globe* office. I suggested that he should allow me to go
to his office. In the interview which followed he stated
that he had been offered the position of Minister of
Justice by Sir Charles Tupper and had declined for
only one reason. I suggested that no doubt the reason
was that he could not defend the Remedial Bill before
the country. He said, "No. I was not asked to do so.
I had the positive assurance from the Prime Minister
that he would abandon the bill if I would enter the Government." He said, further, that he would have
accepted save for the single reason that he was regarded
as a Liberal. He had neglected to explain his position
to the country. It was not understood that aside from
the school question, he had greater confidence in Sir
Charles Tupper than he had in the Liberal leaders. If
he joined the Cabinet he would be suspected of betray-
ing the Liberal party for office and exacting a price,
which would confuse the issues before the country and
possibly aggravate the bitter racial and sectarian
quarrel which the school question had produced.
When I recall this statement by Mr. Osler I cannot think that Tupper was happy in the position
which he had inherited, and I wonder that he did not

insist upon a modification of the Remedial Bill or a
complete withdrawal of the challenge to Manitoba
when he accepted the office of Prime Minister and set
himself to reorganize and re-unite the Conservative
party. If he believed that the Remedial Bill was
strategically unwise or constitutionally unsound, he
should not have attempted to force it through Parliament. If he thought there was a constitutional obligation upon the Government to give such full measure of
relief to the religious minority of Manitoba as the bill
provided, he should not have bargained with Mr. Osler.

I think of an incident of the campaign in Toronto.
In the Centre Division Mr. William Lount, K.C., was
the Liberal candidate against Mr. G. R. R. Cockburn.
Mr. Lount rode "the Protestant horse" not perhaps
with great skill, but with extreme ardour. When it
was suggested that Mr. Laurier should hold a meeting
in Toronto, Lount declared that if the proposal were
not summarily abandoned he would withdraw from the
contest. Two weeks before polling Mr. J. K. Kerr,
K.C., and I spent Sunday with Mr. Laurier at London,
where he was the guest of Mr. C. S. Hyman. Laurier
intimated his desire to speak in Toronto. We agreed
that it was necessary that he should do so, and that the
effect throughout the country of a successful meeting in
the chief city of the Province would give inspiration
and confidence to Liberal candidates and workers in
the last days of the contest, and do something to create
in other Provinces the impression that Ontario would
give a substantial majority against the Government. I
had *The Globe* announce next morning that Laurier
would speak in Toronto, and during the day a meeting
of Liberal workers was held to fix a date and arrange

details. Mr. Lount protested that to bring the French Catholic leader to the city where sectarian feeling was so acute was a fatal error, that he would be denied a hearing, that there would be organized interruption, tumult and disorder, and that the effect throughout the country would be infinitely damaging to Liberal prospects. When Laurier came there was such a demonstration in his honour as he can have had but seldom, even in his own Province. Hundreds who could not get into Massey Hall cheered with irrepressible fervor as he made his way to the meeting. Hundreds were still around the building when he reappeared two hours later. There was continuous cheering as he was escorted slowly and laboriously through a narrow lane of excited people to an overflow meeting at the old Queen Street Auditorium. Inside Massey Hall there was a meeting as memorable for its spontaneous and explosive enthusiasm as any ever held in Toronto. Sir John Macdonald himself never could have had a more tumultuous welcome in the Orange and Protestant stronghold of Canada. While he spoke there were frequent long rolls of applause, but not a whisper of dissent or protest. Indeed, I cannot think that I remember any other meeting in which there were such manifestations of an intimate and almost affectionate relation between the speaker and the audience, such ardour of emotion, such unity of sentiment. There was only one incident of less happy import. Mr. Lount, who was among the first speakers, held the floor so long that the audience became restive and indicated by persistent shuffling and stamping that its patience was exhausted. Thus for a few moments there were symptoms of disorder to justify Mr. Lount's prophecy. As we passed through the crowds from Massey Hall to the Auditorium, Laurier exclaimed: "Is this Tory Toronto?" It was, and Tory Toronto never more clearly expressed itself than in that remarkable demonstration over the French Catholic leader of the Liberal party.

Only mischief results when political expediency governs in the interpretation of a statute or the reading of a constitution. We have had in the educational clauses of the British North America Act a source of misunderstanding and confusion which has not made for national solidity and more than once has filled the country with the angry clamour of sectarian controversy. We have had during the whole period of Confederation a resolute and unceasing effort to read into the Constitution a guarantee of sectarian schools for every Province of the Confederation, and a steady denunciation of those who insist upon a different interpretation, and contend for the right of the Provinces to control over education, subject to their conception of the constitutional limitations, as zealots and bigots, and mischievous traders in racial and religious prejudices. It may be desirable, therefore, to investigate the origin of Separate schools in Canada and to trace the evolution of the Canadian Constitution.

As early as 1841, when the first attempt was made to establish a system of schools in Upper Canada, the right of Separate schools was obtained by the advocates of dogmatic religious teaching. This privilege was recognized in the first Common School Act for the Province which was passed five years later. But it was not until 1852 that the Roman Catholic ecclesiastics entered upon an active struggle for the extension of the Separate school system. Up to that year only fifty

Separate schools had been established, and thirty-two of these had lapsed in the three years preceding. Thirteen of those remaining were Roman Catholic Separate schools; three were Protestant, two of these in French districts; and two were maintained for coloured children in Kent and Essex. In 1853 the provisions for Separate schools were revised and extended and all supporters of such schools were exempted from local or municipal school rates. Hitherto they had shared only in the Legislative grant and County school taxes; but no part of the municipal assessment could be applied for separate school purposes, and no municipal officer could be employed to collect rates for their support. The whole separate school movement was strenuously opposed by George Brown and his allies, while Bishop Charbonnel was as determined to secure absolute authority over the education of Catholic children and to establish separate schools wherever they could be supported. In 1856 the Bishop declared in a Pastoral letter that "Catholic electors who do not use their electoral power in behalf of separate schools are guilty of mortal sin; likewise parents who do not make the sacrifices necessary to secure such schools or send their children to mixed schools."

From year to year the school law was amended in minor particulars, separate schools increased in number from thirteen in 1852 to one hundred in 1858, and the clerical agitation for still more generous facilities for their support and organization was maintained with unabated vigour. Dr. Ryerson protested against the interference of priests and bishops belonging to Lower Canada with the school system of Upper Canada and denounced "this double aggression by Roman Catholic

257

Bishops and their supporters in assailing on the one
hand our public schools and school system, and invad-
ing what has been acknowledged as sacred constitutional rights of individuals and municipalities, and on
the other hand demanding the erection and support at
the public expense of a Roman Catholic hierarchical
school system." Finally, in 1860, Hon. R. W. Scott,
then representing Ottawa in the United Parliament,
introduced a Separate School Bill which, after three
defeats in successive years, was adopted with modifications in 1863 and is the general basis of the law which
now exists. In the final vote the representatives of
Upper Canada gave ten of a majority against the measure, and it was thus imposed upon Ontario by a majority
from Quebec. This in Ontario was the position at
Confederation, while in Quebec Protestant public
schools were maintained by the non-Catholic elements
of the population.

According to Pope's Confederation Documents, the
question of Education was first raised at the Quebec
Conference on October 24th, 1864. On motion of Mr.
Oliver Mowat it was resolved "That it shall be competent for the local Legislatures to make laws respect-
ing (1) Agriculture, (2) Education, (3) Emigration,"
and various other subjects thereinafter enumerated. On
the next day Mr. D'Arcy McGee moved that "The
following words be added to item 2—Education—'sav-
ing the rights and privileges which the Protestant or
Catholic minority in both Canadas may possess as to
their denominational schools at the time when the Constitutional Act goes into operation'." This was the final
deliverance of the Conference on the subject of Education, and it seems therefore to be conclusively estab-

lished that the constitutional limitations upon Provincial control over Education were meant to apply only to Ontario and Quebec. It must be remembered also that the Conference which recommended this clause for insertion in the constitution made provision for the incorporation of British Columbia, Rupert's Land and the Northwest Territory in the new Commonwealth.

But to Sir A. T. Galt, not to McGee or Mowat, we trace the educational clauses in the Confederation settlement. Galt was a resolute foe of hierarchical pretensions, a vigilant champion of the rights and interests of the English minority in Quebec, and throughout all his public career a formidable figure in the political life of the country. He was Minister of Finance in the Coalition Government which was organized to carry Confederation, but resigned office in 1866 on account of its failure to pass legislation securing to the English minority of Lower Canada a fair share of the public funds for Protestant schools and a Protestant Board of Education. It must be remembered that no system of public schools existed in Quebec as in Ontario. In Ontario the schools of the majority were non-sectarian and open alike to Protestant and Catholic without offence to religious susceptibilities. In Quebec the schools of the majority were strictly Roman Catholic, devoted to the teaching of Roman Catholic dogma, and under the practical, if not the complete, control of the Roman Catholic hierarchy.

The position was clearly stated in a petition to the Throne from the Provincial Association of Protestant Teachers of Lower Canada which was forwarded while the Canadian delegates were in London advising with the Imperial authorities upon the terms of the Confederation settlement. They represented that "under the educational law of Lower Canada, and in consequence of the denominational character of the schools of the Roman Catholic majority, your Majesty's subjects professing the Protestant faith are subjected to serious disadvantages; first, in being deprived of the benefits of a general system of education similar to that enjoyed by their fellow-subjects in Upper Canada; secondly, in their liability to be taxed for the support of Roman Catholic schools; and thirdly, in the difficulties which they experience in establishing non-denominational or separate schools and seminaries of higher education for themselves." They argued that the result of this condition of affairs was to discourage the settlement of Protestants in Lower Canada and to cause many families to leave the country. They pointed out that pledges were made by members of the Government that the grievances under which they laboured would be remedied by parliamentary action, and that though a bill for that purpose was introduced by Government at the last session, it was almost immediately withdrawn, and that unless provision to this end was introduced into the Imperial Act of Confederation, there was grave fear that their educational rights would be left to the control of the majority in the local Legislature without any guarantee whatever. They declared frankly that they would prefer a general and non-denominational system of education, but that "so long as the present system of separate schools shall continue in Lower Canada," they must claim as constitutional rights that all direct taxes for the support of schools paid by Protestants should be applied to Protestant or non-denominational education, that all public money given for the same purpose should be divided between Protestants and Roman Catholics in proportion to population, and that just and proper safeguards for the effective protection of their educational interests should be introduced into the Act of Confederation. This was the situation with which Galt had to deal and this the position of the minority for whose interests he was concerned. In Ontario, if a school section contained only a single Roman Catholic child, it could attend the Public School without impediment or embarrassment; in Quebec there were, as there still are, whole counties where absolutely no provision exists for the education of isolated Protestant families. Galt, too, was distrustful of the Quebec Legislature and fearful that the securities required by the Protestant minority would not be established under the local constitution, or would be established under conditions which would not give the necessary guarantees of permanence. Hence, at the London Conference on December 5th, 1866, Galt moved that "the following words be added to and form part of the 6th subsection of the 43rd clause: "And in every Province where a system of separate or dissentient schools by law obtains, or where the local Legislature may hereafter adopt a system of separate or dissentient schools, an appeal shall lie to the Governor-in-Council of the general Government from the acts and decisions of the local authorities which may affect the rights or privileges of the Protestant or Catholic minority in the matter of education. And the general Parliament shall have power in the last resort to legislate on the subject." Thus were developed the guarantees for the Protestant minority in Quebec where, as has been said, no public schools existed, and hence the clauses which the Roman Catholic hierarchy have employed in the endeavour to secure certain constitutional rights under the Public School law of New Brunswick, to create and perpetuate separate schools in Manitoba, and to establish a separate school system in the Western Territories.

The first appeal taken under these clauses of the new constitution came from the Roman Catholic minority of New Brunswick. This Province at Confederation had no separate schools, but religious teaching under liberal regulations was permitted in the schools established in Roman Catholic communities. In 1871 the Legislature passed a law prohibiting such religious teaching in the common schools, and under Galt's clauses, providing for appeal to the Central Government against any act or decision of local authorities affecting the rights or privileges of a Protestant or Catholic minority, the disallowance of the Provincial legislation was demanded. The Legislature resisted the demand, passed resolutions asserting the exclusive authority of the Province over education, insisting that its jurisdiction and powers should not be curtailed without express sanction of the people at the polls, and declaring that without the consent of the Legislature the Imperial Parliament or the Parliament of Canada ought not to interfere. Upon appeal to the constituencies, the local Government was decisively sustained. Sir John Macdonald, as Minister of Justice, in answer to the demand for disallowance, said: "The Act complained of is an Act relating to common schools and the Acts repealed by it relate to parish grammar, superior and common schools. No reference is made in them to separate, dissentient or denominational schools, and the undersigned does not, on examination, find that any statute of the Province exists establishing such special schools." This position was sustained by the law officers of the Crown, and while the controversy extended over several years, and the clerical demand was insistent and importunate, there was no serious attempt at Federal interference with the Province, which clearly was the intention of Sir John Macdonald from the beginning.

The second appeal was from the Roman Catholic minority of Manitoba. In 1870 the Province of Manitoba was created with the educational clauses of the British North America Act incorporated in its constitution. In 1871, not by voluntary action of the people, but in obedience to the Federal authority, a system of separate schools was established. It must be remembered that there was no public system of education in Manitoba prior to the organization of the Province in 1870, and that such denominational schools as existed were supported by the voluntary contributions of the various communions. But under the system of education established in 1871 the Roman Catholics of Manitoba received as liberal treatment as the Catholics of Ontario. The first subsection of the twenty-second section of the Manitoba Act declares that the Province shall not have power to pass any legislation which "shall prejudicially affect any right or privilege with respect to denominational schools which any class of persons have by law or practice in the Province at the Union." This was doubtless intended to give a constitutional guarantee for separate schools in Manitoba; but when the appeal taken by the Catholic minority had made its way through the Canadian courts to the

Judicial Committee of the Privy Council, it was there decided that the legislation of 1890 abolishing separate schools was constitutional inasmuch as the only right or privilege which Roman Catholics enjoyed was the right or privilege of establishing such schools as they preferred and maintaining them by their own contributions.

A second appeal was then taken under sub-section two of the twenty-second section of the Manitoba Act, which provides that: "An appeal shall lie to the Governor-General-in-Council from any act or decision of the Legislature of the Province, or of any provincial authority, affecting any right or privilege of the Protestant or Roman Catholic minority of the Queen's subjects in relation to education." The Supreme Court decided that even under this section no right of interference was vested in the central Government, and mainly upon the grounds that every presumption must be made in favour of the constitutional right of a legislative body to repeal the laws which it has itself enacted, and that an enactment irrevocably held by the Judicial Committee to be *intra vires* could not have illegally affected any of the rights and privileges of the Catholic minority. The Judicial Committee, however, reversed this judgment and found that the Governor-General-in-Council had jurisdiction in the premises, but added: "The particular course to be pursued must be determined by the authorities to whom it has been committed by the statute. It is not for this tribunal to intimate the precise steps to be taken. Their general character is sufficiently defined by the third sub-section of section twenty-two of the Manitoba Act." This sub-section provides for action by the Governor-General-in-Council in case a Provincial Government fails or refuses to remedy grievances of a religious minority occasioned by Provincial legislation, and authorizes the Parliament of Canada to make remedial laws for the due execution of such measures as may be adjudged necessary in the circumstances. But while the Judicial Committee declined to give explicit direction to the Federal authority, it closed its judgment with these pregnant sentences: "It is certainly not essential that the statutes repealed by the Act of 1890 should be re-enacted, or that the precise provisions of these statutes should again be made law. The system of education embodied in the Acts of 1890 no doubt commends itself to, and adequately supplies the wants of, the great majority of the inhabitants of the Province. All legitimate ground of complaint would be removed if that system were supplemented by provisions which would remove the grievances upon which the appeal is founded, and were modified as far as might be necessary to give effect to these provisions."

Fortified by this judgment, the Liberal Government of Manitoba declared that under no circumstances would it sanction the restoration of the separate school system, and refused absolutely to obey the remedial order issued by the federal authorities. The Provincial ministers, however, professed every disposition to consider and remove any grievance or injustice under which the minority could be shown to labour, and to modify any harsh features in the existing regulations of the Provincial Department of Education, if such could be discovered. All efforts to effect a compromise between the Federal and Provincial authorities proving unsuccessful, the Remedial Bill re-establishing separate schools in Manitoba was introduced in the House of Commons, opposed by the Liberal party and, as has been said, defeated by obstruction, in which its opponents persisted until by effluxion of time the legal life of Parliament expired. It is remarkable that the party ranged behind the Remedial Order commanding the restoration of separate schools in Manitoba was led by the statesman who had abolished separate schools in Nova Scotia, while the leader of the forces opposed to the coercion of Manitoba was the statesman who, nine years later, guaranteed separate schools in Alberta and Saskatchewan. It is not necessary now to consider the terms of the settlement agreed upon by the Laurier Government and the Greenway Administration, since its provisions have been abrogated by the Liberal Government which now holds office in Manitoba and English made the only language in the schools of the Province. There is no doubt, however, that during his term of office Sir Wilfrid Laurier pressed again and again for concessions to the Roman Catholic minority of Manitoba beyond those yielded in the settlement of 1896, but at least in the letter nothing substantial was conceded by the Provincial authorities.

When I left *The Globe* in 1902 I had no thought of a political separation from Sir Wilfrid Laurier. I knew that he desired to guarantee separate schools in Alberta and Saskatchewan when the Western Territories were divided into Provinces, but I doubted if he would ever give effect to his intention and doubted more strongly if the Liberal party would agree to establish in Alberta and Saskatchewan a system of schools which it would not restore in Manitoba. But during the electoral campaign of 1904 I became convinced that the new Parliament would concede the demand of the Western Territories for Provincial autonomy and that separate schools would be guaranteed to the religious minority. In articles in *The Daily News* I asserted that this was Sir Wilfrid Laurier's intention and argued that the country should not be left in ignorance of what was contemplated. But Laurier would neither affirm nor deny and the country was uninterested. When the Autonomy Bills were introduced in 1905 establishing separate schools in Alberta and Saskatchewan and Federal control over natural resources, no one who has read my History of Sir Wilfrid Laurier and the Liberal Party can think that I had any choice but to oppose the measures. Even with the guarantees provided by Galt's educational clauses in the British North America Act, it seems to be settled by the deliverance of the Privy Council in the Manitoba appeals that a Province—always excluding Ontario and Quebec—cannot be forced to establish a separate school system, and that all the fair obligations of the constitution are fulfilled by provisions in the Public School law which protect a minority from offence to their faith or infringement upon their religious susceptibilities. Galt held that under the exceptional conditions which surrounded the English population in Quebec this protection for Protestants was essential, but it is inconceivable that he would have taken this ground if there had been any prospect that Lower Canada would establish and maintain a non-denominational Public School system such as exists in Ontario, in Manitoba, in British Columbia, and in the Atlantic Provinces. In 1875, when the Act establishing the Territorial Government was before the Senate, George Brown protested against the extension of the separate school system to the Territories. He contended that: "This provision was quite contrary to the British North America Act." "Nothing was more clear," he said, "than that each Province should have absolute control over education." He thought that was the only principle upon which the Union Act could continue. If the Dominion Government interfered with local matters we would get into inextricable confusion with the Provinces. The safe way was to let each Province suit itself in such matters. This country was filled by people of all classes and creeds, and there would be no end of confusion if each class had to have its own peculiar school system. It had been said this clause was put in for the protection of the Protestants against the Catholics, the latter being the most numerous. But he, speaking for the Protestants, was in a position to say that they did not want that protection. In this case it was proposed that the national machinery should be used for the imposition and collection of taxes upon persons of peculiar denominations for the support of schools of their kind. It was an attempt to force upon that country peculiar views with regard to education.

It is true Brown contended that from the moment the Act passed and the Western Territories became part of the Union, "they came under the Union Act and under the provisions with regard to separate schools." But we are concerned with his statement of the intention of the founders of Confederation rather than with his legal opinion. Besides, his position was not sustained by the judgment of the Privy Council in the Manitoba cases. It was surely an extraordinary contention that the Canadian Parliament could not

268

repeal a statute which it was under no compulsion
to enact, and a still more extraordinary assumption
that the four millions of people in older Canada who
maintained separate school systems should undertake
to determine for all time what should be the character
of the local institutions over territories which in half a
century will probably have a greater population than
the older Provinces. There is a story of a Tammany
politician who lobbied a Senator in order to secure his
support for a particular concession, and when told by
the Senator that the act would be unconstitutional,
insisted that the Constitution should not be allowed to
interfere between friends. In this spirit we have often
interpreted the Constitution of Canada, bred among the
people bitter enmities and endangered the very foundations of the Commonwealth. Through the resolute
intervention of Mr. Clifford Sifton the Autonomy Bills
were vitally amended, although his attitude involved
his resignation from the Cabinet. The Bills were opposed by the Conservative Opposition under Mr.
Borden, but the party which a few years before had
attempted to restore separate schools in Manitoba was
not in a favourable position to resist separate schools
for Alberta and Saskatchewan. Ever since these Provinces were created their affairs have been administered
by Liberal Governments, and this perhaps could be
offered as evidence that the educational provisions of
the Autonomy Acts are consonant with Western feeling
and adapted to Western conditions. It has to be said,
too, that aside perhaps from unwise concessions to "foreign" elements, the educational departments of the two
Provinces have been conducted with courage and efficiency and in appropriations alike for elementary and

higher education the Legislatures have been liberal and
far-sighted. One still thinks, however, that the educational provisions of the British North America Act
should have been incorporated in the Provincial Con-
stitutions and the people permitted to determine the
character of their educational institutions. Parliament, however, decreed otherwise, and what was the
concern of Canada when the Provinces were created is
now the sole concern of the Western people. I opposed
the reservation of the natural resources by the Dominion
as strongly as I opposed the educational clauses of the
Autonomy Acts, and in support of that position the
Liberal Governments of the three Western Provinces
are now united.

Over language, as over education, there have been
bitter and dangerous political quarrels in Canada. The
French population constitutes nearly one-third of the
total population of the country. There are more than
1,750,000 French-speaking people in Quebec, nearly
250,000 in Ontario, and between 110,000 and 125,000
in the Atlantic Provinces. There is a compact French
settlement at St. Boniface in the old Red River Territory and French groups in the Western Provinces of
Saskatchewan and Alberta. The Dominion is divided
into 235 Parliamentary constituencies. Quebec elects
65 members to the House of Commons, and there is not
a single division in which French voters are not influential. At Confederation the Eastern Counties of Quebec were a reserve for English-speaking people. But
the pressure of thrifty French farmers and changing
social and educational conditions drove out the English
element. The French advance was gradual, but irresistible. The ultimate conquest was decisive. Twenty-

five years ago eleven Quebec Counties had an English majority. In all these the English-speaking Protestants have become a minority. There are groups of French voters in ninety out of the 235 Parliamentary constituencies, and in at least seventy of these the French constitute a majority of the electors. The facts constitute an impressive appeal for unity between the French and English elements. But if the Constitution is observed there can be no legitimate ground for conflict. The British North America Act clearly provides that French and English shall have equal status in Quebec, in the House of Commons and Senate and in Federal courts and documents. Sir Wilfrid Laurier said when the Western Autonomy Bills were before Parliament: "The fathers of Confederation did not pretend to authorize the French language in any part of the Dominion except in this Parliament and in the Province of Quebec. Everywhere else the people were left free to deal with the matter as they thought fit." As Sir Wilfrid Laurier interpreted the Constitution, so it is interpreted by the Imperial Privy Council. Clearly outside of Quebec French has no equal constitutional status with English. What recognition French may obtain elsewhere is by consent and not by right or privilege. On the other hand, French should not be treated as an alien language in Canada. It is desirable on this English-speaking continent that French people should be able to speak the English language in order that they may have equal advantage and opportunity in commercial and industrial pursuits, in the services of the State, and in all activities and offices where English is required. But it is desirable also that, after English, French should be a preferential language in the high schools, colleges and universities of the English Provinces. How much misunderstanding would be avoided and how many misconceptions removed if the public men of the English Provinces could speak to the people of Quebec in their own language. It is vain to think that the French of Quebec can be made to speak English by pressure from outside. It is just as certain that pressure from Quebec in the strain of menace prejudices the position of French in the English Provinces. Demands for which no constitutional warrant exists provoke resistance. A concession extorted may be yielded in the letter and defeated in the practice. A concession yielded in amity endures and produces the fine fruit of sympathy and understanding.

We talk much in Canada about the rights of minorities and the duties of majorities. Much of what is said in this connection is wise and wholesome. But there are other considerations. There are the constitutional rights of majorities and the constitutional duties of minorities. The obligation to respect and observe the Constitution lies as clearly upon minorities as upon majorities. A habit in Canada, which has produced infinite mischief, is that we think of the unwritten Constitution of Great Britain and imagine that we, too, have an unwritten Constitution. But as a matter of fact, we have a Constitution as arbitrary and inflexible as that of the United States. It is the charter of every Province and of every element of the people. When we desire to alter its provisions, to impose new obligations upon a majority, or to restrict the privileges of a minority, we should submit the proposal to all the Legislatures or to the sovereign people and abide by the result. It has been said that "unsettled questions have no pity for the repose of nations." In Canada, education and language have been unsettled questions for a century and chiefly because we have sought to effect constitutional changes by political manoeuvring and bargaining. The feature of the American Constitution which provides a method for constitutional changes stabilizes the compact of States and ensures popular sovereignty. One cannot but think that strict constructionists of the Canadian Constitution are the best friends of minorities, as fidelity to the Constitution is a supreme obligation upon all those who are responsible for the orderly working of Canadian institutions. When all is said, no people in the world have better learned the lessons of toleration than those of Canada. There is no necessary conflict between Ontario and Quebec or between French and English. It has to be admitted that the compact with the Protestant minority has been generally observed and respected by the Legislature of Quebec, but it is just as true that the Governments of Ontario have scrupulously observed and liberally interpreted the provisions of the Constitution affecting the French and Roman Catholic minority. In neither Province is the minority benefited by pressure from outside for concessions which are not required by the Constitution or by agitation which excites the prejudices of the majority and endangers privileges which, even if they exceed the strict requirements of the Constitution, conciliate diverse elements, nourish good will, and solidify the national structure.

CHAPTER XII

OFFICE AND PATRONAGE

There is a touch of tragedy in the illusion of office. For a political party Opposition is a school of virtue. In office there is danger that ideals will lose their lustre and principles their rigidity and authority. The influences which control a party in Opposition are far less powerful when the party has assumed the responsibilities of government. There is all the difference between human nature tempted and human nature untempted. In Opposition, the idealists and reformers within a political party struggle for eradication of abuses, while all the forces which fatten upon patronage, contracts and subsidies beat upon the doors of Cabinets. As it is at the seat of Government, so it is in the constituencies. Those who sought office for their leaders in order to secure reforms in legislation and administration are thrust aside by those who are concerned with very practical objects. Honest, economical and efficient government comes only by the grace of God and the eternal vigilance of ministers.

The character of a political party is established and its standards determined not by the easy and irresponsible professions of Opposition, but by its power to resist evil influences and its fidelity to principles and convictions when its leaders control the Treasury and command a majority in Parliament. It will be clear if one goes back to Confederation, that neither Canadian party has had any peculiar reserve of virtue or any pre-eminence in evil. The vices of office have been as plainly revealed in one party as in the other. If this could be admitted and all the nauseous Pharisaical trumpeting of press and platform over degrees of corruption and relative standards of morals could be silenced, the corruptionists of one party would find less shelter behind the corruptionists of the other, and devotion to party would not require toleration of rascality, defence of moral treason and protection of public brigandage. In a free country men will divide, and should divide, on questions of policy and methods of administration, but the public judgment should fall as sternly and inflexibly upon ministers of the Crown and representatives of the people who subordinate the public interest to private or party advantage, as the sentences of the judges fall upon lesser criminals who rob private houses or swindle the shareholders in commercial companies.

In Canada the vicious notion has prevailed that the journalist associated with a political party was under peculiar obligation to defend dubious transactions and suspected ministers. If he faltered or hesitated, the whisper ran that he was disloyal to the party, afflicted with inconvenient scruples, and subject to dangerous moral impulses. The press of Canada, however, like the press of Great Britain and the United States, now generally revolts against such unhappy servitude, and nothing is more certain than that administrative and electoral corruption become less common if evil practices go undefended. What can be more humiliating and discreditable to any country than continuous attack upon the integrity of its political leaders? The effect is not to elevate, but to debase public morals, to bring free institutions into contempt, and

275

to make a seat in Parliament, which should be the chief place to which a citizen may aspire, a dubious and equivocal distinction. For thirty years I have had a close relation to political leaders in Canada. I saw something of the inside of both the old national political organizations. Looking through the files of Canadian newspapers, one is distressed to find how much space has been devoted to charges of corruption and how closely the practices of one party in office resemble those of the other. Every species of offence of which Conservative Governments were guilty was committed by Liberal Governments. Liberals who were intolerant of corruption under Conservative Governments became submissive and placable when like methods were employed by Liberal Administrations. The masses of both parties hated corruption, but as between success in the constituencies and retention of office upon the one hand and decent electoral and administrative methods upon the other, the appeal of party often prevailed, political standards were debased and the nation defamed. It is true that there was gross exaggeration of the actual degree of corruption which prevailed alike under Conservative and Liberal Administrations; but it is just as true that for long periods in Canada we have had government for party rather than government for the country, and inevitably the moral and material consequences were represented in a devitalized public opinion and gross waste of public money.

When the Liberal party succeeded to office in 1896 there was expectation of a moral and political revival. One feels that the standards were set above the level of human nature. Among the achievements of the Laurier Government are many measures of enduring value to

Canada. There was, too, a redistribution of constituencies distinguished by fair consideration for the political minority. For this example of decent equity, which has been influential in subsequent redistributions, Sir Wilfrid Laurier was greatly responsible. One feels that the "Gerrymander" will never again be a tolerated instrument of political warfare in Canada. But there was no such regeneration of electoral methods nor any such fresh infusion of integrity in the administration of public affairs as a complete redemption of Liberal pledges in opposition required. All the literature of the Liberal party produced in Opposition could have been adopted by the Conservative party from 1896 to 1911, for there was a strange likeness between the methods of the men in office from the fall of the Mackenzie Government in 1878 down to the second restoration of the Conservatives a third of a century later. In the Mackenzie Government Cauchon was the object of pursuit, and he, indeed, was as strongly attacked by Liberals before he was taken into a Liberal Cabinet. Under Sir John Macdonald there was constant attack upon Caron and Langevin and Pope and Tupper, and the Conservative leader himself, as the chief pillar in the edifice of Tory corruption which Liberal writers erected with so much industry and enthusiasm. Under Sir Wilfrid Laurier, Tarte and Blair and Sifton and Prefontaine and Pugsley were denounced as "corruptionists." I single none of these out for attack or aspersion. I am thinking rather of public men who escaped attack, but through whose hands money poured into the constituencies as naturally and freely as water falls at Niagara. I am thinking, too, of those who received but did not collect. Possibly in the other world the balances will be adjusted. History makes George Brown a purist and Sir John Macdonald a corruptionist. But it was George Brown who suggested a "Big Push" and insisted that it was necessary to "Come down handsomely." Curiously, "Big Push" became an insignia of discredit to the Conservative politician who exposed George Brown's appeal for political subscriptions. Both Macdonald and Brown, however, stand high above their detractors, even though they used the political instruments of their time with greater courage than conscience.

One has more respect for the bold front of the doer than for the feeble hypocrisy of the receiver. It is true, as Mr. Tarte said, that elections are not won by prayer. Even the legitimate cost of an election in Canada is heavy. When the allowances made out of the campaign fund for doubtful purposes are taken into account, the total runs into millions. A few men raise the money for elections. Too often candidates who gouge the last dollar out of the fund are the first to roll their eyes at the collectors. The ward politician is often a nauseous and noisy nuisance, but he is a patriot compared with the obnoxious pharisees of the clubs who defame "politicians," and deplore corruption but never give a day of honest service to the country or a decent subscription to meet the necessary expenses of elections. Nineteen out of every twenty men in the Parliaments and Legislatures of Canada are honest and anxious to advance and protect the public interest. No doubt they often betray excessive zeal for party, but they do not steal or get rich. Democracy is a shabby paymaster. We bleed members of Parliament for the churches, for sporting organizations, for social entertainments, for fairs, concerts and testimonials, and for a multitude of other projects by which busy people think they benefit the community. To some people the indemnity or the ministerial salary may seem to be excessive. But ask those who have had actual experience in politics and they will tell you what it means to go to Parliament. If they do not spend and give, they cannot be re-elected; if they do, in a few years they are beggared. The people of Canada get better government than they deserve. We can reduce the cost of elections. We can do something to compel publication of all campaign subscriptions. We can leave the courts no option but to sentence to imprisonment for giving or taking a bribe. We can imprison officers and directors of corporations and companies which make improper contributions for political purposes. But no laws will be effective unless the people themselves show unselfish patriotism and feel responsibility for the cost as well as for the result of elections. How few of the moral, social and commercial leaders ever appear at a ward meeting or interest themselves in the nomination of Parliamentary candidates. But the ward meetings and the party conventions do more to determine the standards of public life and the character of our institutions than the superior people who regard "politics" as mean and sordid.

In the trial of controverted elections the judges have been impartial and courageous. But we have much evidence that when they sit upon political commissions they are as human as other people. Judges, like ministers of the Crown, are underpaid. There is much public work that they can do, and they are peculiarly fitted for many public commissions. But they should be disqualified for service on commissions which have to give political judgments. At least they should only receive and report evidence, and should get no additional remuneration in such cases. The people will take law from the Bench, but on political questions they have no more respect for judges than they have for laymen. One thinks of many commissions of judges appointed and instructed to investigate charges of political corruption, but in very few cases was the truth revealed or a judgment delivered which satisfied either Parliament or the country. It is clear that no judge reporting against a Government by which he was appointed could hope to be re-employed. Moreover, there is the element of favour in judicial appointments and promotions. In the discharge of its regular functions there is high integrity in the Bench of Canada, and there should be emoluments adequate to sustain its dignity and exemption from all services which compromise its impartiality.

The evils of patronage have been as virulent in Canada as in any other country. For many years, however, we have had no absolute application of the spoils system. It is true that with every change of Government many office-holders were removed for political reasons, and down to twenty years ago public officials were so active in political contests that they received at least as much mercy as they deserved. But gradually civil servants have ceased to be the organizing agents of party and their tenure of office has become more secure. Under successive Governments, however, there were dismissals which could not be defended, as there was a rigid reservation, as far as the regulations would permit, of all public places for supporters of the governing party. There was, too, a system of purchase of public supplies and distribution of public contracts which effectually excluded political opponents from any profitable access to the treasury. The evils of the system of patronage were illustrated again in the. construction of public buildings, breakwaters, harbours, and local railways, not as the public interest required, but in calculating submission to the importunities of members of Parliament and the demands of favourable or doubtful constituencies. In all this there was much waste and not a little corruption. From the privileged dealers in supplies political subscriptions were taken, and from many contracts there was a generous return to the party fund. The whole system was venal and ugly, vicious in practice and demoralizing in results. But the tempest of war shook the fabric to its foundations and a public opinion seems to have been created which should make its restoration difficult. So if the people are alert the ascendancy of the traders in patronage and the civil service should never be re-established. To the inside service the competitive system with judicious modifications has been applied. Over the outside service the Civil Service Commission, subject to a preference for war veterans, has independent jurisdiction. There are, however, groups in Parliament and in the constituencies eager to recover control over supplies, contracts and appointments, and unless the Civil Service Commission displays energy, courage and wisdom and an active public opinion is maintained in the country the ground won by long and arduous fighting may be retaken by the mercenaries. The experience of other countries demonstrates that the forces which contend for patronage are never finally conquered. But if we are to have efficient and economical administration of the public services and control and operate a great national railway system ,the independence of public servants must be maintained and the obligation to the State set high over any obligation to party.

The Senate is the great reserve of patronage for Canadian Governments. When Confederation was established three senatorial divisions were created, (1) Ontario, (2) Quebec, (3) the Atlantic Provinces. To each of these twenty-four representatives in the Senate were assigned. The object was to give a guarantee of constitutional stability and a proportionate balance of political power to the three great territorial sections. Later, as population warranted, senators from the West were appointed until a fourth division with twenty-four representatives was completed. Only once has the test of party been ignored in an appointment to the Senate. In that single instance Sir John Macdonald was the culprit, and it is believed that he was actuated by a feeling of personal gratitude. In connection with the Fenian Raid of 1866, the Conservative leader was charged with improperly using Secret Service money. It was a charge he could not absolutely disprove, inasmuch as he could not disclose the purposes for which the money was expended. Among the members of the Assembly was Mr. John Macdonald, one of the successful pioneer merchants of Canada, and a Liberal of moderate opinion. He condemned the attack on the Conservative Prime Minister as cruel and unjust, since he was not free to produce evidence in his own defence. It is known that Sir John Macdonald was grateful for this unexpected support, and it is suspected that his gratitude was expressed in Mr. John Macdonald's appointment to the Senate. But this violation of a sacred precedent stands alone. Never since has any Canadian Government admitted a man to the Senate who could not give the password of the party in office.

The Union Act of 1840 provided for an appointed Legislative Council and an elected Legislative Assembly. But from the first there was profound dissatisfaction with the constitution and character of the Second Chamber. There was indeed such constant and intemperate criticism of the Council that many of the members rarely appeared in the Chamber, and it was often impossible for the Speaker to obtain a quorum. In those days there was much of personal rancour in Canadian politics and a savagery both in press and platform of which we now have rare examples. In Lower Canada the Council was treated with angry and ferocious contempt. In Upper Canada criticism was only less immoderate. As was said during the Confederation Debates ,"the nominative system was a standing grievance in Lower Canada as well as in Upper Canada." The system of nomination was abandoned in 1856 and an elective Council substituted. The act of 1856 defined the districts to be represented and provided electoral machinery, but there was no summary removal of life members. There was provision for an election every two years when twelve members were automatically retired. At Confederation the Legislative Council had twenty-one life members and forty-eight elected members. There is reason to think from a careful reading of the Confederation Debates that Parliament was not favourable to a nominated Senate. Over and over again it was represented that the decision in favour of nomination was a concession to the

Maritime Provinces, and a necessary condition to the project of union. Sir John Macdonald, George Brown, and Alexander Mackenzie were resolute advocates of appointment. George Brown, indeed, had opposed the application of the elective principle to the old Legislative Council of the Canadas. They held that the Upper House could be valuable only as a court of revision. A body of equal jurisdiction with the House of Commons was not required. By the elective principle operating to fill both Houses the jurisdiction of both branches of the Legislature would be co-ordinate.

Sir John Macdonald admitted that the elective principle had not been a failure in Canada, but there were causes, not taken into consideration, when the system was adopted, why it did not so fully succeed as they had expected. "One great cause was the enormous extent of the constituencies and the immense labour which consequently devolved on those who sought the suffrages of the people for election to the Council. For the same reason the expense—the legitimate expense—was so enormous that men of standing in the country, eminently fitted for such a position, were prevented from coming forward. At first, I admit, men of the first standing did come forward, but we have seen that in every succeeding election in both Canadas there has been an increasing disinclination on the part of men of standing and political experience and weight in the country to become candidates; while, on the other hand, all the young men, the active politicians, those who have resolved to embrace the life of a statesman, have sought entrance to the House of Assembly." He argued that the independence of the Upper House would be preserved by limitation of the membership. It would be "a separate and distinct Chamber, having a legitimate and controlling influence on the legislation of the country." He did not believe that it was necessary to grant the right of unlimited appointment in order to prevent a deadlock between the two branches of the legislature. "There would be no use of an Upper House if it did not exercise, when it thought proper, the right of opposing or amending or postponing the legislation of the Lower House. It would be of no value whatever were it a mere Chamber for registering the decrees of the Lower House. It must be an independent House, having a free action of its own, for it is only valuable as being a regulating body, calmly considering the legislation initiated by the lower branch, and preventing any hasty or ill-considered legislation which may come from that body, but it will never set itself in opposition against the deliberate and understood wishes of the people." He held that there would be an infinitely greater chance of deadlock between the two branches of the Legislature should the elective principle be adopted than with a nominated Chamber chosen by the Crown and having "No mission from the people."

There was much contention to the contrary and much accurate prophecy of just what has happened. Mr. Sanborne, for example, during the debate in the Legislative Council pointed out that members of the Senate would be chosen not by the Sovereign or the Sovereign's representative, but by a party Government, that in the Commons Governments would be defeated, while the Upper House would have a far more permanent character, and since it would be the creation of party recurrence of deadlocks would be inevitable. This was the general reasoning of the opponents of the system of nomination, and, while we cannot know what results would have developed under an elective Senate, there is no doubt that throughout its whole history the nominated Upper Chamber has been at least as devoted to party as the House of Commons. Mr. Cardwell, the Colonial Secretary, foresaw the danger in a fixed membership. In a message to the Canadian ministers he said: "Her Majesty's Government appreciate the conditions which have influenced the Conference in determining the mode in which this body, so important to the constitution of the Legislature, should be composed. But it appears to them to require further consideration whether, if the members be appointed for life and their numbers be fixed, there will be any sufficient means of restoring harmony between the Legislative Council and the popular assembly, if it shall ever unfortunately happen that a decided difference of opinion shall arise between them." This and other similar representations and arguments were not wholly without effect. It is interesting to trace the proceedings of the Union Conference in Sir Joseph Pope's Confederation Documents until we discover evidences of uneasiness over the arbitrary limitation of appointments to the Senate. Finally it was provided that in the event of deadlock the Imperial Government, on application from the Government of Canada, could grant power to appoint six additional senators, but that these should fill succeeding vacancies in order to prevent any permanent increase of membership. No Government has obtained power to make these additional appointments, although the Mackenzie, Laurier and Borden Governments were temporarily embarrassed by a hostile Senate.

Senate reform has been on the lips of Canadian politicians for a generation. We had much violent criticism of the Upper Chamber by the Liberal press and the Liberal leaders during the long ascendancy of the Conservative party. At the National Liberal Convention of 1893 it was declared that "the present constitution of the Senate is inconsistent with the federal principle in our system of government, and is in other respects defective, as it makes the Senate independent of the people and uncontrolled by the public opinion of the country and should be so amended as to bring it into harmony with the principles of popular government." But the Senate was not reformed by the Laurier Administration. There were attacks upon the Upper Chamber while it was destroying Liberal legislation and a proposal for joint sessions of the two Houses in cases of deadlock, but when death had done its work among Conservative Senators and a Liberal majority was secured in the Upper Chamber there was a great acquiescence among Liberals and soon a murmuring among Conservatives. In what has been called the Halifax platform of the Conservative party, Mr. Borden demanded "such reform in the mode of selecting members of the Senate as will make that Chamber a more useful and representative legislative body." It is not easy to devise a Senate exactly adapted to the functions which such a body should exercise. We cannot turn to the system which the United States discarded a few years ago and perhaps the chief evil of which was to force national issues into State politics. Already we have instructive lessons from Australia in the incompatibility of two elective Chambers. Once there was a formidable feeling in Canada for total abolition of the Senate. But it is gravely doubtful if the country would have government by a single Chamber, and save by consent of all the Provinces the Senate could hardly be destroyed. It is not believed that Quebec would favour abolition, and possibly the three Atlantic Provinces would also be hostile.

If any revolutionary amendment of the constitution should be attempted, probably the balance of opinion in the country would substitute an elected Senate for the nominated Chamber. But as against the Senate popular feeling will not easily find effective expression. Nor can such a vital condition of the compact of union be rashly disturbed. To abolish the Senate by common appeal to the people would be as revolutionary as to abolish French as an official language or to repeal the guarantee of Protestant schools in Quebec or of Catholic schools in Ontario. Mirabeau said there was no tyranny like the tyranny of a single Chamber. "I protest," he declared, "that I can conceive nothing more alarming than the despotic oligarchy of 600 individuals." Since all countries under responsible government maintain two Chambers, it is manifest that the wisest leaders of democracy distrust popular impulses and unregulated sovereignty. Parliament does not always express the sober judgment of the people, nor is it desirable that 235 citizens in the House of Commons should have final and absolute authority under all circumstances to impose measures upon millions of citizens outside as to which they have not been consulted. It may be said that any measure is subject to reversal by the people, but serious confusion and disaster might be produced before the reversal could be effected. In Canada the Senate itself, or those responsible for its character and performances, have furnished the strongest available argument for a single Chamber. Substantially, we have had a single Chamber ever since Confederation, except for those short periods when the majority in the Senate was out of accord with the majority in the Commons. In other words, when there was a Conservative majority in both Houses, the Senate was substantially the obedient echo of the Commons. So it was if there was a Liberal majority in both Houses. But when there was a Liberal majority in the Commons and a Conservative majority in the Senate, the Upper Chamber was the echo of the Conservative minority in the Commons. So with a Liberal minority in the Commons and a Liberal majority in the Senate, the Upper House was the agent and mouthpiece of the minority in the popular Chamber. This is only distinguishable from government by a single Parliamentary body, because the system is more vexatious and cumbersome. If, therefore, the Senate should perish, political practice rather than constitutional defects will have wrought its destruction.

It is not a fatal objection to the Senate that many members of the Commons receive promotion to the Upper Chamber. Such long political training and experience as many of these possess should be of value in the Senate. Moreover, the sacrifices inseparable from service in the Commons often constitute a sound claim for recognition. Through the Senate we have a system of superannuation, unrecognized in legislation, but in many cases justifiable as compensation for those whose businesses and incomes have been sacrificed in the public service.

An enormous patronage is vested in ministers in Canada. If the President and Cabinet at Washington appointed all senators, all judges, local and federal, and all Governors of the States, one would not easily believe that the Republic could have free, responsible and responsive government. That, however, is exactly the situation in Canada. We are also organizing a national railway system, with an army of public employees. If these should have any close political relation to the Government probably no Administration could be defeated unless 65 or 70 per cent. of the unofficial electors could be consolidated against its candidates. This apprehension is not supported by the experience of Australia, which has a national railway system, and far more frequent changes of Government than we have in Canada. But the conditions of Australia are not reproduced in this country. In emphasizing these considerations, no attack upon national railways, direct or indirect, is intended. The only object is to establish the necessity for elimination of patronage from the public services and to illustrate the tremendous reserve of political power which a Government possesses under the Canadian constitution. In only a few instances has the country suffered when the Senate has acted as a revising or amending body. More often doubtful measures have been improved or rejected. But whether the Senate obstructed the measures of the Mackenzie, Laurier or Borden Governments, the country believed that the proposals amended or rejected would have been accepted if they had come down from an Administration in political sympathy with the majority in the Upper Chamber. For this unfortunate impression the Senate itself cannot escape responsibility. There is a curious assumption that the Senate should merely register the decrees of the Commons, but if that is its whole duty, there is no reason that it should exist. If the Upper Chamber is open to criticism it is because it has not exercised its functions. It has a power to initiate legislation which it could afford to use more freely. Its constitutional right to reserve revolutionary legislation for the judgment of the people cannot be challenged. There is a story that a senator, greatly anxious for the disappearance of the Liberal majority which embarrassed the Borden Government, was greeted by a friend in the lobby with the cheerful report that another Liberal senator had passed away. "Who," he asked, with anxious interest. But when the name was furnished, he said: "Oh h——, he died yesterday." Still the processes of decay were rapid—for the Senate.

In land policy and in railway policy in Canada we have been prodigally wasteful and grievously short-sighted. We had in the West such a landed estate as few countries have possessed. But we wasted with the irresponsibility of a graceless spendthrift, alternately fattened and impoverished speculators, squandered upon political favourites the heritage of a nation, and developed conditions and problems which even now perplex Governments and impose heavy obligations upon the public treasury. Probably the ultimate judgment of history will justify the original contract with the Canadian Pacific syndicate. For the builders of the pioneer transcontinental railway committed themselves to a tremendous undertaking. Great faith, signal resource and high courage were required to construct the road, to overcome reluctant money markets, and inveterate and incessant political attack, and to sustain the enterprise while settlers came slowly, local traffic was inconsiderable and neither sun nor stars in many days appeared. In 1895 two men in the West, one a Liberal and the other a Conservative, both of naturally confident temperament and extensive knowledge of Western conditions, and perhaps the very foremost of its political leaders, told me that they did not believe the Canadian Pacific Railway could ever earn a living revenue or the prairies ever be settled with people who would remain in the country. I like to think that they could not subdue my optimism, although I was fortified by faith rather than by knowledge. I declared my faith in a survey of Western conditions and prospects which filled two or three pages of *The Globe,* and of that issue Sir William Van Horne ordered 250,000 copies, and the Department of the Interior, under a Conservative minister, 100,000 copies. From that time Van Horne was my friend, and I had many evidences of his regard and good-will. But occasionally there were differences. Once *The Globe* had an article emphasizing the complaints of Western farmers over delay in moving the wheat crop to market. He pasted the editorial on a sheet of foolscap and wrote across the page: "Don't you know that God wouldn't let the farmers do their threshing until October."

But whether the first transcontinetal railway project was wisely conceived or not, it is certain that the railway system of Canada is a remarkable product of individual courage, national confidence, sectional cupidity and political necessity. It was perhaps unfortunate that the federal Government ever undertook to subsidize local railways. There could be no other result than competition between provinces, between constituencies and between parliamentary candidates for largess from the treasury. It is true that these evils would have appeared under a provincial system of subsidies, but there would have been more rigid selection of projects and more direct responsibility to the people. It is said that a Conservative member for a Nova Scotia constituency, pleading for a subsidy for a local railway, was told by Sir John Macdonald that he doubted if the road could develop any traffic if it was constructed. The answer of the member was, "Traffic be d——. I want the road to carry me back to Parliament." There was, however, a substantial advantage in assumption of local railways by the Dominion if otherwise the federal Commission could not have exercised control over the whole railway system of the country. The conflict between state and federal authority has made just and effective regulation of American railway charges exceedingly embarrassing and difficult.

In 1897 I wrote and printed a pamphlet on the Railway Question in Canada. I argued for effective regulation of freight charges and against unnecessary duplication of railways. "Canada," said the pamphlet, "is a country of enormous distances, of length rather than breadth, and trade between the provinces is difficult and transportation charges very heavy. In these facts we have conclusive arguments against the rash multiplication of through roads and the consequent maintenance of needless transportation facilities. In truth, to construct another great through road in Canada would be very like adopting a fiscal measure imposing a tax of fifteen or twenty per cent. on all inter-provincial trade." I said: "We must not forget that freight rates are a form of taxation, and that if the tax bearers be few the burden must be heavy. If we divide the traffic between competing roads the load must be heavier still. If we increase and concentrate the traffic and multiply the population we have a right to reduction of charges and improvement in service. Railway monopoly under efficient regulation will give lower freight charges than any system of unregulated competiton, or even a system of competition regulated by public authority." I believed that we should double-track the Canadian Pacific along Lake Superior and across the West as traffic should require, that branch roads should be constructed as population increased, that the system should be designed to effect compact settlement, and that traffic from all the branches and extensions should feed the through road, and freight rates be reduced by public authority as revenues should warrant. Possibly the proposals were impracticable. At least the country would not listen.

The common criticism was that I was a subsidized agent of the Canadian Pacific Railway Company. If so, there never has been any recognition of the contract nor any payment on account. The pamphlet was written twenty-two years ago, and no doubt as settlement increased and population spread over greater areas a second transcontinental road became necessary. But there never was any justification for long stretches of duplication and three through systems. It was believed when the Grand Trunk Pacific was projected that an amalgamation with the Canadian Northern would be effected. But the rival interests could not be reconciled. Purely sectional and political considerations explain the duplication of the Intercolonial. We built in Canada as the railway lobby demanded and as political exigencies dictated. It may be that as the country develops a great railway system built with cheap money may become a valuable national asset, but for the time the burden is heavy and we could have builded with greater wisdom even if we had had no other object than to endow future generations with an adequate system of transportation.

CHAPTER XIII

LAURIER AND THE EMPIRE

Mystery surrounds the decision of the Laurier Government to establish a fiscal preference in favour of imports from Great Britain. It is certain that no such action was contemplated by the Liberal leaders before they took office. In 1892 Mr. L. H. Davies, of Prince Edward Island, had offered an amendment to a motion by Mr. McNeill, of North Bruce, in favour of reciprocal preferences, in effect that, as Great Britain admitted the products of Canada free of duty, the scale of Canadian duties levied on goods mainly imported from Great Britain should be reduced. But, while this proposal probably expressed the sincere conviction of Mr. Davies, many of his parliamentary associates were chiefly concerned to embarrass the Government and the Conservative Imperialists who were as rigid protectionists for Canada as any other group in Parliament. Indeed, the Liberal parliamentary party was still committed to unrestricted reciprocity with the United States. There was even a disposition to declare more definitely for direct discrimination against Great Britain. As editor of *The Globe,* I represented to Mr. Laurier that any such course would be fatal to Liberal candidates in the constituencies and that it was necessary to recede from the position which the party had taken rather than to persist in flagrant defiance of the British sentiment of the country. I had knowledge that this was a common feeling among Liberals. I knew that there would be a formidable revolt against any proposal for open and deliberate discrimination against British imports. The true feeling of the party was soon revealed and, as has been said, was expressed in the resolution subsequently adopted by the National Liberal Convention.

The leaders also became convinced long before the general election of 1896 that it would be impossible to "eliminate the principle of protection from the tariff." Whether the country understood or not, there was deliberate adjustment of the party to a moderate and practical fiscal policy in many of the speeches and much of the literature of the campaign. One recalls the letters exchanged between Mr. Laurier and Mr. George H. Bertram, of Toronto, and many private and public assurances that there would be no revolutionary fiscal changes. This was so clearly the attitude of *The Globe* that it was doubted by Conservative candidates if the paper expressed the actual spirit and intention of the Liberal leaders. Nor was the chief object to conciliate protectionists. It was recognized by the official leaders of the party that any radical reduction of duties was impracticable and impossible, and that it was desirable to prepare the country for the position which would have to be taken should they succeed in the election.

A curious story attaches to a speech which Mr. Laurier delivered at Winnipeg. In the report as published there was a declaration in favour of "free trade as it is in England." He told me later that he had refused, despite great pressure, to use the phrase which was beloved of Western Liberal candidates and that an eager and importunate colleague, distressed at his caution, had incorporated the sentence in the report of his address. He could not challenge the accuracy of the report without a practical repudiation of the position of the free trade extremists in the party, nor could he expose the associate who had revised the address without authority. But he would sometimes recall the incident when he was denounced for apostasy to his platform pledges. Mr. Borden once said that Laurier had promised prohibition as it was in Maine, and free trade as it was in England, but had maintained protection as it was in Maine and prohibition as it was in England. The truth is that Laurier did not declare himself in favour of prohibition nor did he believe that complete free trade was practicable in Canada. The whole argument of the Liberal party in 1896, however, was for lower tariff, although in the speeches of the leaders there is no definite forecast of the British preference. But when the leaders attained office and redemption of the fiscal pledges became the immediate concern, it was recognized that substantial duties against American imports must be maintained and that even upon goods from Great Britain the tariff could not be greatly reduced without depleting the revenue and endangering the position of Canadian industries. In these circumstances the suggestion of lower duties upon British imports was the happy solution of a perplexing problem.

It will be remembered that in the campaign the Patrons of Industry and the Third Party, under Mr. D'Alton McCarthy, had candidates in various constituencies. Between the Patrons and the Liberal party there was organized co-operation. So Mr. McCarthy was concerned to damage the Government and assist the Opposition. But in consideration of Mr. McCarthy's attitude towards Quebec the true relation between Mr.

Laurier and himself was not disclosed. At a meeting at Owen Sound, Mr. McCarthy was asked to say what he thought of Laurier. He smiled and suggested softly that he doubted if a frank answer to the question would be of advantage to the Liberal leader. What he had in mind was that praise from McCarthy in Ontario would not help Laurier in Quebec. Mr. McCarthy was an advocate of Imperial fiscal preferences, while the Patrons of Industry demanded a revenue tariff and transfer of taxation from necessaries to luxuries. All three groups supported the British preference when the proposal was submitted to Parliament. Possibly Mr. McCarthy suggested the cardinal principle of the Fielding Tariff, but as to that I cannot speak with knowledge. I never sought to discover the origin of the preference, although I was consulted before the proposal was considered by the Cabinet.

Through Mr. George H. Bertram, who came to me with a message from Laurier, I had the first intimation that the economic practicability and the political advantages of discrimination in favour of countries which admitted Canadian products free of duty was a subject of consideration at Ottawa. Naturally, I gave instant support to the proposal as politically advantageous, as agreeable to Canadian and British feeling, and as a method of escape from the position in which advocacy of free trade with the United States had involved the Liberal party. It was clear that the country would approve preferential treatment of British manufactures and that no general feeling in favour of equal treatment of American manufactures could be developed. Thus the British preference was an Act of Extrication, of Emancipation, and of Indemnification for pledges which could not be fulfilled. Liberal Ministers, however, in establishing the preference, were not implementing any unholy compact with manufacturers, but were governed by industrial and national considerations which in the actual situation of the country could not be disregarded by practical and responsible statesmen.

There was singular boldness in the determination of the Canadian Cabinet to offer the preference to Great Britian and compel the Imperial Government to reject the concession or denounce the German and Belgian treaties which prevented discrimination by the Dominions in favour of the Mother Country. Indeed, the preference was imposed upon Great Britain, and there were British statesmen who denounced the old treaties with reluctance and in slumberous wonder over the serene audacity of an inconsiderate colony. Laurier was attacked for not exacting a reciprocal preference from Great Britain. But he was convinced that no such preference could be obtained except upon conditions which Canada could not accept. As it was, the Canadian offer was regarded with suspicion by rigid British free traders. Mr. Chamberlain had not yet adopted "tariff reform," and among Unionists and Liberals alike there was uncompromising adhesion to the teaching of the Manchester economists. While Laurier was in London, in 1897, Mr. Chamberlain declared that, except on the basis of free trade within the Empire, he would not touch preference "with a pair of tongs." This, however, was said in a conversation between Laurier and himself and was not available as a defence for the Canadian Government against the attacks of opponents. In the autumn of 1897 there was a bye-election in Centre Toronto. Mr. George H. Bertram, the Liberal candidate, was opposed by Mr. O. A. Howland. At every Conservative meeting there was criticism of Laurier for "the free gift" of preference to the Mother Country, when preferential treatment of Canadian products could have been obtained if the Liberal leader had not been more anxious to secure the "Cobden medal" than to initiate a system of Imperial protection. During the contest Laurier came to Toronto and was at pains to give me an exact statement of Mr. Chamberlain's position. He did not authorize me to make any public use of the statement, nor did he suggest that there was any obligation of discretion or silence. For a day or two I hesitated, but the Conservative attack persisted and I persuaded myself that Mr. Chamberlain's position should be stated. *The Globe's* explanation was cabled to England and became the subject of a question in the Imperial Parliament. In reply, Mr. Chamberlain frankly admitted its accuracy and thus gave the confirmation which was required. Shortly afterward I suggested to Laurier that I was probably in disfavour for using Mr. Chamberlain's statement without authority. His answer was, "My dear fellow, that is what I wanted you to do." I thought I had read his mind, but one cannot always be certain that a statement communicated in private is intended for publication.

Once I asked Laurier how the famous letter from Father Lacombe, intimating that the Roman Catholic bishops were united in support of the Manitoba Remedial Bill and would be as united against any public man who opposed the measure, came to be published. He said, "I do not know, but it was wise to have the letter appear in *The Montreal Daily Star* instead of in a Liberal newspaper." It was necessary that his political associates should have knowledge of the letter, and one doubts if he emphasized its confidential character. He held that there was moral and public justification for its publication, and clearly there are circumstances in which a political leader has the right to call the people to his defence against groups or interests which present private ultimatums. In this instance, nothing but the letter itself could have disclosed the actual situation. But, ordinarily, Laurier was very scrupulous and no one could more resolutely retain what he did not choose to reveal.

It is doubtful if there ever was exact accord between Laurier and Chamberlain. The one was as resolute as the other and each had a vitally different conception of the Imperial relation. Laurier regarded free trade within the Empire as impracticable and impossible. Nor was there complete agreement between the two when Chamberlain became an advocate of tariff reform and Imperial preferences. It is true that when Laurier desired to have the food duties imposed during the war in South Africa retained against foreign countries and remitted in favour of the Dominions, he would have had Chamberlain's support; but they were repealed during Chamberlain's absence in South Africa. When this was refused he finally abandoned effort to obtain preferential treatment of Canadian products in British markets. But there was irritation over the refusal and even serious thought of actual withdrawal or substantial modification of the Canadian preference in favour of British manufactures.

Mr. Chamberlain's proposal to establish a consultative Imperial Council, Laurier opposed and defeated.

He was reluctant to send contingents to South Africa and submitted at last only to a manifestation of public feeling which he could not safely resist. He was embarrassed by the attitude of Mr. Tarte and disturbed by the vehement counsel of Mr. Bourassa. As editor of *The Globe,* I was in a difficult position. I told Laurier that he would either send troops or go out of office, but gave a rash pledge that *The Globe* would not suggest the despatch of contingents in advance of the decision of the Cabinet. A few days before war was declared Laurier had to go to Chicago and he insisted that I should go along. In the party also were Mr. L. O. David and Mr. Raymond Prefontaine, of Montreal. For three days we discussed the Imperial obligation of Canada and the possible political consequences of a decision against sending contingents in all its phases, if not with unanimity, at least with good temper and complete candour. I shall not forget the wise discretion of Mr. David and his grave concern that nothing should develop to affect Laurier's position or disturb the relations between Canada and Great Britain. It is fair to explain that Sir Wilfrid contended the war in South Africa, if war there should be, would be a petty tribal conflict in which the aid of the Dominions would not be required, and that over and over again he declared he would put all the resources of Canada at the service of the Mother Country in any great war for the security and integrity of the Empire. When we reached London on the homeward journey we learned that the South African Republics had precipitated the conflict. Laurier had not believed that war was inevitable and he was greatly comforted by assurances received at Chicago, through British sources, that the Republics would submit to the demands of Great Britain or the conditions would be so modified as to avert hostilities and ensure a settlement by negotiation. During the journey between London and Toronto he was very sober and silent. He recognized that the Canadian Government must reach an immediate decision, but he would not admit that the fact of war necessarily involved Canada in the conflict.

When we parted at Toronto, I urged that as soon as he reached Ottawa he should announce that the Government would send troops to South Africa. But he was still reluctant, unconvinced, and rebellious. Next day, however, I received this despatch: "Am sending contingents. Will be in Toronto in the morning.—Wilfrid Laurier." When we met again he frankly admitted that public feeling in the English Provinces was too strong to be opposed and that under all the circumstances the Government could not afford to challenge the sentiment of the country and withhold Canada from a struggle in which the other Dominions would be engaged. He explained that there would be no serious division in the Cabinet, but he doubted if the Liberal representatives from Quebec could be united in support of the action of the Government. Unfortunately there was no such unanimity of feeling in Quebec as existed in Ontario, and probably his influence among the French people would be sorely tested. Over the decision of the Government Mr. Bourassa resigned his seat in Parliament and was re-elected. But the intimate personal and political relation which had existed between Laurier and Bourassa never was restored. The war in South Africa produced the Nationalist movement. The seeds of Nationalism lay long in the ground, the growth was reluctant, the harvest ripened slowly.

But at last Bourassa gathered many sheaves in Quebec from the sowing which began when his counsel was rejected and Laurier sanctioned the organization of contingents for South Africa. I think I never doubted that Laurier's ultimate decision would be in favour of contingents. For that among other reasons *The Globe* said nothing to embarrass the Government or to excite public feeling.

The Globe's first deliverance in support of contingents was not written in the office. One day Mr. Justice Street offered a letter for publication. He explained with much courtesy and equal hesitation that *The Globe's* position was detached and indefinite and that doubtless there were legitimate political considerations behind its discretion and reticence. As a judge he was not clear that he should speak in his own name, but he had written a letter which would not compromise the paper and which he would like to have published without his signature. When I had read the letter I intimated that if he did not object I would make a few minor changes and print it as an editorial. He was agreeable and grateful. There was judicial caution in the statement which *The Globe* required at the moment and it is doubtful if Mr. Justice Street would have been censured even if he had written over his signature.

In the general election of 1900, rash utterances by Mr. Tarte were exploited with deadly effect by the Conservative Opposition. There is no doubt that Tarte was opposed to the organization of contingents for South Africa and believed that his position would be sustained by the Cabinet. In this confidence he made statements which were singularly inconvenient and embarrassing in the English Provinces. He explained

305

20

that he had gone no farther than to insist that troops should not be sent out of the country without the direct authority of Parliament. But in a political contest there is no reverence for a qualification. Tarte was gibbeted in every Conservative journal and from every Conservative platform. For the time he displaced Mr. Sifton as "the master of the Administration," and a very fervour of passion was excited in the country against the contumacious and aggressive French Minister. There was much sheet lightning in the display, but even sheet lightning is dangerous when it is associated with racial feeling and Imperial patriotism. Tarte was the issue, and the jawbone which he wielded too freely slaughtered many Liberal candidates. Eight or ten days before polling Laurier was in Toronto, and naturally there was anxious consideration of the political outlook. At a conference which I attended, the leader was assured that Ontario would give a majority of at least twenty for the Government. I alone insisted, despite the angry protests of the optimists, that the majority against the Government would be twenty. I gave my reasons, of which Tarte was the chief, and Laurier agreed that my forecast would probably be justified by the result. The returns gave the Opposition a majority of twenty-two in Ontario.

The defeat of Laurier in Ontario in 1900 had long consequences. No doubt he had hesitated to involve Canada in the war in South Africa, but he had yielded to public feeling, had imposed his decision upon Quebec, had alienated cherished associates, had frankly confessed his reluctance to involve Canada in a British quarrel, and had defended the British position and the final intervention of Canada with vigour and eloquence.

But despite the British fiscal preference and the action of the Government in relation to South Africa, despite recognition of Imperial sentiment and despite disregard of the protests of elements in Quebec, he sustained a decisive defeat in the chief English Province of the Confederation. He coveted the goodwill and the confidence of Ontario. He had doubted if a French Roman Catholic could lead a national party. In any evidence that this was a misinterpretation of the Protestant majority, he rejoiced. He believed in 1900 that he deserved a greater measure of support from Ontario than he received. Thenceforth he turned to his own Province and his own people. He never wooed Ontario again. It may be that he never was willing to lose Quebec. He would often insist that at any cost he must have the confidence of his own Province. There is reason to think that Bourassa became a spectre in his pathway. He often said that if Bourassa had not separated himself from the Liberal party and had cultivated a national outlook he would have been his natural and inevitable successor. But from 1900 he saw Bourassa as an ever-present menace, against which he believed he could not rely upon Ontario.

No one who knew Laurier could believe that he was an Imperialist. Economically he was a continentalist and politically he was an autonomist. At Imperial Conferences he resisted all proposals leading towards federation of the Empire or even involving any rigid machinery of co-operation between Great Britain and the Dominions. It is not surprising to learn from letters published by Mr. J. S. Ewart, K.C., that he was in sympathy with the movement to establish Canada as an independent kingdom under the British monarchy. What the position would be of a common sovereign over five equal and independent nations if a domestic quarrel should develop, taxes the imagination. We talk of the Sovereign as the bond of Empire, but an Empire united by a sovereign who would be bound by the advice of his Ministers at five separate capitals would be feeble and fantastic enough. Laurier thought of Canada as a nation. He made Canada a nation according to the panegyrists. Indeed with every change of Government, Canada is made a nation over again. But the new pattern much resembles the old, however the artificers may labour to remould and rebuild. It is not easy to see how we can be an Empire for commercial purposes and five separate nations for diplomatic purposes. If we think of separate nations instead of Empire, the ultimate result may be separation. Equal citizenship in the Empire cannot be achieved by extension of autonomy so long as an Imperial Parliament at London exercises authority over war and peace which is not possessed in equal degree by the Parliaments of the Dominion. War Cabinets and Oversea Ministers and Imperial Conferences are perhaps convenient agencies of co-operation, but they cannot give the Dominions co-ordinate authority in emergencies, or even in the regular adjustment of relations with other nations. Where the parliamentary power reposes the real authority rests. A fractional majority in the Parliament at London will have greater power than the Governments and Parliaments of the four Dominions to commit the Empire to war which may involve the Dominions in great sacrifices of blood and treasure. What actual responsibility had Canada for the Great War which cost 60,000 lives and over a billion of money? No one doubts what our decision would have been if we had possessed co-ordinate authority, but an issue may arise in the future over which vital differences may produce disruption. It is idle to pretend that under the existing organization of the Empire the people of the Dominions can have equal citizenship. Autonomy is consistent with the ideal of ultimate separation, but not with the fact of Empire. On the other hand, it is inconceivable that Canadians will be forever content with an inferior citizenship or with a divided loyalty. They must have an equal voice in the Empire with the people of England or Scotland, or ultimately they will establish a separate and independent nation. This voice can be obtained only through a sovereign Imperial Parliament exercising authority over the foreign relations of the Empire and in which the Dominions will have actual direct and equal representation.

Who believes that the American colonies, if they had not separated from Great Britain, would now be tolerant of war cabinets and periodical imperial conferences? Would they regard representation in an Imperial Parliament as a sacrifice of autonomy? In the near future the Dominions which now have a population of 16,000,000 or 17,000,000 will have thirty, forty or fifty millions of people. Even to-day they would have a third of the representation in an Imperial Parliament. The autonomy of Prince Edward Island is not impaired by representation in the Canadian Parliament, nor that of Montana or Oregon by representation in the American Congress. There is an answer to the anxious autonomists in the cry of the world for a League of Nations. If the United States and the

British Empire can agree to the assumption of common international obligations, Great Britain and the Overseas Dominions can safely establish a common Parliament for the protection of interests and the adjustment of affairs common to all portions of the Empire. The world has had a new revelation of the vital need for understanding and organization and the lesson has its significance for the British communities. For either organization or disruption is the fiat of destiny. By one method or the other, equality of citizenship must finally be established. One believes that the Empire will not dissolve and that the genius of British statesmen will find and the British peoples in their sanity and wisdom accept the inevitable solution.

Nor is it true, as is so often contended, that free trade within the Empire is an essential condition of organic federation. There is no vital reason why Canada should not maintain protection for national and industrial reasons or that Great Britain should not do likewise. It is not even necessary to establish preferences within the Empire, so long as there is not discrimination in favour of foreign countries. Control over fiscal policy, as over immigration, would naturally and wisely be vested in the domestic Parliaments. Each portion of the Empire would be concerned to develop its own resources and determine its own methods of production and standards of living. There need be neither friction nor conflict under a system of Imperial organization which would clearly separate domestic from Imperial interests and reserve alike for Great Britain and the Dominions unchallengeable control over domestic concerns. It is not essential either that any absolute power to levy taxation should be reposed in an Imperial Parliament. There is reason to think that effective organization for defence would be less costly through the operation of common machinery, and since by the very evolution of the Empire to which we have consented the Dominions have become partners in defence, they would provide the contributions required to maintain and stabilize the partnership. Undoubtedly the whole problem is complex and difficult in many of its phases, but at least the chances of misunderstanding and confusion are greater under an unorganized than they would be under an organized Empire in the new relation which has involved the Dominions in common obligations for the support of the Imperial structure. The details of federation could only be settled by the statesmen of the Empire in conference around a common table, as any project of Imperial union would require the free and decisive assent of the Parliaments and peoples of all the British Commonwealths.

Sir Wilfrid Laurier was not a federationist. As he grew older he became inflexible in his attitude towards the Empire. He often seemed willing to extend autonomy to the verge of separation. For his day he could acquiesce in the existing relation. He was not anxious for the future. But he thought he could see the ripe fruit falling from the parent tree. He was not hostile to Great Britain and he had reverence for British traditions and British institutions. But he believed that there was no advantage to Canada in closer connection with the Mother Country. He regarded projects of federation not only as visionary and impracticable, but as inimical to colonial freedom and self-government. He could see the vision of a League of Nations. He could not see the vision of a League of Empire. Look-

ing into the future he probably saw an independent
Canada, not separated from Great Britain in interest
and sentiment, but politically dissociated from problems
which are the necessary condition and inheritance of
an Empire. He was indeed a Canadian nationalist,
and grew ever more convinced that between nationalism
and Imperialism there was a necessary conflict. He
was deeply impressed by his first visit to Great Britain.
But he grew weary of London Conferences and the
insurgent Imperialism and diplomatic precipitancy of
Australia. He was closer to Botha than to any other
representative of the Overseas Dominions, convinced
perhaps, that Botha was his natural ally in opposing
doubtful Imperial enterprises. But there is no reason
to think that he ever had to resist pressure from any
British statesmen except Chamberlain, or that the autonomy of Canada that he so dearly cherished was ever
menaced by any secret design, covert manœuvre, social
attack, or political cabal. British statesmen have long
recognized that any impulse towards Imperial organization must proceed from the Dominions and that any
suspicion of British coercion would excite only irritation and resistance. The future of the Empire lies with
the Dominions. Downing Street is a legend. No system of Imperial organization incompatible with
national sentiment in the Dominions could endure. It
is inconceivable that British statesmen would imperil
the whole structure even by consent to any unequal cen-
tralization of authority in London. But Laurier was
doubtful and apprehensive. Possibly his apprehension
only expressed his attitude in domestic affairs. There
were phrases and catchwords that were useful in Canada, and he was careful not to reduce their value on the

political exchange. Possibly he resented the pressure of Imperial officials in Canada when an offer of troops for South Africa was desired, and over certain proposals for the organization of the Canadian forces. But he never could have doubted the position of responsible British statesmen, misrepresented sometimes perhaps by functionaries and officials, who could not understand place without power and were reluctant to acknowledge that they had no actual responsibility for the decisions of the Canadian Cabinet and the Canadian Parliament. And there was Bourassa.

From all the fretful agitation of Australian statesmen in England for preference in British markets, Laurier held coldly aloof. He conceded to the United Kingdom all the freedom which he demanded for Canada. He did not believe that colonial statesmen could wisely intervene in the movement for tariff reform in Great Britain or appear on British platforms as advocates of preferential treatment of colonial products. In that he was upon ground which could not be challenged. The strength and sanity of his position would be convincingly established if British statesmen should appear on platforms in Canada as advocates of free trade for the Dominion. Changes in British fiscal policy imposed upon the British people at the demand of the Dominions would subject the Dominions to angry political attack in Great Britain, produce a situation not unlike that which led to the revolt of the American colonies, and endanger the unity and stability of the Empire.

The naval controversy in Canada had many strange and ugly manifestations. It may be that Sir Wilfrid Laurier was as reluctant to establish a navy or commit

Canada to any direct obligation for sea defence as he was to send troops to South Africa. But public opinion demanded and he submitted. In 1909 the Canadian Parliament adopted unanimously a resolution in favour of a Canadian navy or other speedy and adequate contribution to the defence of the Empire. Laurier opposed any direct contribution to the Admiralty, but after consultation with the Imperial authorities it was resolved to create a naval college and to organize a fleet of cruisers.

This programme was opposed by Mr. Bourassa, as imperiling Canadian autonomy and exposing the Dominion to compulsory participation in the wars of the Empire all over the world. Mr. Bourassa ultimately was joined by Mr. Monk, the French Conservative leader for Quebec, and an inflammatory appeal was made to the French constituencies against the naval policy of the Government. On the other hand, the Conservative Opposition, under the leadership of Mr. Borden, contended for an emergency contribution of Dreadnoughts and urged a further consultation with the Admiralty in order to frame a measure which would be of greater immediate service to the Empire and of greater ultimate value in the defence of Canada, and which should be submitted to the Canadian people for ratification. Against his French assailants, Laurier argued that the proposals of the Government were a just and necessary assumption of responsibility to aid in the defence of the Empire, but insisted that the fleet should be under the control of Canada and should engage only in such wars as the Canadian Parliament might approve. As against his Conservative opponents, he contended that a contribution of Dreadnoughts would infringe upon the autonomy of the Dominion and that the demand for a referendum was a manœuvre to delay action and to exploit feeling in Quebec to the advantage of the Conservative party. At stages of the controversy the fear or the lure of Bourassa was behind the action of both parties. There was no danger to the Empire in a Canadian navy. There was no menace to the autonomy of Canada in a contribution of Dreadnoughts or in the naval proposals subsequently placed before Parliament by the Borden Government. There was reason, perhaps, to enlarge the Laurier programme. There was no sound reason that it should be opposed. When all is said, Laurier committed Canada to naval defence, and in consequence sustained heavy political losses in Quebec. It is understood that Mr. Borden himself was anxious to maintain the unanimity secured in support of the original naval resolution. But he could not hold Mr. Monk, and there were forces within the Conservative party which could not be withheld from assault upon the Laurier programme. For this there was a time of visitation and vengeance when parliamentary ratification of the Borden proposals was required. There was burning anger among Liberals over the substantial alliance between Conservatives and Nationalists in the general election of 1911, and the character of the attack upon Liberal candidates in the French Province. The truth is that Monk and Bourassa thrust Borden aside in Quebec. For the time the official Conservative party did not exist. Conservatives adhering to the traditions of Cartier and Macdonald could not be nominated, and not a few would not have accepted nomination under the conditions prescribed by the Nationalists. The old Bleus, under Bourassa, were in even worse fortune than the old Rouges under Mercier. Whatever responsibility lies upon Borden, it is certain that he regretted Monk's desertion and never submitted to Nationalist domination. Exclusion of Nationalists from the Borden Cabinet would have been equivalent to denial of French representation. In a country with Canada's history and with 2,500,000 French people in a total population of 8,000,000 or 9,000,000, counsels of patriotism and prudence forbid such a decision, as any deliberate resolve by Quebec upon self-exclusion would be singularly unfortunate and undesirable.

There are few less attractive chapters in Canadian history than that which covers the parliamentary debate on the Borden naval programme. One feels as he reads through Hansard that there was an insensate and incurable determination to misjudge and misunderstand. It is hard to think that anyone believed the purchase and transfer of three Dreadnoughts to the Royal Navy, subject to recall if the country should determine to create a home navy, was reconcilable with any jingo conspiracy to destroy self-government and restore the ascendency of Downing Street in Canada. But there was much passionate rhetoric to that effect and danger of actual physical violence in the crises of the debate. One feels that the action of the Nationalists in Quebec in 1911 affords the explanation. At least they could not complain of the ardour with which their doctrine was proclaimed to the detriment of Conservatives who had temporarily profited by their inflammatory agitation in the French constituencies. Nothing was more startling than the metamorphosis of the leader of the Senate. From urgent advocacy of closure to force the Naval Aid Bill through the House of Commons to spokesman for the majority of the Upper Chamber, who rejected the measure, or at least demanded a referendum, which was practically equivalent to rejection, was a remarkable demonstration of political devolution. But in a few weeks Sir George Ross passed through all these phases and was still fresh for new achievements. It was a triumph in transformation of which perhaps there are few like illustrations in practical politics. But Sir Wilfrid prevailed, and when the Great War came, no Canadian Dreadnoughts rode the seas under the ensign of Canada. One reads the story from the original unanimous resolution of Parliament, through the controversy over the Laurier proposals and down to the rejection of the Borden programme, and feels that a great issue was enmeshed in party strategy and that neither party is to be congratulated upon the result to which they mutually contributed.

It is said that Laurier, at a dinner at Windsor Castle, found a card at his plate inscribed, "Right Honourable Sir Wilfrid Laurier," and that in this fashion he was subjected to the honour or indignity of Knighthood. It is a pretty story. It may or may not be true. One can hardly conceive of a Laurier manœuvred or coerced into acceptance of a title if his will was not to accept. If ever there was a man who was master of himself, it was Laurier, although the country was slow to understand how vitally resolute he was. There is no doubt that before he left Canada for the Diamond Jubilee, he had considered acceptance of a title and was chiefly concerned over the fact that he had proclaimed himself "a democrat to the hilt," and by acceptance of any Imperial recognition would expose himself to criticism and misunderstanding. We talked together in London shortly after he had accepted the title, and he explained frankly that refusal would have been ungracious and that he could not think there was any valid objection to the decoration. It is inconceivable that he would seek a title. Nor had he then any feeling that he should not have accepted. It is certain that he was not less a democrat, but not even the bonfire which he suggested, when titles were under attack in Parliament, could have purged him of the high social fastidiousness which was a vital element in his character. He was not indifferent to wealth or social position. Laurier belonged to the old Whig group of England, or to the old Court circle of France, gracious, restrained, of serene spirit and simple tastes, hating noise and swagger and loving culture and the surroundings of beauty and plenty. But, titled or untitled, he was himself, as is every other man who has native quality, to whom a decoration can give no distinction, nor invest with virtue or authority which are not his by character and achievement. Titles give no social precedence in Canada. Precedence belongs only to members of the Senate, members of the Parliaments, the Church, the Bench, and the Army and Navy. From recognition of faithful civil service to the State no evil can proceed. It is doubtful if wealth alone should mould and dominate society. For there will be society, however legislators level up or level down. Hereditary distinctions belong to the past, and titles, too, may be banished. Whatever the decision is of no vital consequence to those who have or to those who have not. It is vain to think that honours will always be worthily bestowed or the fact universally admitted when they are so bestowed. This is a human world and often envy is as powerful to

318

destroy as ambition is to build. One cannot desire that all the distinctive badges of British civilization should disappear, nor can one admit that the State will be endangered by recognition of civil service according to the traditions and customs of an Empire which through centuries has been the cradle of free institutions. Very rarely have Canadians deliberately sought Imperial honours. There is no evidence that they have been awarded in recognition of service to the Empire as distinguished from service to Canada. For half a century there has been continuous extension of freedom and authority to the Dominions, and Imperial honours have fallen chiefly upon colonial statesmen who have organized and directed the forces by which this result was accomplished. Besides, however we may regard the King's honours, is it a reproach to a colonial statesman that he concerns himself with the affairs of Empire? Is Imperial patriotism repugnant to domestic patriotism? Is devotion to the common interest treason to Canada? Laurier was not affected in his attitude towards Great Britain by Imperial recognition, nor has any Canadian statesman since Confederation succumbed to the mysterious social influences in London which we are so often told seduce representatives of the Dominions from their natural allegiance, and forever prey upon weak and complacent colonials for evil purposes which never take the form of action.

When Great Britain declared war against Germany, Laurier gave ungrudging and unequivocal support to the decision of the Government to equip and despatch contingents for service in Europe, and the Opposition voted as a unit for the appropriations necessary to make the participation of Canada in the conflict influential and effective. In Parliament and on the platform he denounced German aggression, extolled the heroism of France and Belgium, and maintained with convincing argument and luminous eloquence the justice and righteousness of the cause of Great Britain and the allied nations. It may be that at vital moments personal and partisan consideration prevailed, but again there was Bourassa.

> Like some old miser, Rustum hoards his fame,
> And shuns to peril it with younger men.

From his youth Laurier was a politician. He became more utterly and incurably a politician as he grew older. He could take defeat, but he loved power, and meant to regain power before he died. No one who knew the man could believe that he would resign the office of leader while his strength lasted, and no one who knew the Liberal party as it was fashioned under his hand could believe that he would ever be displaced except by his own decision. Whether an Imperialist or not, he made no quarrel between Great Britain and Canada, he established the British fiscal preference, he first sanctioned the organization of Canadian regiments for Imperial service abroad, and he first committed Canada to a definite obligation for naval defence. It may be that he answered to public opinion, but he did answer, and that was something.

CHAPTER XIV

WHAT WAS LEFT OVER

The Liberal party of Ontario was on the edge of the grave when Sir George Ross became Prime Minister. For the condition of the party he was not chiefly responsible. His fault was that he tolerated desperate expedients in the endeavour to resuscitate a body whose hold upon healthy and vigorous life could not be renewed. In successive bye-elections there was organized personation, violation of the sanctity of ballot boxes, intimidation, coercion and direct purchase of voters. It is a profound pity that such a chapter should have been written, for there is no other in the history of Ontario of which its people need be ashamed. The demoralization began under Mr. Hardy, although he was even less responsible than Ross for the calculated plottings and activities of the agents of corruption. A guerilla organization with connections at Ottawa, Toronto, and London, recruited a body of personators for service in provincial and federal bye-elections, and carried constituencies in defiance of public sentiment. One could produce the evidence, but there is nothing savoury in the rehearsal of scandal nor any profit in reviving incidents which would involve the dead and the living in discredit and dishonour.

Many of the active agents in these discreditable practices never were discovered. Some of those upon whom condemnation fell most heavily were not the chief culprits. It is best sometimes that the veil should not be lifted even if one cannot agree that there is any obligation of personal or party loyalty which requires defence of conspiracy and rascality. The time came when even Ross was convinced that office could be retained only by methods which were beyond toleration and by dependence upon instruments which could not be employed without complete humiliation and disgrace. But he was not willing to resign nor convinced that the outlook was hopeless. He persuaded himself that it was better to save something by negotiation than to lose all in a battle which was going badly. With the sanction, therefore, of Sir Wilfrid Laurier and Sir Richard Cartwright and two or three of his own colleagues, he approached Sir James Whitney with proposals for a coalition. Mr. Goldwin Smith in *The Weekly Sun* had suggested coalition, and he was persuaded to revive the agitation on assurances that Ross had become a convert and that *The Globe* would support *The Sun's* argument. *The Globe's* first article in accordance with this agreement was an appeal for union as unequivocal as Mr. Goldwin Smith could have desired, but which in the judgment of many Liberals emphasized too strongly the hopeless position of a Government with only three of a majority in the Legislature. A second article followed, more guarded in language, but in definite advocacy of coalition.

Sir George Ross foresaw that the position would be embarrassing if Whitney should not entertain his proposals, and he was anxious that neither *The Globe* nor himself should be irrevocably compromised. For my part I was convinced that the Government should resign, and I had no thought that Whitney would coalesce. Ross and Whitney were incompatible in temper and method. The Conservative leader was open and eruptive. The Prime Minister was adroit and acute. Ross was often brilliant, Whitney seldom. But Whitney had more quality than he ever revealed in Parliament or on the platform. Whitney trusted Hardy, and they were much alike; he distrusted Ross, and they were greatly unlike.

Among Liberals there was a common conviction that the Conservative party never could attain office under Whitney. This, too, was the impression of many Conservatives. I remember that a few days before polling in 1905, when I was convinced that the Conservatives would have a majority of forty, an active and influential Conservative met my confident prediction with the blunt but unflattering rejoinder that "only a d—— fool would think that Whitney could ever beat Ross". This curious undervaluation of Whitney perhaps partly explains Ross's confidence that the project of coalition would be entertained and explains also the favourable attitude of some Conservatives towards the proposal. But there was never even a momentary prospect that Whitney would enter a coalition. If he ever seemed to hesitate it was because he desired to understand fully the position of his opponents. When this was disclosed he rejected the offer with decision and emphasis, as he resolutely resisted subsequent attempts by a group of influential people outside the Legislature to bring the leaders of the two parties together in a union cabinet.

Sir Wilfrid Laurier sanctioned the advances to Whitney, but he cannot have believed that Ross would succeed. He was greatly concerned over the

323

situation in Ontario, and very urgent when the Union proposal was rejected that Ross should resign office and enter the federal Cabinet as Liberal leader for Ontario. Laurier contended that if Ross were to persist in the attempt to govern with an inadequate majority he would destroy his own reputation, bequeath the party an accumulating heritage of scandal, and provoke a public feeling which would not discriminate between the Government at Toronto and the Government at Ottawa. He was anxious for Ross, anxious for himself, and anxious for the Liberal party, but the Provincial leader would not listen nor would he ever believe that he could be defeated in a general election. When a party has governed continuously for a third of a century it is not surprising if its leaders become convinced that they have an hereditary title to office. Even during the electoral campaign of 1905 Ross believed that he would hold the Province, and he infused his courage and confidence into many of his candidates. But the defeat was overwhelming; the ruin so complete that the wreckage still embarrasses and encumbers.

When Sir George Ross was in London for the coronation of King Edward VII. Mr. Joseph Chamberlain through a casual inquiry learned that he was the fourth successive Liberal Premier of Ontario, and that for more than thirty years the Conservative party had been excluded from office in the Province. Turning upon Ross with courtesy but with energy, the Imperial statesman insisted that the British system of government required regular alternation in office between the political parties, and that only by such changes could the initiative and capacity of rival statesmen be fully employed in the public service. But Ross was not affected by the advice of Mr. Chamberlain, nor would he listen to the appeal of Sir Wilfrid Laurier, although he admitted that questionable expedients and corrupt expenditures were necessary at the moment to success even in constituencies which were historic strongholds of the Liberal party. If he had resigned in deference to wholesome public sentiment he would have protected his own reputation and dignity, and the restoration of the Liberal party in Ontario would have been a far less onerous undertaking for his successors. But he had an excess of courage, and he was so effective in debate and so persuasive and convincing on the platform that he could not forsake the field and refuse a battle in which he did not doubt that he would prevail.

There was nothing spontaneous in Sir George Ross's speeches, and yet there was a simple, easy, natural spontaneity in their deliverance. Although he prepared with infinite labour, his sentences were spoken as simply and impressively as though they were the coinage of the moment. When he read a speech, as he did sometimes, he was heavy and unimpressive. If he made the same speech without production of the manuscript he was happy, alert, stimulating and inspiring. Few public men speak without exact and laborious preparation. Blake, Cartwright, and Mowat were as dependent upon manuscript as was Ross, but they never achieved his natural spontaneity. Sir John Macdonald, Sir Wilfrid Laurier, and Alexander Mackenzie avoided verbal preparation, but they never spoke more naturally than did Ross when he was using the literal language of the manuscript. There was spirit in his sentences, occasional flashes of satirical or impudent humour, a suggestion of complete candour, passages of orderly eloquence, not so perfect when dissected, but singularly impressive as delivered with appropriate inflextion and gesture. His voice was not musical, but there was a penetrating quality, a curious sharpness in attack and an intimate cadence in appeal and defence. Few men could handle a public meeting with such skill, or so restrain and conciliate hostile elements. He was so nonchalant, so reliant, so easily confident in his message and in himself that only the irreconcilable suspected and only the unwary interrupted. If his speeches were prepared his humour was spontaneous enough, and when he could not subdue with banter he would silence and humiliate with contemptuous ridicule or a sudden savage retort from which there was no recovery.

His speeches reveal an amazing power of absorption. They suggest greater knowledge than he possessed. He read many books and something of all remained in his memory. He could expound the science of banking better than the bankers. He could advise manufacturers and instruct farmers. He had an instinct for assimilation and exposition. He had language for the other man's knowledge and expression for his experience. He let off cargo as easily as he loaded. There is not much in his speeches that will survive, for the true flavour of literature is missing, as is almost inevitable in material for the platform. But for immediate effect Sir George Ross was the best speaker of his time in Canada or at least Sir George Foster alone among his contemporaries was as uniformly attractive and effective on the platform and in Parliament. 326

WHAT WAS LEFT OVER

Sir George Ross was not fortunate in his term of office as Prime Minister of Ontario, nor was his reputation enhanced in the Senate, but these are incidents in a career which was distinguished for patriotic service and a living interest in movements of high social and national value. There were tests he did not meet, but he was not narrow in sympathy or outlook. His reconstruction of the educational system of Ontario may have been faulty, but the defects were insignificant in a solid body of achievement. He was eager to stimulate native literature. He made valuable contributions to biography and history. A gallant spirit prevailed over severe physical affliction, and he held for thirty years without a single defeat the constituency by which he was first returned to Parliament.

For years after he became leader of the Conservative party Sir James Whitney was a lonely figure. He lived in a village between sessions of the Legislature. Even while the House was sitting he had few friends outside the Chamber. He was seldom seen at a club or at a private dinner. He would go often to the theatre, and he could enjoy a harrowing melo-drama. He read the Sunday editions of the American newspapers, from the first page headlights to the comic supplements. But he also read many books, and few men had a wider or more exact knowledge of British political and constitutional history. In social intercourse he could be charming and companionable, generous in judgment, and tolerant of differences of opinion. When he first appeared in the Legislature his speeches were singularly moderate and judicial. But in the long struggle for office he developed irascibility. He became convinced that the balances were weighted against Conservative candidates, that the returns of the ballot boxes did not express the intention of the voters, that there was careless toleration of evil political practices by the comfortable classes, and that even the churches were acquiescent and cowardly. One suspects that he also resented the attitude of many Conservatives to whom his personality made no immediate appeal and who withheld the sympathy and support which was so freely accorded to Sir William Meredith and Sir John Macdonald. It cannot be said that he had strong support in the Legislature, although the Opposition under successive Conservative leaders was not so contemptible as the country was led to believe. For years there was a general impression that the Conservative party in the Legislature could not form a Cabinet out of the material available and that there was no alternative but to prolong the tenure of Liberal administration. Conscious of this feeling, Whitney often displayed resentment and anger in his speeches. Indeed he was often heartily abusive but never grossly personal in attack. He was never so abusive as when he defended an associate or repelled aspersions upon his own motives. Unlike Sir George Ross, he spoke without preparation and was often carried into violence and extravagance of statement. But he was so transparent that the people understood and rejoiced in his tempestuous ebullitions. He travelled the Province over, without parade or pretension, often alone and unsupported, often weary but aggressive, resolute, independent and defiant.

From day to day while I was its editor *The Globe* reported his speeches as fully as they were reported by any Conservative newspaper, to the distress of Liberal

ministers, who often protested that if the paper would
treat him with salutary neglect he never would rise
above his natural insignificance. But I was concerned
only for *The Globe's* reputation as a newspaper and
could not be convinced that the speeches of the Conservative leader should be ignored. There was no
thought of conciliating Conservatives nor any desire to
assist Whitney into office. The time came when
defence of the methods employed in behalf of the Ross
Government was impossible, but there would have
been a suspicion of betrayal if, as editor of *The Globe,*
I had attempted to exercise the freedom which I believed the circumstances demanded. Connected with the
sensational incidents in which Mr. Gamey was the
central figure there is much that has not been disclosed.
Neither upon the one side nor upon the other was there
a complete revelation, and if the judgment of the Royal
Commission was according to the evidence the investigation was incomplete and inconclusive. There could
not be a more tangled story, and it was just that Mr.
Gamey and the Ross Government should have suffered.

As Prime Minister, Sir James Whitney required
and enforced simple integrity in administration and in
legislation. He came into office unfettered by pledges
to any group or interest. In appointments to office he
did not forget the faithful workers of the party, but he
protected and trusted the permanent Civil Service.
He provided liberally for the University of Toronto.
The appropriations for primary and secondary education were substantially increased. He was not too
generous towards agriculture nor was he very sympathetic towards revolutionary panaceas for the re-

generation of mankind. He suspected the idealists and hated evangelical profession and pretension. He thought he was a Tory, which he was not; he was stern in word and compassionate in action. He guarded his own integrity with such anxious vigilance that his colleagues were sometimes subjected to inconvenient restraint. For he fully trusted only himself, not so much in doubt of associates, as in the resolute determination to know every detail of administration and the reason for every departmental decision. Although he distrusted "public ownership" he sanctioned a great project of municipal co-operation which has been of undoubted advantage to Ontario. He was not a prohibitionist, but he required stringent enforcement of the license regulations and agreed that if a public sentiment should develop strong enough to assure general respect for a prohibitory enactment the Legislature must give effect to the will of the people. He was a British subject of intense conviction and devotion. He would flame into anger over any suggestion of withdrawal from the Imperial connection. He was deeply anxious that Canada should grow closer to the Mother Country and bear its legitimate proportion of the burden of Imperial defence. He said to me just after the general election of 1908, in which the majority for the Government was overwhelming, "Ontario does not think I am a great man. It does think I am honest. And honest I must be." But that was not a hard task for Sir James Whitney. He was invincibly and belligerently honest, and his character and example, whether or not he was a great man, are among the best possessions of the Province.

There died the other day a colleague of Sir James

Whitney of remarkable quality. Hon. W. J. Hanna was less than sixty years old, and five years ago he would have been said to have a great reserve of strength and energy. But the strength was exhausted too soon by the energy which could not be restrained. He was not perhaps an orderly worker, but at times he had almost a demoniac power of concentration. At his best he stood to the level of great men, but he revealed himself reluctantly, and much that the gods offered he cast aside. He could have been counsel for the Grand Trunk Railway, but he chose instead the fretful irritations and the meagre emoluments of public office. He could have been Chairman of the Federal Railway Commission, but Sir James Whitney would not agree, and Mr. Hanna in simple loyalty to a political comrade accepted the decision. When he took the office of Food Controller he expected that criticism and unpopularity would be his portion. He did not attempt to conciliate critics by promises of immediate reduction in prices. Believing that the chief objects were to increase production and provide food for the allied countries and the allied armies he was unmoved by all the clamour for arbitrary regulation of producers. He was primarily concerned to increase production not to reduce prices, and although his office exercised a greater control over prices than was generally believed it was by open co-operation and quiet pressure rather than by vexatious and repressive regulations that effective results were secured. The statement he issued when he resigned office was a conclusive vindication of the system of control which he devised and a message of high significance for the future.

There was a quality in Mr. Hanna which few men possess. He could labour and sacrifice and conceal what his hand was doing with infinite reserve. He was restless when he was praised but grateful when he was understood. For the causes to which he was devoted he had enthusiasm that could not be controlled. These causes were chiefly connected with the erring and the unfortunate, the maimed and the broken in the battle of life. No man ever saw more good in those upon whom the strict moralists laid their censure, or ever was more eager to restore the penitent who would not look towards the uplands. He believed in the essential divinity of man and in compassion saw the law of justice. On the prison farms which he established he was happy as he was nowhere else, and these are his praise and his monument.

As he sought to restore those who had come under social and legal condemnation, so he was anxious for the estate of women and the dignity and independence of labour. Of idleness and inefficiency he was intolerant. Perhaps he hardly distinguished laziness from actual criminality. But he could not be reconciled to social conditions under which work was denied to those who were willing to do it, which condemned men and women to live in unwholesome surroundings, and which laid upon the backs of honest and thrifty people burdens greater than they could carry. It may be that he had no great reputation beyond Ontario. More than once he stood upon the threshold of national politics. If he had greatly desired he could have sat in the Federal Cabinet. But it was ordered otherwise, and he was content. He disliked the meaner side of party warfare, the littleness and ugliness of personal controversy, the demagogic ranting which disgusts honest men with public service. But he could have been a great Minister of National Welfare, if by abuse and misuse that term has not become misleading and unattractive. He was peculiarly, perhaps, the servant of Ontario, but his achievements, little as he did to attract attention to himself, have national significance and should have national recognition.

As I reach the end of this story I think of men for whose friendship I am grateful, of incidents insignificant in themselves which linger in the memory, of things said that one cannot forget, of things written that one would not recall. Alexander Russel, the famous editor of *The Edinburgh Scotsman,* declared that the life of a journalist is a warfare upon earth. But the conflict is absorbing and if one advocates many causes which deserve to succeed and do not, one also fights many battles which he deserves to lose and does not. The journalist must develop philosophy. He must harden his hide and soften his heart. If he lets the sun go down upon his wrath he will have much sorrow and will make much sport for his contemporaries. He must learn that "wisdom lingers" and that prophecy is the pastime of fools.

For thirty years I looked every day through scores of exchanges. Nothing in the day's work was more interesting, more instructive or more effective in reducing conceit and restraining arrogance. I was often told that I wasted time upon the exchanges. I do not think so. They expressed Canada, town, village and country, and often in an unpretentious weekly publication one found a word of inspiration or a revelation of feeling of national significance. Often, too, there was humour in the exchanges, conscious or unconscious, as interpreted in different surroundings or from a different outlook. I recall an account in a Brampton paper of a wedding which ended with the impressive sentence, "The happy couple took the Chicago flyer for Guelph." Once a Fort William paper stated that a Pole had been shot in the foreign quarter. A Durham exchange reported the farewell sermon of a Methodist minister from the text, "Sleep on now and take your rest." Another journal published in Grey County had this item, "Mr. John Albrecht, Mr. George Schenck's hired man, had the misfortune of cutting off one of his big toes on Thursday. We think it was an axe that did the terrible work. Dr. McLean was called and dressed the wound." A Nova Scotia exchange gave the prayer of a little girl, apparently belonging to a Liberal family, who said, "Now, O God, take care of yourself, for if we lose you we shall only have Laurier left to take care of us and he is not doing as well as papa expected he would do." *The Kincardine Review* mentioned a colonel who could not join the Strathcona Horse because he was an ass. The *Catholic Record* of London, expressing regret for the death of a bank director, through the eccentricity of a typesetting machine was made to say that he had been "added to the rest account." A Winnipeg paper intended to say "women clothed with sanctity," but actually said, "women clothed with scantity." There was the Montreal story of a dispute between a French Roman Catholic and a Scottish Presbyterian. Finally the exasperated Scotsman said, "To hell with the Pope." The Frenchman retorted, "You say, to hell wis zee Pope, den I say, to hell wis Harry Lauder."

WHAT WAS LEFT OVER

One acquired, too, a beautiful collection of anonymous letters. It is, perhaps, not easy to be reconciled to such letters, for only an irredeemable coward, unfit for the decent earth which he encumbers through the mercy of an indulgent God, sends even to an editor unsigned letters which are meant to wound and fester. But one does become reconciled to the ways of such creatures and as the years pass there is genuine delight in rereading their curious messages. I find an old envelope addressed to "J. S. Willison, proprietor of Cox and Jaffray's morals and daylight editor of *The Globe.*" A letter which preserves the balance reads, "The daily sight of the knightly editor defending Rogers is enough to make angels weep." Another letter reads, "You can beat Ananias; better not yell political purity so long as you have stinking fish in your own basket." Of like implication was a letter I received four or five years ago, just a few minutes before I had to address the Canadian Club of Vancouver, "You are the biggest liar in Canada. It is a wonder you were not shot long ago." At least there is comfort in the reflection that one is not an amateur. Another of which I have lost the connection but which is signed "A Conservative," reads, "It must be something of a wrench to have to do this sort of thing, so long as one retains any pretensions to decency in public affairs. Surely the Prussian taskmaster could not be harder than this indicates. I take it that there was no escape, or you would have ignored the rascal in politics, even if you could not call your soul your own sufficiently to deal with him as the general interest dictates. And, believe me, the policy of our party so dictates, whatever may be your instructions from your immediate masters." But I could multiply such letters into a volume and possibly other editors with greater virtue than I possess have not been neglected by these curious guardians of the public morals.

How many vagrant stories, gathered in a third of a century, lie at the back of one's memory. Many years ago Mr. David Glass was prominent in political contests in London and Middlesex. Once he was speaking in London South and was interrupted by a man in the audience of very diminutive stature, with the remark, "Cut it short, Dave, cut it short." Glass retorted, "The Lord in His wisdom saw fit to cut you short." I recall that when I was in the Press Gallery of the House of Commons a Liberal member who was reading his speech was called to order. Interrogated by the Speaker, the member confessed that he had "copious notes." He was, however, allowed to proceed. Not long afterwards a Conservative member was reading his speech, and Dr. Landerkin stood up, and, addressing the Speaker, said, "I rise to a point of order." "You mean," interrupted the Speaker, "that the honourable gentleman is reading his speech?" "No," said Dr. Landerkin, "my objection is that he is reading it so badly." During the campaign of 1887 Hon. Edward Blake, speaking at Barrie, pictured Riel as insane and the Western halfbreeds as driven into revolt by a feeble and corrupt Government. When he had fully developed his argument he sternly questioned, "Should this man have been hanged?" Some one at the back of the hall shouted, "Yes, what else would you do with the scoundrel?" Mr. Blake retorted, "I hope the Judge will take a more merciful view when you appear for sentence." In

WHAT WAS LEFT OVER

1876 Sir Richard Cartwright was addressing a meeting in South Ontario. A well-known political worker interrupted while he was denouncing Tory corruption with the question, "What changes have you made in the law to ensure purer elections?" Sir Richard answered savagely, "One change will make it more difficult for you to sell your vote next election." The blow was mortal, for it was believed that the interrupter had "keen commercial instincts."

Sir George Ross never was more happy than at a meeting in Toronto when he applied the old Jacobite epitaph for George Frederick, Prince of Wales, to Mr. George Frederick Marter, for a very short time leader of the Conservative party in the Legislature :—

"Here lies Fred,
  Who was alive and is dead;
  Had it been his father,
  I had much rather;
  Had it been his brother,
  Still better than another;
  Had it been his sister,
  No one would have missed her;
  Had it been the whole generation,
  Still better for the nation.
  But since 'tis only Fred,
  Who was alive and is dead,
  There's no more to be said."

Once in the House of Commons, when Hon. William Paterson was speaking, a Conservative member, who had measured his liquor carelessly, muttered between sentences, "Rot," "Rot," "Rot," Mr. Paterson paused, removed his glasses, beamed upon

22

the offender with placid benignity and whispered as much in appeal as in reproach, "If the honourable gentleman thinks it is rot, why does he take so much of it."

Looking backward a few figures appear in the shadow with whom I walked side by side or followed at a distance. In my first years as editor of *The Globe* no one gave me wiser counsel than Principal Grant of Queen's University. He could be a politician if occasion required and he often needed to exercise political genius in behalf of the University. But he had none of the docility of the partisan nor ever cringed to the majority. As a young man in Nova Scotia he stood boldly with the minority for Confederation. He never hesitated to defend Quebec and its institutions if they were unfairly attacked. He was as ready to resist any extreme demand by the French Province or to oppose any public man of Quebec who sought through appeal to Race or Church to elevate himself or aggrandize a faction. He could resist the glamour of Sir John Macdonald. He was equal to negotiation with Sir Oliver Mowat. An advocate of the Gothenberg system of control over the liquor traffic, he bore with serenity the denunciations of prohibitionists from pew and pulpit. Perhaps only Colonel George T. Denison among Canadians was so influential in opposing every movement towards separation from Great Britain, in strengthening Imperial sentiment, in fashioning the structure of Empire. For they were the teachers of British statesmen, and the evangels of a gospel which even the British people were slow to understand. Derided and misrepresented, they persisted, and Dr. Grant lived as Colonel Denison has lived, to see an abundant harvest from the seed which they scattered in lonely furrows thirty or forty years ago. They said that Dr. Grant was a "trimmer," but that sentence falls upon all men who will not be the servants of party unless the service goes with conviction. I think of no career in Canada which was more distinguished for simple and resolute patriotism. It is true that he was often dexterous in pursuit of his object, but the object was worthy and the diplomacy objectionable only to those who were overcome and who used more clumsily and ineffectively the instruments by which he achieved. If he had been governed by personal ambition only he would have turned his back upon Queen's University, entered the federal Cabinet and stood foremost among the statesmen of the Empire.

Another man of remarkable personality, of whom I saw little but knew much, and whose confidence it was my privilege to enjoy, was Sir William Van Horne. Few men have had a greater thing to do or in the doing displayed more signal resource and courage. He had to build a railway across an uninhabited country, through wastes of rock and over high mountain ranges, with the people greatly divided as to the wisdom and practicability of the undertaking. The Canadaian Pacific Railway Company had to go to the public treasury again and again for relief. In 1885 the stock sold as low as 35¾. Its position was assailed in the London money market. It was the object of inveterate political hostility. Within the company itself there was friction, angry criticism, and suspicion of mismanagement. Against all this Van Horne had to contend, and he showed superb self-control and inflexible purpose. He kept the confidence of the Board and had the devoted loyalty of subordinates. His own activities were various and numerous almost beyond computation. He had to deal with ministers, often timid, and for years profoundly apprehensive concerning the ultimate issue of the undertaking. If Sir Charles Tupper never flinched it is not certain that so much could be said for Sir John Macdonald. He had to concern himself with problems of immigration, to consider the more desirable fields for settlement, to conciliate angry municipalities, to establish terminals, to organize a system of elevators, to acquire steamships for the lakes and the Pacific, to superintend crop reports, to devise attractive advertising and to maintain, subject to the authority of the directors, the credit of the company against political attack at home and sullen money markets abroad.

In all these things he concerned himself, in all he advised, in much he was absolute. Perhaps his courage was most signally displayed in 1891 when, feeling that the company would be fatally damaged by free trade with the United States, which was the central feature of Liberal policy, he organized its forces against the Liberal party and perhaps was chiefly instrumental in the decisive victory which Sir John Macdonald obtained in his last contest. He said afterward to the late Carrol Ryan, who was writing a sketch of his career: "I am no politician. I have no time to give to politics, even were I inclined that way, which I am not. I am only a plain business man. All my time is given to the Canadian Pacific. I never interfered in politics in my life but once, and I hope I will never have to do so again. I care nothing about parties, and the company is under no obligation to either

Government or Opposition." This was sincere, and it is curious that he never reappeared in a political contest until 1911, when again a measure of free trade between Canada and the United States was the issue.

Van Horne was a gracious host who talked much but was never dull or commonplace. Decisive in judgment and confident in opinion, his sentences were so picturesque and so penetrating that even his rasher statements were seldom challenged. His career was of the very genius of this continent, and yet there was a sense in which he belonged to the Old World. There is no evidence that he read many books, but art was his playmate. He had no diplomacy. He was unhappy on a public platform. Before Parliamentary Committees he was peculiarly ineffective. Face to face, in single combat, he was invincible. In one man there were many men compounded. Fortunately he outlived all strife and contention and saw the railway which he was so instrumental in building develop into a system of transportation beyond even his original conception.

There is a last word to be said about one other man whose friendship I greatly cherished. One thinks of Mr. T. C. Patteson, for many years postmaster of Toronto, as the last survival of Toryism in Canada. He was, however, not so much a Tory as he thought he was for he had a tolerant conception of creeds and systems which he could not accept. But he disliked the telephone. He would not dictate a letter. Against all sumptuary enactments he revolted. He would choose his own company and live in his own fashion. He was a Squire at Eastwood, a genial autocrat at the Albany Club. Strong in his dislikes he was incapable of deceit or treachery. He played cricket as became a student of Eton and Oxford. The race track had for him just such fascination as it had for Charles Greville. If he had kept a diary or written memoirs, which unfortunately he did not, they would have shown as wide knowledge of public affairs, as keen and as shrewd judgment of men, and at least as sound, prophetic reading of events. He had a passionate love for horses. His whole being responded to the excitement of a great race. Far distant as he was, his heart was across the sea on successive Derby days, and he seemed to see the very horses sweeping around the course. He was a familiar figure on race tracks all over America, and it is doubtful if any other man on the continent knew so much of racing and breeding or spoke with equal authority. He was fond, too, of riding and rode out daily almost down to the day of his death. So he loved gardening, and the hours which many give to the club, to golf, or to some other outdoor recreation, he gave to his garden, and in this intimate touch with nature his life was mellowed and enriched.

He was intimate with successive Governors-General, and many friends in England with whom he maintained a regular correspondence. As editor of *The Mail* during the "Pacific scandal" and the formulation of the National Policy, he had material at command which would have illuminated vital incidents in Canadian history. It is no secret that he believed history was perverted in the common understanding of the events of that period but he left nothing behind. Indeed he wrote only for the moment and never at length or with material collected by laborious investigation. Under Mr. Patteson's control *The*

Mail's editorial page had distinction and dignity. He wrote freely and clearly, but in his style there was no pomposity. It was the English of the essayists, simple, straightforward and unaffected. He was sometimes merciless in political attack, but there was often a touch of generosity which restored the balance of sanity. The page, too, was far-reaching in its survey and catholic in its sympathies. Books, music, sport and Old World affairs received careful and regular treatment, much after the method of the chief British journals. We have had no better editorial writing in Canada, and Mr. Patteson had the genius to preserve the unity of the page, no matter by how many hands the work was done. He wrote while he lived, for he never grew old but died at seventy-one, as buoyant of spirit as most men of forty or fifty. I have a letter written a few hours before he died. He was jaunty and confident. In the few sentences there is a chuckle at those who thought he was dying. But he was never to see his garden again nor ride again along the valley of the Humber.

INDEX

INDEX

INDEX

ference to Tories, 35; famous letter to Thomas Hodgins, 36; attitude toward protection, 37; last years in Parliament, 35.

Martin, Hon. Joseph, 247.

Murder, The Thomas Scott, 251.

McGee, Hon. T. D'Arcy, 258.

Minorities in Canada, 272.

Money in elections, 277.

Macdonald, Hon. John, 282.

Monk, Hon. F. D., 314, 315.

Marter, G. F., M.P.P., 337.

McGreevy charges, The, 145.

Marchand, Hon. F. G., 168.

Masson, Hon. L. R., 191.

Macdonald, Rt. Hon. Sir John: foresees defeat of Sandfield Macdonald, 17; loss of friends, 24; Ministry resigns, 25; defeat in 1874, 27; restoration to office, 28; tribute to George Brown, 30; tactics in opposition, 31, 36; dubious about protection, 38, 39, 198; public ownership of C.P.R., 71; agitation against Jesuits' Estates Act, 140; The Riel issue of 1885, 148; wins back the Bolters" in 1887, 159; the Anti-Jesuit agitation, 175; qualities as leader, 177; opinion of Sir W. Laurier, 176; his humour, 178; his habits, 179; relations with Sir R. Cartwright, 181; ancedotes of, 179-189; tributes by W. F. MacLean, M.P., and Nicholas Flood Davin, 185, 187; compared with Disraeli, 187; alliance with Cartier, 191; opinions of Sir John Abbott, 193; relations with French colleagues, 195; his reliance upon men, 196-7; grief at his death, 199; election campaign of 1891, 227-8; separate schools, 262; secret service money, 282.

Macdonald, Baroness, 71.

Mowat, Sir Oliver: qualities as leader, 92-96; political policies, 93; attitude toward Prohibition, 95; on patronage, 96; supported by Catholics, 97; debating skill, 101; personal qualities, 102; Presbyterian support, 150; withholds eulogy of Laurier, 173; the Blake letter against Unrestricted Reciprocity, 232-3.

Meredith, Sir William, 100; opposition leader, 108; attitude toward Catholics, 109; a true public servant, 110; appointed to the Bench, 111, 176, 207, 328.

McQuade, M.P., Mr., 155.

National Policy, The, 30, 38.

Newspaper finances, 45.

News, The Toronto, 38, 111, 267.

New Brunswick school case, 262.

Naval Controversy, The, 313-17.

National Club, Toronto, founded, 74.

Oronhyatekha, Dr., 48.

Ontario constitutional issues, 89-90, 101.

Office-holders in politics, 93.

Orange Association in 1871, 97, 251.

Owens, T. P., 120.

O'Brien, Col. Wm., M.P., 174.

Ontario Convention called, 228; cancelled, 233.

Osler, B.B., 253, 254.

Office and Patronage, 274.

Obligations of party journalists, 275.

Political meetings in 1872, 13.

Patteson, T. C., 38, 39, 207, 341-43.

Pirie, Alex., 45, 48, 51, 86, 120.

Pawning the office safe, 45.

Phipps, R. W., 52.

Paterson, Hon. Wm., 19, 63, 337.

Prohibition issue in Ontario, 93.

Patronage in politics, 95.

Protestant Protective Association, 99, 174.

Pardee, Hon. T. B., 103-104.

Payne, J. L., 119.

349

INDEX

Carthy opposed to, 139; power as a debater, 141; speech on the Riel issue, 144; office declined by D'Alton McCarthy, 176; advice of Sir John Macdonald, 193; Blaine and reciprocity, 234; Manitoba school issue, 252.

Telegram, The Toronto, 48.
Times, The London, 54, 237.
Times, The Exeter, 57.
Times, The Hamilton, 62, 63, 64.
Times, The St. Thomas, 63.
Tribune, The Winnipeg, 119.
Turner, Ald. John, 184.
Tilley, Sir Leonard, 207.
Taylor, Chas. W., 223.
Titles in Canada, 318-19.
Tooley, M.P.P., Mr., 111.

United States press paragraphers, 46.
Use of patronage, 95.
Unrestricted Reciprocity, 225-244.

Value of contemporary writings in history, 12.
Varna, The village of, 13, 15.
Voices of Brant County orators, 18.
Vindicator, The Oshawa, 212.
Van Horne, Sir William, 213, 221, 292, 339-41.

Willison, Sir John: youthful days in Huron County, 9; rural life in the Sixties, 10; leaves the farm for Journalism, 11; first political meeting in 1872, 13; father a Conservative, 22; value of rural libraries, 22; writes verse for the press, 41; efforts to join *The Globe*, 52-54; appointed to *Advertiser* staff, 55; Ontario Press Gallery, 89; Ottawa Press Gallery, 113; association with Hon. Edward Blake, 153; visits Sir W. Laurier at Arthabaskaville, 162; chairman of Laurier meeting in Toronto, 174; appointed editor of *The*

Globe, 201; relations with Edward Farrer, 206-15; reports of party meetings, 216; threat of dismissal, 217; advocates federal railway commission, 220; leaves *The Globe,* 223; letter from Mr. Blake, 228; refuses to publish it, 230-3; pamphlet on the railway question, 293; the Imperial relation, 308-11; political and other sketches, 321-343.

Wilson, M. P., Dr., 163, 201.
Wood, Hon. E. B., ("Big Thunder"). at Varna, 14; his effective oratory, 15; Provincial Treasurer, 17; leaves the Cabinet to join Edward Blake, 18; the "speak now" incident, 18; his humorous appeal to Edward Farrer, 19; campaign story of John Charlton, 20; Chief Justice of Manitoba, 21.

Wright, A. W., 44.
White, Hon. Thomas, 49, 62, 114, 195.
White, W. J., 58.
Wilkinson, Jonathan, 63.
Wood, A. F., M.P.P., 107.
Whitney, Sir James: attitude toward minorities, 99; first speeches in Legislature, 108; press news, 122; proposed coalition, 322; his personal qualities, 327; his policy and character, 329-30.

White, R. S., M.P., 114.
Wallis, A. F., 118.
Wallis, Horace, 120.
Wright, Alonzo, M.P., 122.
Wallace, Hon. N. Clarke, 124, 250, 251.
Weldon, Dr., M.P., 147.
World, The Toronto, 45, 118.
Watchman, The Tiverton, 55.
Wiman, Erastus, 166, 212.
Watson, Hon. Robert, 185.
West Durham Letter, The, 240.
White, Hon. Peter, 251.
Written Constitution, A., 272.
Young men and politics, 44.

351

Warwick Bro's & Rutter, Limited,
Printers and Bookbinders, Toronto, Canada

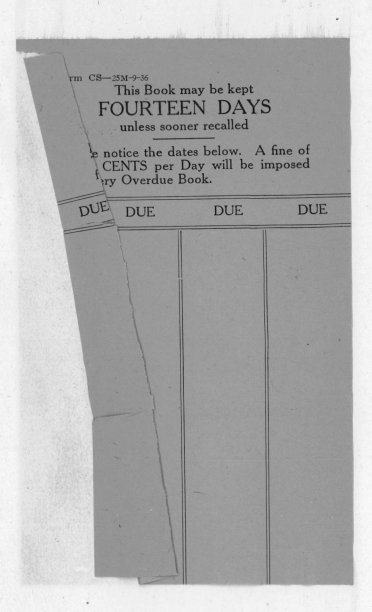

rm CS—25M-9-36

This Book may be kept

FOURTEEN DAYS

unless sooner recalled

e notice the dates below. A fine of
CENTS per Day will be imposed
ry Overdue Book.

| DUE | DUE | DUE | DUE |